Al Deere

Al Deere

Wartime Fighter Pilot, Peacetime Commander

The Authorised Biography

Richard C. Smith

GRUB STREET · LONDON

Published by
Grub Street
The Basement
10 Chivalry Road
London SW11 1HT

British Library Cataloguing in Publication Data
Smith, Richard C., 1956-
   Al Deere: wartime fighter pilot, peacetime commander:
   the authorised biography
   1. Deere, Al 2. Fighter pilots – New Zealand – Biography
   3. Fighter pilots – Great Britain – Biography
   4. World War, 1939-1945 – Aerial operations, British
   I. Title
   940.5'44941'092

ISBN 1 904010 48 2

Typeset by Pearl Graphics, Hemel Hempstead

Printed and bound in Great Britain by
Biddles Ltd, Guildford and King's Lynn

CONTENTS

ACKNOWLEDGEMENTS

It has been a great honour and a pleasure for me to have been given permission by Alan Deere's family to write this biography.

I would like to thank them for their time and generosity, as I do other family members and friends, peace and wartime colleagues, and all those for whom 'Al' Deere, as he is generally known, has a special place in their hearts or interests. Sadly, some of those who gave so much during the writing of this book are no longer with us, but their memories included within the book will be a fitting tribute not only to Al Deere, but to themselves.

Squadron Leader Douglas Brown RNZAF
Flight Lieutenant Pierre Clostermann, DFC
Wing Commander John Checketts, DSO, DFC, RNZAF Retd
Flying Officer Max Collett, Secretary of 485 RNZAF Squadron
  Association
Lieutenant General Baron Michael Donnet, CVO, DFC, FR, AE, Retd
Wing Commander Frank Dowling, OBE, RAF Retd
Air Commodore John Ellacombe, CB, DFC, RAF Retd
The late Flight Lieutenant Leslie Harvey
The late Flight Lieutenant John Kemp
The late Air Commodore James Leathart CB, DSO
Wing Commander Hector MacLean, AE
Flying Officer Hugh Niven
The late Squadron Leader Jeffery Quill, OBE, AFC
Flight Lieutenant Jack Rae, DFC, RNZAF
Squadron Leader Nigel Rose
Air Commodore David Strong, CB, AFC, RAF Retd
Flying Officer Howard Squire
Squadron Leader Harvey Sweetman, DFC, RNZAF
Group Captain Edward Wells, DSO, DFC, RAF Retd
Air Commodore Sir Archibald Winskill, KCVO, CBE, DFC, RAF Retd
Mr Jim Barton
Mrs Pat Bishdon
Mr John Cox
Mr Jerry Crandall

6

Mr Brendon Deere
Mr John Deere
Mr M. Druitt
Mrs Erin Englert
Mr F. James
Mr D.J. Keats
Mr John Meddows
Mr Gerry Mobb
Mr Arthur Moreton, chairman of the North Weald Museum
Mr R.W. Needham
Mr Stanley Reynolds
Mr G.F 'Ricky' Richardson
Mr Jack Shenfield
Mr David Smith
Mr A.E. Sweetman

Special thanks go to John Deere for authorising me to undertake this project, to Brendon Deere for all his help with the New Zealand contacts during its research, and to Wing Commander Johnny Checketts for providing the excellent foreword. To aviation artist Jerry Crandall for allowing us to use his marvellous painting for the front cover. Thanks are also due to the Imperial War Museum Sound Archive, London, the Public Record Office at Kew, the Personnel Management Agency at RAF Innsworth, and Christopher Shores for permission to use his record of Al Deere's combat claims. To Peter Arnold, Jim Barton, Andy Saunders, Howard Squire, and David Smith for excellent photographs and information. Thanks also to David Whitham, Historian of the Rosslyn Park Rugby Club.

My thank go also to loyal friends and supporters of my work, for without them there would be no books; to Squadron Leader Peter Brown, AFC RAF Retd, David and Alison Campbell (Lashenden Air Warfare Museum), John and Anne Cox, David and Alison Ross (603 Squadron rules ok?), to Colin and Rose Smith of Vector Fine Art, for their outstanding book launches, hospitality and support, and to Alan and Sue Gosling and all at the Purfleet Heritage and Military Centre who support my work. Special thanks go to John Davies, Anne Dolamore and Amy, Louise King, Amy Myers and Luke Norsworthy, the 'kings' of Grub Street. Finally, to my wife Kim who helped greatly with Al's unpublished manuscript and my two sons, David and Robert for all their patience and love.

FOREWORD

by Wing Commander J.M. Checketts DSO, DFC, RNZAF Retd

Not only do I find writing a foreword to this book about Air Commodore Alan Deere to be an honour, but also one of great pleasure for it brings to mind the wonderful companionship Alan and I enjoyed during our wartime service and the years afterwards.

I knew of him long before he knew of me, for I was aware of the reports of his aerial fights over the beaches of Dunkirk during the sad withdrawal of the British Expeditionary Force from France in May 1940, and then again in the bitter combat period of the Battle of Britain, when he flew with No.54 Squadron.

In November 1941, I was posted to the RAF Station Kenley Wing as a junior pilot officer to join 485 Squadron. I trained on Hurricanes and on my first flight in a Spitfire, I had difficulty in landing it; as a result, I was unhappy and was in this state when Alan Deere made himself known to me. He was commanding 602 Squadron, at that time at Kenley, and soon had me in a different frame of mind. So my confidence returned, to be followed by a firm friendship. Alan's ongoing assistance now covered any aspect of aerial fighter warfare he thought I should know about, and later to fly with him when he commanded the Biggin Hill Wing, which always proved to be a great adventure.

By September 1943, Alan had flown 700 hours on operations, during which he had been involved in the destruction of 21 enemy aircraft, had a total of four probables and 18 damaged. A remarkable score. Tired and ill at the time, he was hospitalised and then taken off active operations. The following November, he was in command of the Central Gunnery School at Sutton Bridge, where we were to meet again soon after, when I was posted to the school to command the air combat squadron. Our recreational interests were similar, so we were often into the wartime countryside for wildfowl shooting in the Wash or just visiting friends. London's proximity when serving at Kenley or Biggin Hill meant taking leave in the city, with visits to the Kemul Club where I was to meet many of Alan's friends.

After the war ended, Alan stayed on in the Royal Air Force, but we still managed to see each other occasionally in England and in New Zealand.

He was a first class rugby player and sportsman, a great leader and an excellent fighter pilot. He was a true friend and I was fortunate to know him.

Johnny Checketts,
Christchurch,
New Zealand,
May 2003

INTRODUCTION

The name and exploits of New Zealand fighter pilot Alan Deere became legendary with his RAF colleagues during the Second World War and to a wider audience after the release of his autobiography *Nine Lives* in the late 1950s. His story of incredible escapes during combat with the enemy and his tireless energy and leadership won him many plaudits. He was a shy and modest man who regarded himself as nothing out of the ordinary and always maintained that as a fighter pilot he had been doing the job for which he had been so effectively trained.

This new book on Al Deere was conceived in 2000, when Deere's son John asked me if I would like to catalogue his father's memorabilia, which were stored in several large boxes and consisted of a vast collection of RAF and family photographs and papers. During this pleasurable task I came across a bound manuscript entitled Escape, a previously unpublished adventure story that might have been the follow-up work to Deere's own autobiography. Having read through the story, I decided to contact John Davies at Grub Street to seek his thoughts and advice on the manuscript. After much debate, we concluded that the short story could not be published by itself, and the idea of a biography on the great man was mooted, to include his unpublished manuscript. Although Deere's autobiography was in its own way excellent, many of the events that took place had only been briefly mentioned, and therefore a more detailed account of the man and his life would be valuable. The project would first have to have the full backing of Deere's family and this was obtained.

The information for the book was researched in three main ways: firstly through interviews with family, friends and wartime colleagues worldwide; secondly by using official records and combat reports; and finally from Alan Deere's own spoken word from various recorded interviews. I was also given free access to many of Deere's original and unpublished photographs and documents. In conclusion, I hope the reader will find this book all that they hoped in presenting a fuller insight into the life of this outstanding man and aviator.

Richard C. Smith,
May 2003

10

PART ONE

CHAPTER 1

THE SPIRIT OF FLIGHT

Alan Christopher Deere was born on 12th December 1917 in the small town of Westport, in the South Island of New Zealand. His parents were second-generation Irish immigrants, whose own parents had left the country due to the Irish troubles in the late 1880s. His father, Terence Joseph Deere, had been born in Greymouth, New Zealand, on 10th May 1893, the son of John and Mary Ann Deere, née O'Brien.

Alan Deere's mother, Theresa Veronica Curtain, was born on 25th May 1895 in Kumara, New Zealand. Theresa Curtain was one of twelve girls and four boys, one of whom was a half brother. Her father Christopher Curtain, who had originated from County Clare, had married, but his first wife had died either in childbirth or shortly afterwards. He later married Nora Gamble who had came out to New Zealand from the village of Rear Cross in County Limerick at the tail end of the potato famine. After being introduced by a parish priest, they married and soon started a family. With hard work, they eventually owned the Empire Hotel in Kumara on the west coast of the island.

Terence Deere had begun his early career as a news reporter, but then went to work for the railways. He met Theresa Curtain in Westport, where she worked in one of the town's stores and after starting a courtship they married on 9th January 1915. He was 21 and she was 19 years old. Setting up home in Westport, they too quickly started a family. Alan Deere was the third of six boys, who would be brought up in the open and healthy climate that New Zealand offers its citizens. He had two older brothers, Patrick and Brian, and three younger, Leslie, Kevin, and Desmond. Leslie was always known as 'Jimmy.'

Alan's upbringing as a child was strict and disciplined, but not overbearing, for it was a close and loving family. The great outdoors held many adventures for children in those carefree days, and they were allowed to wander and seek out their own entertainment and fun. Nearby the Deeres' home ran the Buller River, where during the summer months the boys would spend many hours swimming, fishing and playing in the sand and mud. It

11

was during one of these summers that while playing with his two older brothers, Alan Deere first became acquainted with the aeroplane. They were sitting playing a game of marbles when they heard an unusual sound in the distance growing in volume. Looking towards the source of this strange sound, they could see the unfamiliar shape of a biplane flying overhead.

With their game of marbles now forgotten, the three young boys raced to find out where the flying machine was headed for. The aircraft had flown over the town of Westport and as it began to descend, the three children estimated from its course that it was going to land on the nearby beach, which was ideally suited for this because of its long stretching sands. The beach was nearly half an hour away however, but on his arrival, completely worn out from his exertions, the young Alan Deere marvelled at the silver biplane. Many of the locals were already on the beach to investigate the strange bird. Deere and his brothers spent the next few hours looking at every aspect of the aircraft, studying it from every angle. Alan's greatest thrill was to be hoisted up by an adult and given a quick look into the cockpit to view the layout of the instrument dials and control column.

Back at home that night, the boys' only talk over dinner was that of their adventure with the aeroplane, and Alan was preoccupied with the thought of one day being able to fly such a machine. He would remark in later years:

> As a boy I always wanted to fly, but in New Zealand at that time there was very little opportunity to do so before the last war. Aviation had barely made an impact in my country at that time.

The family remained in Westport, where Alan started his first full time education at the St Canice's School in 1923. In 1926 the area suffered bad flooding, when the Buller River burst its banks. The family home was in jeopardy one night, when the water level increased so much that the Deeres' home was caught in the flood. The family awakened in the early hours to find the home flooded and the water steadily rising. Their father carried the boys to the highest level in the kitchen area, on top of the cupboards. It must have been an incredibly frightening experience for the youngsters, huddled up together in complete darkness with the terrific noise of rushing water and debris outside. Rescue came with the dawn. A small rowing boat was heard outside, and its owner was calling out to ask if there was anybody inside. The family quickly made their way to the boat, where they were given blankets to warm themselves. They were then rowed to the hotel in the town centre, which had escaped the flooding. When the flood had subsided the family home was still standing although all the family's belongings were destroyed. In the true spirit of the colonials, they picked themselves up and started to rebuild their home and lives. Unfortunately on 17th June 1929, Westport was hit by disaster yet again, when shock waves from a severe earthquake, which had its epicentre several miles away, caused much damage. At 10.30 am, when the shock waves hit the town, Alan Deere was in school. He later recalled the Murchison earthquake:

It only lasted a matter of seconds, but the whole earth seemed to be erupting. Children were lying flat on their faces in the schoolyard. I clung on to a school fence and from there I could see the post office clock tower swaying. It suddenly just disintegrated and fell to the ground. Suddenly everything went quiet again and the trembling finished. It was all over. The earthquake had caused quite severe damage to the town's buildings and most of its population, including my own family, had to spend a few nights in tented accommodation before returning to their homes.

In early 1930, the family decided to move to New Zealand's fifth city, Wanganui, which is situated on the west coast of the North Island. Here they moved into No. 43 Plymouth Street. Alan was now 12 years old. His education continued with the Roman Catholic Marist Brothers in 1930 and then at the Wanganui Technical College from 1931 to 1934. At the college he did well both academically and physically. He excelled at sports and represented the school in cricket, rugby and boxing, and for the latter he also represented his town in the New Zealand Boxing Championships. In 1933, he was voted in by the college pupils of Rees House as a councillor, which meant he had a certain amount of authority over his schoolmates. In his acceptance speech, Deere gave an excellent talk on diving, as among his other fortes he was also good at this. Deere's cousin Erin Englert, whose mother was his mother's sister, remembers his visits to their home as a youngster:

During the New Zealand depression, my father and mother lived in Waipawa and my father used to deliver the mail on the run that went around the rural places. Because of the depression the mail run was stopped so my father had to look for work and he managed to get a job as a shepherd on the Bidwall Estate at Pihatea House and Alan used to visit us there. This belonged to the Bidwall family and they took an interest in Alan; I think he probably knew the Bidwall boys because they were the same age. He helped with the haymaking and he would go out on the dray with my father. The nanny who was employed at Pihatea at that time to look after the family children was Jane Chichester, whose brother was Francis Chichester – who would become famous for his aviation and nautical records; he used to fly over in his Gypsy Moth aeroplane. I don't know if Alan was staying with us at that time, but when Chichester flew over, everybody would come out of the house and wave. This was in 1932.

Deere's latent interest in aviation was brought to the fore, when Wanganui's airport became host to one of the pioneering aviators of this period, Sir Charles Kingsford-Smith, who arrived in his aircraft, *Southern Cross*.

Kingsford-Smith was an Australian, born in Brisbane in 1897. At the age of 13, he began studying mechanics and electrical engineering at the Sydney Technical College. At the outbreak of the First World War, he enlisted at the age of 18 in the army where he saw action at Gallipoli and later became a motorbike despatch rider.

He was selected to join the Royal Flying Corps, and flew in operations over France. In one combat he was shot in the foot, which caused him to have three of his toes amputated. To many, his flying days seemed over. He was awarded the Military Cross by King George V and was hailed as a war hero by the people of Australia. After war's end he travelled to the United States of America and sought work in the early film industry as a stunt pilot, but by 1921 he had returned to his native country completely penniless. Fortunately he managed to acquire employment with the new Australian Airways Company, flying mail runs to the outback; but, ever the adventurer, he wanted to fly across the Pacific Ocean and break new records. Managing to find sponsorship, he went back to America, where he purchased *Southern Cross*.

On 31st May 1928, Kingsford-Smith, with co-pilot Charles Ulm, navigator Harry Lyon and radio operator James Warner, took off from San Francisco in an attempt to fly across the Pacific. The journey was made in three stages and was one of the great navigational flights of history. They finally landed at Brisbane after 83 flying hours, and were hailed as heroes. To many this would have seemed the pinnacle of success, but Kingsford-Smith continued to break further records. In 1930 he won the England to Australia Air Race and in 1933 he broke the record for a solo flight from England to Australia. In 1935, however tragedy was to strike, when on 6th November, he took off with Tommy Pethbridge from England on another record-breaking attempt. A few days later, his aircraft was reported missing near Burma, and has never been found. So ended the life of a man who had pioneered more long distance routes than any other pilot in history.

During Kingsford-Smith's visit to Wanganui, he offered passenger flights in his triplane at ten shillings per head. This was one opportunity that the young Al Deere could not pass up and he managed to acquire the money needed for a flight in the aircraft. This was his first flight into the azure blue sky, which would later become so routine for him. During the flight he felt exhilarated and from that day on, he was hooked on the idea of somehow learning to fly and becoming a pilot.

After obtaining his qualifications, he left school and spent a year working as a sheep hand on a local farm at Okoia owned by Mr I. Higgie, before finding more substantial employment in 1935 as a clerk with Treadwell, Gordon, Treadwell and Haggitt, a solicitors' firm at Wanganui.

In 1936, after learning from the Deeres' family doctor, Kendrick Christie, that the Royal Air Force was now recruiting for pilots in the Dominion countries, Deere's aspirations of being able to learn to fly were reawakened. His major concern however was how to get his father to approve his application. Al felt at that time that his father would more than likely refuse to sign the recruitment papers, so he looked towards his mother for help; and she somewhat reluctantly agreed to sign. It was not until he had received a letter notifying him to attend a Royal Air Force selection board that his father became aware of his son's attempt to join up. Al recalls:

> I applied to join the Royal Air Force at the age of eighteen. The Air Ministry sent out from England a selection board, which covered both Australia and New Zealand. I went before this board and undertook a medical and then waited to hear. Fortunately I was one of the lucky first twenty-four selected in New Zealand.

One of the officers on the selection board when Deere applied was Wing Commander Ralph Alexander Cochrane, who after a distinguished career later became Air Chief Marshal The Honourable Sir Ralph Cochrane. Cochrane had been sent to New Zealand in 1936 to assist with the creation of a Royal New Zealand Air Force, independent of the Army. This was inaugurated on 1st January 1937, with Cochrane becoming its Chief of Air Staff. In May 1939, Cochrane returned to England to become Aide de Camp to the King and Deputy Director of Intelligence; by December that year he was commanding RAF Abingdon. He rose to Senior Air Staff Officer Headquarters of 6 (Bomber) Group during 1940 and on 1st July became AOC 7 (Bomber) Group. In 1943, he was AOC of 5 Group and one of his first tasks was to supervise the undertaking of *Operation Chastise*, the Dams Raid, in May 1943, which proved successful, and afterwards he was an advocate of precision bombing against certain German targets. After the war he continued in the RAF until his retirement in 1952. Air Chief Marshal Cochrane died on 17th December 1977.

A few weeks after being notified of his selection for Royal Air Force training, Alan Deere was finally ready to leave, bidding a fond farewell to his mother, father and brothers. It would be 11 years before he would see them all again. His journey to Britain and a career in the Royal Air Force had begun. Travelling to Auckland, he boarded a passenger steamship, the *Rangitane*, on 23rd September 1937. After storing his belongings in the small cabin he would share with a couple of the other RAF hopefuls who were bound for Mother England, he went back up on deck to watch the ship depart from port and finally out of sight of land.

Among the other RAF pilots who Deere befriended on the ship were Kenneth William Tait, Jack McKay, Steve Esson and 'Spud' Miller. The voyage soon became tedious, however, with little to do or keep him occupied. Finally the monotony was broken when the vessel reached Panama City, when the passengers were allowed to spend some time ashore before the next stage of the journey. Here Deere and his colleagues were bedazzled and amazed by the metropolis of sound, sight, and colour and the people they encountered for the very first time in this vibrant city. There was nothing to compare with this in New Zealand.

The ship left port on the early tide the following morning, and no doubt the main subject for discussion the next day would have been the night before. After nearly five weeks at sea, the ship finally berthed at Tilbury Docks, which Deere was afterwards to see many times from the air. From Tilbury, the group of young New Zealanders headed by train to London. The very next day they were greeted by New Zealand's High Commissioner, Bill Jordan, when they arrived at New Zealand House for information and instructions. Before going off to start their new careers, Deere and the others spent a few leisurely days looking around the sights of London, especially the historic landmarks, including visits to the Tower of London and Buckingham Palace.

On 25th October 1937, Deere began his flying training at De Havilland's 13 Elementary & Reserve Flying Training School at White Waltham, Berkshire. Here Deere and other hopefuls underwent *ab initio* flying training to see if they were deemed suitable to continue into the Royal Air Force as future pilots.

As with all new arrivals, the pupils were given a complete medical. For some unknown reason Deere had developed a slight blood pressure problem and although he told the medical officers that he felt completely fit, they sent him off for further tests at the RAF hospital at Halton. After being kept under observation for a few days, he was finally released and given a clean bill of health, putting the blood pressure scare down to over-excitement at the prospect of flying. On his return to White Waltham, Deere was eager to make up the time he had lost while in hospital. He was an enthusiastic pupil and his instructor, Flying Officer Dixon, went out of his way to help him as much as possible, although at times Deere's eagerness overruled his actions in handling the Tiger Moth aircraft on which he was training.

> I began my training immediately and before long a great moment arrived – my first dual instruction flight in a Tiger Moth biplane. I will never forget the thrill of feeling the aircraft rolling and looping at random. As the amount of hours flying mounted, I wondered whether I would ever go solo, and I suspected my instructor of thinking in the same terms. On many occasions I came very near to tears, partly in anger at myself and partly through some of the scathing words, that came from the instructor with monotonous regularity through my headphones.
>
> I vividly remember that beautiful November day, when my instructor suddenly said, 'Deere, you are ready for your first solo.' I was so excited to be off that before my instructor had finished speaking, I banged the throttle open and was airborne. I was master of my own aircraft. How I got down again has always been a miracle to me, but down I got and safely too. After my first solo I undertook spins and then went on to instrument flying and from that to aerobatics and cross-country. By

7th December, I had amassed 25 hours dual and solo and was all set for the more advanced flying training school.

On 9th January 1938, Deere was granted a short service commission. His RAF number was 40370. His next move was to RAF Uxbridge, where he spent the following fortnight on an officers' training course, during which he was also measured for his RAF uniform. After going through various exercises and tests and undertaking some regular parade ground drilling, he was then sent to continue his training at 6 Flying Training School at Netheravon, Wiltshire, on 21st January 1938. A few of the pilot trainees with whom Deere shared the course would later fight in the Battle of Britain; these included Tony Lovell, Kenneth Tait, and Leonard Jowitt. Lovell had been born in Ceylon (now Sri Lanka) and had also joined the RAF on a short service commission in 1937. He later went on to serve with 41 Squadron at Catterick and at Hornchurch during the battle and became an ace with an ultimate total of 16 and six shared victories. He flew operationally throughout the war, surviving the conflict only to die tragically on 17th August 1945, when he crashed his Spitfire after completing two slow rolls following take-off from Old Sarum aerodrome.

Ken Tait, a fellow 'Kiwi' from Wellington, had worked as a stock and invoicing clerk before being accepted for pilot training. He would later join 87 Squadron and take an active part in the Battles of France and Britain, claiming five enemy aircraft destroyed. Sadly, Tait was lost in action on 4th August 1941, while attacking German E-boats. Len Jowitt came from Manchester; he had worked his way from being an aircraft apprentice to engine fitter and seen service on the Indian North-West Frontier with 20 (Army Co-Operation) Squadron. He then decided to apply for pilot training, after which he later joined 85 Squadron flying Hawker Hurricanes, seeing action in France. He was killed at the start of the Battle of Britain on 12th July 1940. While protecting a convoy in the Channel which was being attacked by German bombers, he was shot down into the sea off Felixstowe.

It was during his time at Netheravon that Deere was also free to indulge in his great love of sports, which were available when time allowed. Deere's rugged build and aggressive spirit in all things sporting did not go unnoticed by the RAF, and he was soon asked if he would represent the service in both rugby and boxing. He was a little apprehensive with regards to the boxing, having not really trained for this particular sport for a few years, but he decided to give it a go. It proved successful, and he attained a winning position in the middleweight class. Deere's continued prowess in the ring even pushed him to the level of being selected to tour South Africa with the Royal Air Force team. Fate intervened, however, and it was thought to be more beneficial for Deere to finish his flying training, so he missed the tour, and fortunately also the flight which ended in tragedy. Half of the RAF contingent was killed when their aircraft crashed on the outskirts of Bulawayo.

It was during this period that Deere was befriended by the Dumas family.

It was at this time not uncommon for families to take into their homes servicemen from the Dominions, who would be seeking friendship, feeling alone and separated far away from their own families. Raymond Dumas and his wife decided they would like to help one of these servicemen and invite him into their home. He turned out to be Al Deere. The Dumas's were quite wealthy and owned two properties, Little Missenden House in Buckinghamshire and a cottage in Cornwall. Throughout the next five to six years, Deere would spend some of his leave with this generous couple for whom he had great respect.

At the end of the first term, Deere was told he had passed all his tests and flying exercises and would now receive the prized accolade given to all successful trainees; on 23rd May 1938 he received his coveted wings. The sense of achievement and pride that he must have felt when stepping forward to receive his wings, would have been overwhelming.

As a fully qualified pilot, he progressed to flying more powerful aircraft, which included the Hawker Fury single-seat biplane fighter. The Fury was one of the RAF's most agile and aerobatic aircraft still in service at this time, but it was becoming obsolete after the introduction of the Hawker Hurricane monoplane fighter in 1937. A year later the Supermarine Spitfire, which had been designed by Reginald Joseph Mitchell and had been first flown in March 1936, had also been brought into service with the Royal Air Force.

On 10th August 1938, Deere's training days came to an end and for the next seven days he awaited news of where and to which squadron he would be posted.

It proved to be all he had wished for, because his first unit was to be 54 Squadron based at RAF Hornchurch in Essex. In Deere's autobiography, he mentioned that the posting was a further surprise because he had actually dreamt the previous night of being posted to this particular aerodrome, although he claimed never to have heard of it. It was to see the beginning of Deere's amazing career as a fighter pilot.

CHAPTER 2

THE GATHERING STORM
1938-1940

On 20th August 1938, Alan Deere and Arthur Charrett, a Canadian, arrived by District Line train at Elm Park Underground station to take up their new posts at RAF Hornchurch as acting pilot officers. They proceeded to walk down the hill from the station, then the quarter of a mile down Coronation Drive, before turning right into South End Road, where the aerodrome's main gate was situated a further 300 yards on the left.

RAF Hornchurch had re-opened in 1928, after being originally known as Sutton's Farm. A Home Defence airfield during the First World War, it had been used to combat the threat of the Zeppelin airship and Gotha raids over London during the period of 1915 to 1917.

On arrival the two young men made their way to the station adjutant's office and reported to the officer on duty. Here they were told that 54 Squadron was on two week's leave and that they had chosen to arrive when none of the squadron's pilots was on camp. Deere and Charrett were left deliberating what to do next, stuck in a position with very little money between them to take further time off. They were saved further anxiety, however, when it was suggested that the two of them be temporarily assigned to one of the station's other squadrons, No.74. They were then taken across the road from the camp to the officers' mess and shown to their rooms; Deere's was situated on the top floor of the west wing. The following day, Deere was told he would operate with A Flight of 74, which was commanded by a South African pilot by the name of Adolph Gysbert Malan, whose nickname was 'Sailor' due to his previous employment in the Merchant Navy. Malan was older than most of the pilots in the squadron and took Deere under his wing; when time became available, he arranged for Deere to get some flying in on one of the squadron's Gloster Gauntlets.

When 54 Squadron returned from leave, shortly afterwards, Deere was introduced to his commanding officer, Squadron Leader Toby Pearson, and his flight commander, Flight Lieutenant R.C. Love, known as 'Bubbles'. Deere was not immediately put on flying duties, but was given the unenviable tasks of commanding pay and clothing parades, and of reading daily orders. Finally he was allocated his first aircraft to fly, which was Gladiator 7927. His third trip in the aircraft nearly ended in tragedy, when it developed engine failure while Deere was on a sector reconnaissance. Fortunately, he kept a cool head and landed the aircraft in a convenient field without causing injury to himself or the machine.

The squadron's peacetime activities during this pre-war period included formation flying and practising Fighter Command fighting tactics. Compared to the German Luftwaffe during this period, the latter seemed quite antiquated. For many aerodromes, the highlight of the year was the annual Empire Air Display, when the public could marvel at the aerobatics and simulated ground attacks on the airfield, as well as seeing new aircraft that had come into service with the RAF.

Ever since Germany had annexed Austria in March 1938, the threat of war had been looming, and in September came the Munich Crisis. Prime Minister Neville Chamberlain made several visits to Munich to prevent Adolf Hitler's Nazi regime from forcibly annexing the Sudetenland, which was then part of Czechoslovakia. Chamberlain returned from his final visit on 29th September with an agreement which he announced meant 'peace for our time,' achieved only by virtually concurring with Hitler's demands and abandoning Czechoslovakia. A month later Hitler invaded the Sudetenland. In Britain the three armed services had meanwhile been put on a state of alert. Al Deere recalled when interviewed after the war:

> My first squadron after I had finished my training was 54. It was equipped with Gloster Gladiators at the time and our first piece of excitement was of course the Munich Crisis, when we were all brought up to a state of readiness and we had our lovely silver Gladiators with the squadron crests on. We spent days with buckets of paint, brushing over the silver and camouflaging them ready to go to war. Luckily we had that one year's respite and personally I have always believed that's what saved us. We could have never coped with the Germans in Gladiators, as was proven later during the Norwegian Campaign. At the time, we thought we would be able to take these chaps on; we had very good morale in the squadron and we were very proud. We were a mixed bunch of chaps who were all pretty young; the average age was around twenty-one. We were all very keen on flying and we thought we were all pretty good. Because we had Gladiators it didn't occur to us that we'd be shot out of the sky, but we were pleased later to find out we were going to be re-equipped with Spitfires. It was our first taste of war alertness when all the squadrons were brought on to a war footing. Whatever may be said or written about Chamberlain's journey and the motives behind it, it did provide one year of grace for the ill-equipped fighter squadrons of the RAF in comparison with the German Air Force at this

time. That extra year helped to bring us up to a reasonable strength with the re-equipping of the new Hurricanes and Spitfires.

After war with Germany had seemingly been averted, Hornchurch settled back towards normal peacetime activity. On 28th October 1938, Deere was confirmed in rank as a pilot officer. After he had been with the squadron for four months, he presented his flying logbook at the end of the year to his commanding officer who signed the page with the following:

> Pilot Officer A.C. Deere has qualified as first pilot of fighter landplanes w.e.f 1-1-39

Al Deere continued his sporting achievements by playing for the South London rugby team Rosslyn Park, who played at Old Deer Park, Kew. Here he played the position of inside centre on numerous occasions. On 4th February 1939, he was in the team which beat London Welsh 6 points to 3, then again on 4th March, when the team beat Old Blues 8-0 and on 18th March, when Rosslyn beat St Thomas's Hospital 20-3. In a match report for Saturday 8th April 1939, when Rosslyn Park played University College School Old Boys at Osterley, Deere's name was mentioned. It read:

> S.C. Spriggs put Rosslyn Park in an attacking position with a long punt. A clean heel from the srummage in the centre of the Old Boys' '25' sent Spriggs away, A.C. Deere carried on, and W.J. Peart scored wide out to bring the scores level at 3-3.

Unfortunately Rosslyn Park lost this match by one try, 6 points to 3.

One of their outstanding players during this time was Prince Alexander Obolensky, whom Deere referred to in his autobiography *Nine Lives*. Obolensky was born in St Petersburg, Russia on 17th February 1916, the son of Serge Obolensky, a Russian officer in the Tsar's Imperial Horse Guards, and his family came to Britain after the revolution in 1918. He was educated at the Ashe Preparatory School in Derbyshire and eventually became a student at Oxford University. He began his rugby career at the age of 15 with the team at Trent College; during that time the team only lost one match, with Obolensky scoring 222 points. He subsequently became an outstanding wing three-quarter whilst at Brasenose College, Oxford. During his first season in the Oxford XV, he was picked for England and played in four internationals in 1936, against New Zealand, Wales, Scotland and Ireland. There was much debate at the time on the merits of him appearing for England, but as he had already applied for naturalization, the matter was passed over.

His most memorable performances were against the New Zealand 'All Blacks' at Twickenham and Oxford in the 1935/36 seasons. He scored one try while playing for the University, who posted a record win against the New Zealand touring side by 15 points. At Twickenham, he scored two spectacular tries enabling England to win 13-0. In 1938, Obolensky was granted a commission in the RAF Volunteer Reserve; earlier he had been a member of the Oxford University Air Squadron. He continued to play rugby with Rosslyn Park and Barbarians. He was commissioned as a pilot officer, but on 29th March 1940, he was killed in a flying training accident in Norfolk. He was buried with full military honours at the New Cemetery, Ipswich; the New Zealand Rugby Football Union and the All Blacks team of 1935-36 sent wreaths in a sign of respect.

It was during December 1938, that 54 Squadron received three new pilot officers, each of whom Alan Deere would get to know closely in peace and war. The first was John Lawrence Allen; born in 1916 he had joined the RAF in 1937 on a short service commission. He had been sent to 8 Flying Training School at Montrose in August 1937 and whilst still there on 18th January 1938 had escaped death when his aircraft had crashed due to bad visibility on the Glen Dye Moor, Kincardineshire. Although badly injured, he survived after being trapped for hours within the cockpit until a rescue aircraft picked him up. After spending many weeks in hospital, he resumed his training and was posted to 54 Squadron. Allen was a thoughtful, quiet and religious type, a chap who sometimes seemed aloof, but was always reliable.

The second was George Dorian Gribble, born in Hendon, London on 18th June 1919. Gribble had been brought up on the Isle of Wight and on finishing his education had joined the RAF on a short service commission in March 1938. After completing his training at 11 FTS he was posted to 54. Gribble was your typical Englishman of that period; a gentleman, the squadron joker and always full of amusing stories or one-liners. An excellent pilot, he was to become one of Deere's closest friends during the early part of the war.

The third was Basil Hugh Way, born in 1918 in Hinton St George, Somerset. He was educated at Malvern College before entering into the service as a flight cadet at the RAF College at Cranwell in January 1937. During his time there, Way won the Groves Memorial Prize in 1938 for the best all-round pilot on the course. On completion at Cranwell, he was posted to Hornchurch and 54. Way was extremely tall and lean and his stature and awkwardness of walk earned him the nickname of 'Wonky,' but he was extremely intelligent and also had a very good sense of humour. None of these three fine men would survive the oncoming war.

On 3rd March 1939, the first Spitfire, K9880, arrived at Hornchurch aerodrome, flown in from Eastleigh by Flight Lieutenant James Leathart of 54 Squadron. During the next few days other pilots from the squadron would fly their new aircraft back from the Supermarine Works at Eastleigh in Hampshire. On 6th March Al Deere climbed into the cockpit of a Spitfire for the first time. What thoughts must have gone through his mind as he ran through the operating procedure and checked the cockpit layout? On starting that powerful Merlin engine the change from biplane to powerful monoplane must have been awesome. Deere related that memorable day:

My first impression of the Spitfire was I thought it was marvellous. Before that we were on Gladiator biplanes and they were no aircraft to go to war in. We had affection for the old biplanes, but [we now] realised that in terms of fighting the German Air Force who had Messerchmitt 109s, we wouldn't have stood a chance. We hadn't had any experience on monoplanes of course and there was no such thing as a dual monoplane aircraft in those days, so you just learnt the cockpit drill and read the pilot's handbook carefully and then you flew it. But right from the word go the aircraft felt right. The Spitfire was amazingly tough, although it looked fragile with its narrow undercarriage, and you had to get used to crosswind landings. It really didn't have any vices. Also at that time we were not allowed to put rear view mirrors on the cockpit; some of us did later though. We were allowed to have logos; I had a Kiwi, which is the New Zealand bird that doesn't fly, and I had this painted on the cowling.

The era of the biplane at Hornchurch had ended, and 54 Squadron flew its Gladiators up to Turnhouse, Scotland on 30th March, where they were handed over to 603 'City of Edinburgh' Squadron. The squadron had now completely been equipped with the new Spitfire aircraft. Deere and the rest of the pilots spent many hours getting to know the Spitfire's capabilities as a fighting machine, undertaking fighter formation and practice dog fights with cine-gun attacks.

It was while out on an exercise that Deere nearly became a casualty due to his own forgetfulness. While climbing up to an altitude of 27,000 feet, he suddenly blacked out, and the aircraft rolled over and headed down. Deere could have only been unconscious for a few seconds, as, when he came to, he suddenly realised that the blue he thought was the sky above him was in fact the sea rushing up closer and closer. He instantly pulled as hard as he could on the control column to get the Spitfire out of its dive, in which he succeeded.

Somewhat shaken from the ordeal, he landed back at Hornchurch and was checked over by the medical officer who informed him that he had burst the eardrum of his right ear. The cause of this near tragic episode was that while he had been so intensely concentrating on his instrument panel, Deere had forgotten to increase his oxygen flow as he climbed to a higher and higher altitude. The incident and the damage to his eardrum was to keep him off flying duties for a short period.

Deere's Summary of Flying and Assessments Form 414 (A) was signed by his flight commander, Flight Lieutenant 'Bubbles' Love, on 1st June 1939 with the following remarks:

1. *As a fighter pilot – Above the average*
2. *As pilot -navigator – average*
3. *In bombing – N/A*

4. *In air gunnery – not known*

During the first eight months of 1939, Germany continued its aggressive expansion, rejecting all attempts at mediation. It was clear when Russia signed its non-aggression pact with Germany on 22nd August that the writing was on the wall. On 1st September Germany invaded Poland, and France and Britain had no option but to declare war on Germany on 3rd September 1939. At 11.15 am that Sunday morning, fifteen minutes after the expiry of Britain's ultimatum to Germany, Prime Minister Neville Chamberlain had the sad duty of telling the British nation that it was now at war. At Hornchurch, as everywhere else, pilots and station personnel gathered around wireless sets awaiting the grim news. Al Deere remembers that momentous day that would change his life and many others forever:

> I can recall we all gathered around the wireless set in the officers' mess, listening to Chamberlain's speech. The response was 'Let's get at them'. We were all quite keen, being young and adventurous, but later on, it didn't take much to make us realise it wasn't going to be as much fun as it might be.

Meanwhile back in New Zealand, four of Deere's brothers would all soon be in uniform and fighting on all fronts. Patrick joined the army, as did Brian and Leslie ('Jimmy') while Kevin joined the navy. Erin Englert recalls the Deere brothers' call to arms:

> Alan's eldest brother was Patrick, who was a trained motor mechanic. Before the war he owned his own garage in a partnership in Kawarra. He went in to the army and served in the Tank Corps in Italy (possibly Monte Cassino) and he was wounded.
>
> The next brother, Brian, lived in Wanganui, went to the technical college and played rugby for them. He joined the railways and made his career there. He volunteered into the army very early in the war, joining the 25th Battalion as a Bren gunner. He was taken prisoner very early on in the war in Greece – he was in the first battle with the infantry and on the first night he was wounded and taken prisoner. The next brother was Leslie, who was married with two children; his third son was born when he was overseas. He was taken prisoner at El Alamein. Kevin Deere was the gentlest person in the family. He joined the navy and was on the convoys to Russia. Unfortunately he spent some time in the water in the North Sea, which did not lengthen his life because it ruined his kidneys, which was what killed him in the end. Desmond was the youngest; he was hoping all the time while he was at college that the war wouldn't end before he could join the air force while his family were hoping it would.

It was just three days after the outbreak of war, that the Hornchurch squadrons were called into action on 6th September 1939, to investigate an unidentified aircraft plot, which had been picked up by a radar station. Unfortunately, in doing so 74 Squadron mistakenly shot down two Hawker Hurricanes of 56 Squadron based at North Weald, with one of the Hurricane pilots being killed. This unfortunate incident was later to be known in RAF circles as the 'Battle of Barking Creek'. It did however, promote better cooperation between the ground control and air defences, and sharpen awareness of procedure when identifying hostile or unidentified plots on radar and visual sightings. Deere had been flying that day:

> All I remember about it was that we were at readiness and we were scrambled to what we were told was an X-Raid. This was the terminology used during this time in the operations plotting room for an unidentified aircraft. The Controller vectored us all around our Sector, but in the event we didn't see anything. Anti-aircraft guns were firing and aircraft were going around in circles. We came back and it wasn't until we got down on the ground that we learnt that 74 Squadron, which was also based at Hornchurch, had mistaken some Hurricanes from North Weald, which was a neighbouring fighter station, and thought they were 109s. It seems incredible that they would have done so, but one has got to remember we were all very keyed up and didn't think about the fact that a 109 could not have got as far as England from the borders of Germany.

During those early months of the war, there was little action for the squadrons at Hornchurch to undertake except the odd convoy patrols or to investigate enemy radar plots of single German reconnaissance aircraft over the south-east coast. One operation, which was unpopular with the fighter pilots, was night patrols. The Spitfire was not suited to this particular role. Taking off into the darkness of a black night sky was forbidding to say the least, for the pilot had no radar aids within the aircraft to help him. He would have to rely and fly on instrument readings and messages from ground control to search around the sky. He would have no visual bearings of towns and cities on a dark night, made even worse with the blackout restriction in force throughout the country. Another problem was the glare from the aircraft's engine exhaust stubs, which unless the aircraft was provided with an anti-glare plate mounted just over the stubs, meant that the pilot could see even less looking out from his cockpit. It was on one such patrol that Al Deere volunteered to undertake an extra operation one night, when an important merchant convoy was sailing off Harwich, Essex.

Deere took off with another pilot officer, the Canadian Don Ross, at around dusk, and by the time they had patrolled around the convoy and were getting ready to return to base, it was very dark. On their return, they were given headings by the Hornchurch Controller to guide them back to Hornchurch. Both pilots were fully concentrating on their instruments, when they were suddenly distracted by the bright illumination of the ground defence searchlights as they crossed back over the coast. However, Deere was aroused to a more immediate and far more dangerous problem, when Don Ross warned him that there was a barrage balloon dead ahead. Somehow they had been directed into the Harwich barrage balloon defences, but Deere and Ross both pulled hard on their control columns and managed to climb high enough to clear the balloons. Deere let out his feelings about the Controller's error with a few expletives, but he had forgotten his R/T transmission was on auto, so everything he said was picked up in the Operations Room.

As if the patrol had not been already eventful, when they arrived over Hornchurch, they found that the aerodrome was now fogged in. With their fuel very low and with only minutes left before they would just fall out of the sky, they decided to try to land. The ground crews had already lit a path of goose-neck flares to assist the pilots with their landing approach, but the fog had thickened so much at around 200/300 feet that the flares could not be seen.

Don Ross went down first and was fortunate to make a successful landing without incident. Deere however misjudged his approach and landed the wrong side of the 12- foot Chance Light which was situated near the end of the flightpath. As his aircraft touched down, it immediately bounced heavily back into the air before settling down again and coming to an undignified stop, entangled with pieces of wire and wooden poles belonging to the perimeter fence. Deere stepped out of his aircraft alive, but somewhat annoyed. On arriving back at 54 dispersal, he was further frustrated to learn that he had been reprimanded by the station commander for the use of bad language over the radio.

During April 1940, a young fresh-faced blond haired airman arrived at the aerodrome: his name was G.F. 'Ricky' Richardson. He became Al Deere's flight mechanic and they built up a friendship, which lasted until Al's death in 1995. Ricky remembers his first days at Hornchurch:

> I first arrived at Hornchurch in April 1940. I was then a flight mechanic and later I went on a course and came back as a fitter. Al was a pilot officer when I first arrived on the squadron and he was quite a lad. Along with Colin Gray, they were the only colonials we had in the squadron at that time. The colonial boys were different to our chaps in the RAF; there was no side at all to them, it would be 'Ricky this' and 'Ricky that'. My job entailed checking the Spitfire's plugs and magnetos and any complaints the pilots had. Alan Deere had quite a few. He always insisted on 'B', which was his aircraft and this had to be serviceable all the time as far as Alan was concerned. All the other pilots would take any other machine if theirs wasn't serviceable, but with Alan you had to work till two or three o'clock in the morning. We would shove his aircraft into the hangar to work on it. In the summer I would come out at 3.00

am in the morning and at 4.00 am, I would have to go and then run up the aircraft on A Flight.

The so-called 'Phoney War' came to an abrupt end on 7th April 1940 when German warships left their harbours to invade Denmark and Norway. In early May, Hitler turned his attention closer to home. On the 10th, he launched his Blitzkrieg, and German forces poured over the borders of Belgium and Holland. By mid-May the British Army was forced to retreat back towards the French coast, with the consequent threat of being caught in a pincer grab as von Rundstedt's forces swept through France from the Ardennes towards Amiens, Boulogne and Calais.

Churchill and his Chiefs of Staff decided that there was no other option but to save what was left of the British Expeditionary Force and evacuate from France. The point of evacuation would be the port town of Dunkirk. The command and planning of this great task was given to Vice-Admiral Sir Bertram Ramsay; under his guidance the navy along with many civilian-owned vessels would undertake Operation Dynamo, which by its conclusion on 4th June had taken as many British and Allied troops off the beaches at Dunkirk as possible; the official number was 338,226.

On the evening of 15th May 1940, the pilots at Hornchurch had gathered for a briefing in the officers' mess games room. Here they had been informed by the Station Commander, Group Captain Cecil Bouchier, of the serious situation regarding the position held by the British Expeditionary Force and its French and Belgian Allies. More air cover was needed than could be provided by the squadrons then in France, particularly to cover the probable retreat by the BEF.

The next day 54 Squadron carried out its first offensive patrol over the continent. Taking off from base at 10.35 hours, the squadron patrolled over Ostend in Belgium for 30 minutes, but no enemy were sighted. All aircraft arrived back at Hornchurch safely at 12.23 pm. Those who flew the patrol that day were Squadron Leader Douglas-Jones, Flight Lieutenant Leathart, Flying Officers Pearson and Linley, Pilot Officers Deere, Way, Allen, Gribble, McMullen, Gray, Couzens and Sergeant Phillips.

As the days passed, with Boulogne falling to the Germans on the 24th and Calais under attack, Dunkirk became the only refuge for the retreating BEF. Alan Deere recalls those early patrols over to Dunkirk, which for many pilots would be their baptism of fire:

> When the British Army started retreating and Dunkirk was going to be the point of evacuation, fighter squadrons from East Anglia as well as from 11 Group were sent on patrol to cover the beachhead and we did two or three trips a day. It was the first time we fighter pilots had crossed the Channel to make combat and then come back. The endurance factor of the Spitfire at that time was fairly critical; you couldn't stay too long, and we weren't accustomed to finding our way back so to speak, and so we patrolled the coast from Boulogne up to

Dunkirk, and up as far as Antwerp trying to support the evacuation of the British Army.

We met the Germans in combat; they had moved some of their bases forward and they were able to get their fighters as far as the bridgehead. We came into contact for the first time with Dorniers, Heinkels and Messerschmitt 110s and 109s.

One of Al Deere's early reports on a flight over to France records:

> Intercepted Heinkel 111 10-miles west of Dunkerque. Red 1 fired 160 rounds when enemy escaped in clouds 10/10 at 2,000 feet. Contact was not re-established. No known result of engagement.
> Red1 F/Lt Leathart: Red 2 Self: Red 3 P/O Allen.

On the morning of 23rd May 54 Squadron had taken off for its first patrol over the Dunkirk beachhead, and during this eventful day Al Deere became part of aerial wartime history. The morning patrol was uneventful, but 74 Squadron returned with the loss of its commander, Squadron Leader 'Drogo' White. He had been forced to land his damaged Spitfire at Calais-Marck airfield, and it was suggested that a rescue be attempted to retrieve White from the airfield before the advancing German army overran that area. Group Captain Cecil Bouchier obtained permission from 11 Group Headquarters to attempt the rescue mission, and in turn authorised Flight Lieutenant James Leathart of 54 Squadron to take a Miles Master twin-seat trainer aircraft with an escort of two Spitfires across to France. Leathart chose Al Deere and Johnny Allen to accompany him, and when interviewed by the author in 1993, recalled:

> We flew low across the Channel to Calais-Marck. I landed and waited for Squadron Leader White to come and jump into the back; after about ten minutes, my engine began to overheat so I decided to take off again, without a passenger. However I had scarcely got my wheels up, when tracer bullets came racing past me; I was being attacked! So I broke the seal on the throttle, to allow extra power from the engine, and did the steepest turn in my life. Two Messerschmitt 109s flashed past me, pursued by my escort. I dropped the Master back on the airfield and jumped out, running for the nearest ditch, and landing right on top of Squadron Leader White who had been hiding there, watching the aerial battle overhead.
>
> We stayed there for some time watching the battle and seeing two Me109s being shot down by Al Deere. During all this time the German tanks and lorries were going along the road at the edge of the airfield towards Dunkirk. Why they never put a shell through the bright yellow painted Master, I will never know.
>
> After about an hour, things looked all right to go back, but it

was only then that I realised that we had no battery starting trolley. We had only had the Master a few days and I did not know if it could be started by hand; however searching through all the likely places we found two starting handles, one fitted on each side of the engine. We cranked furiously with one eye on the German traffic along the road. Eventually, it started and we jumped in with great relief; however, I'd forgotten that the safety seal on the throttle was broken. Giving it full throttle for take-off, the aircraft went up and, to my great surprise, climbed almost vertically. Nevertheless we got home safely and were not shot down by the Navy, when flying at nought feet back across the Channel. We stopped at Manston for fuel and landed at Hornchurch in time for lunch.

Johnny Allen and Deere, who had been circling above the airfield, tackled the German fighters above Calais-Marck; Allen was at 8,000 feet above cloud, and Deere at a lower altitude. Deere recorded the following events in his flying logbook:

P/O Allen and self while escorting Miles Master containing S/Ldr White and F/Lt Leathart were attacked by at least 12 Me109s. P/O Allen was attacked by at least five at once, but managed to come out with three unconfirmed and at least one certainty.

I was fortunate enough to be attacked by only one at a time and got one confirmed, two unconfirmed, one of which was practically certain to have crashed.

We both returned safely. P/O Allen was hit four times and I, luckily enough escaped unharmed. S/Ldr White and F/Lt Leathart returned safely. I used 2,500 rounds of ammunition.

Later that day a signal from Air Vice-Marshal Keith Park, commander of 11 Group, was sent to Hornchurch and read to the pilots of 54 Squadron:

Air Officer Commanding sends congratulations to No.54 Squadron on the magnificent fight put up by Flying Officers Deere and Allen who so severely punished superior numbers this morning.

Years later, Deere still remembered the event in great detail:

It is now recorded history that I was the first Spitfire pilot to have combat with a Messerschmitt 109, and that was over Calais-Marck. While over there, suddenly some 109s appeared. There were two of us at the time. I managed to get on to the tail of one of the 109s and shot him down. He went down into the sea just on the edge of the coastline, and the pilot didn't bale out, he was too low. This all took place at about 500 feet. But of perhaps more interest was the prolonged dogfight I had with a second 109 almost immediately after.

The second 109, with its sleek grey body entrancingly silhouetted against broken white cloud from which it had emerged, flashed in front of me just as I broke from my first engagement. The pilot must have spotted me, for immediately he went into a steep turn clearly intent on getting on my tail. But I had other ideas. I easily maintained my position behind by turning inside him and although out of range I let him have a quick burst – a sort of warning. He reacted instantly as he violently hurled up in a steep climbing turn. Suddenly, he levelled out and as he did so he bunted into a steep dive. In order to follow him I had to roll onto my back; unlike the 109, the Spitfire lacked direct fuel injection and I was unable to follow this unexpected ploy. Pulling hard through the subsequent dive, I lost valuable distance as he dived to low-level. I followed, now somewhat behind.

With full throttle and the gate on extra boost, I gradually closed in again. Clearly the fleeting 109 pilot had his eye on me because as soon as my closing Spitfire threatened, he commenced a series of violent evasive manoeuvres. The adrenalin now in full flow, I hung on grimly.

I could now clearly see the pilot's face as his helmeted head darted from side to side, intent on keeping me in sight. Again I hopefully tried a burst, but it was not possible to bring my guns to bear as, weaving and yawing, he flung his 109 about the sky. And so it went on until sweating from exhaustion, I was forced to accept that I was not going to kill this bird. Also by this time I was a long way from home; I was low on fuel and I had no wish to land in France. Reluctantly, I broke off combat mouthing a silent salute to the worthy opponent who had escaped seemingly unscathed. I landed back at Hornchurch having been airborne for two hours and fifteen minutes, about the maximum for a Spitfire.

Undoubtedly, the 109 in the hands of a good pilot was a tough nut to crack. Initially, it was faster in the dive, but slower in the climb; the Spitfire could out-turn, but it was at a disadvantage in manoeuvres that entailed negative G forces. Overall, there was little to choose between the two fighters.

On 24th May 54 Squadron were patrolling between Dunkirk and Calais when they sighted three large enemy formations consisting of Heinkel He111s, Messerschmitt Me109s and Me110s. James Leathart led the squadron in to attack the bombers, but in doing so was attacked from above and behind by the 109s. Deere, who had already opened fire on one of the bombers, was unable to continue and had to break away from the danger from behind. He engaged one of the fighters and followed a 109 through cloud from 12,000 feet down to 1,000 feet without firing a shot. The enemy fighter then climbed up to 14,000 feet, but Deere was able to stay with his opponent and fire off some short bursts. After Al's fourth burst of fire, the 109 began to stream smoke and flames. He continued to fire short bursts at 150 yards until the German fighter eventually crashed 10 miles north-east of St Omer.

The squadrons at Hornchurch had been exceptionally busy that day and although they had inflicted heavy casualties on the Germans, they had also suffered several pilots killed or taken prisoner of war. 54 Squadron had lost Flying Officer T.N. Linley who had been shot down in Spitfire P9455 and Sergeant J.W.B. Phillips was shot down after strafing a German lorry convoy; he managed to bale out, but was captured.

Keith Park again sent a congratulatory signal to the Hornchurch squadrons:

> By shooting down thirty-seven enemy aircraft today, the four Spitfire squadrons at Hornchurch set up a magnificent record that is especially creditable with such small losses. The Air Officer Commanding sends sincere congratulations and hopes that most of the missing pilots will turn up again shortly. Immediately the critical military situation in France has passed, the squadrons will be given a well-earned short rest.

Operation Dynamo was put into effect at 6.57 pm on Sunday the 26th. 54 Squadron had once more been up early that day on dawn patrol. The Form F below is the Fighter Command Combat Report for it:

F.C.C.R/63/ 40   FORM "F".   SECRET.

FIGHTER COMMAND COMBAT REPORT

To: Fighter Command.

From: No.11 Group.

Composite report.

54 Sqdn patrolling Calais-Dunkirk 0505-0645 at 15,000 feet sighted two Me.110's above. These were attacked, one being shot down. The Squadron were then ordered to rendezvous Calais at 10,000 feet; a destroyer was being bombed by two lone Ju 88's whilst a formation of 20 E/A (14,000 ft) appeared in the distance. 1 Ju88 was shot down and the Sqdn by now split up attacked the Me110's, which formed into a circle making it difficult for our a/c to attack, whilst a number of our a/c found 2 E/A on their tails when attacking a Me110 . . . i.e. once again the enemy rely upon local superiority of at least 2-3 to one, and whilst a number of fighters are lost, the bombers are able to carry out their task with little interference from the air. Towards the end of the combat 12 Me.109s appeared in a line astern circling above Dunkirk.

Only one of our pilots encountered these (no result). It would appear that reinforcements had been called up although one Squadron of our aircraft could not have accounted for the large numbers of a/c present and the Me's themselves made no attempt to take the offensive.

Enemy Casualties.

1 Ju.88 shot down in the sea by F/Lt Leathart (confirmed by P/O Deere)
2 Me.110 (one in flames) by F/Lt Leathart (confirmed by F/S Tew)
1 Me.110 certain by McMullen.
2 Me.110 certain by P/O Deere.
1 Me 110 possible by F/Lt Pearson
1 Me.110 possible by F/S Tew
1 Me.110 possible by P/O Way

Several further E/A were attacked without known results. All our A/C returned safely, one damaged (but serviceable), by cannon fire – which E/A shot from both front and rear guns.

Evasive tactics of E/A during combats were to dive and turn.
1 Me.110 was chased to Lille by F/Lt Pearson before he left (it) in a distressed condition.
R. 1123 26.5.40.

Alan Deere's own combat report covering his action against the two Messerschmitt 110s relays the following:

On approaching Gravelines at 17,000 feet, two enemy aircraft were sighted. Red Leader and I gave chase using 12 boost. These aircraft were identified as Me110s.
Red Leader shot one down in flames. On returning to Gravelines we saw enemy bombers attacking destroyers off Calais. On going into the attack we were in turn attacked by Me110s. I shot one of the Me110s down in flames after three bursts and immediately became sandwiched between two more Me110s, experiencing considerable fire. I steep turned and got on to the tail of one Me110. After three short bursts both of his engines commenced smoking and the enemy rapidly began losing height to the north of Calais. I then returned to base as my port wing was badly shot away.

Deere claimed the two Messerschmitt 110s as destroyed.

It was during this tense exhausting period that Deere met a pilot who would become famous both during wartime and later even more so after the war had ended. While chatting with James Leathart, who was his flight commander, but promoted that day to command the squadron, they were suddenly interrupted by a brash individual, who then proceeded to ask them questions regarding the tactics and combat action over Dunkirk. After a couple of minutes, the RAF officer walked away, looking unimpressed with the answers he had been given. Both Deere and Leathart noticed the strange walk as the pilot went away. This had been their first encounter with Douglas Bader, who had just flown in to operate from Hornchurch with 222 Squadron.

According to Bader's biographer, Paul Brickhill, the 222 Squadron pilots were not impressed with their first sight of those 54 Squadron pilots, some of whom had pistols tucked in their flying boots, or displayed beard stubble. Given the fact that they would have been up by 4 am during the Dunkirk crisis and been flying more or less continuously, this was hardly surprising, however.

Bader was very soon to find out for himself that there was very little time for line-shooting – the pilots at Hornchurch and other airfields involved over France were putting in tremendous flying time over the battle area and indeed were suffering from extreme tiredness. For Bader to suggest that, because a chap had not had time to shave before going into action, it was unacceptable behaviour, was ridiculous. Was this just typical Douglas Bader arrogance or simply ignorance of the facts?

Pilots would have undertaken early dawn patrols and would have continued flying at least two or three more sorties during the day. Under normal circumstances they would have had time to shave and take regular meals etc, but this was far from normal and was an extremely busy military operation.

As Operation Dynamo proceeded, with all available warships and boats evacuating the forces, the situation over the Dunkirk beaches was worsening day by day. There was intense aerial fighting over Dunkirk as the Royal Air Force attempted to reduce the bombing of the troops by the Luftwaffe within the small Allied-held pocket of resistance. On the 27th, 54 Squadron took off on its first patrol at 4.30 am and encountered a Junkers Ju88 at 20,000 feet south-east of Dunkirk. It was attacked, and was last seen heading inland back over France with its starboard engine badly smoking. Its flight commander Max Pearson was seen chasing after it, but was not heard from again, and was listed as missing in action. During the afternoon, the squadron was again patrolling over the Calais/Dunkirk area, when Deere, James Leathart and Johnny Allen sighted several Junkers 88s attacking a white hospital ship. They went into the attack and engaged the German aggressors. Deere claimed one of the bombers destroyed, and a shared victory with Leathart and Allen on another enemy machine. In his combat report, he writes:

> I was flying as No.2 Red Section, which attacked a Junkers Ju88 bomber off Calais at 17,000 feet, when my leader broke away. I went into attack, fired two short bursts and in breaking away saw another Ju88 6,000 feet below me at 4,000 feet.
>
> I dived to the attack (460 mph indicated) and overtook so fast that I had to use all my remaining ammunition in one burst

– using full deflection. The enemy bomber caught fire and
crashed wheels up in fields 15 miles south-east of Calais.

Because of the strength of enemy opposition, RAF Fighter Command
Headquarters decided to try using squadrons over Dunkirk in wing strength,
which might have more impact against the big German formations of escort
fighters, and accordingly on 28th May 19, 54 and 65 Squadrons took off
from Hornchurch at 4.30 am. Unfortunately due to the thundery cloud
conditions and poor visibility, the squadrons soon lost contact with one
another. One of the pilots flying that day with 54 Squadron was Pilot Officer
John Kemp, he had been posted from 609 Squadron at Northolt with another
squadron pilot named Garton. Kemp recalls:

> We travelled down together on 27th May, arriving at
> Hornchurch the same evening. We were introduced to 'Prof'
> Leathart, the newly promoted commanding officer of the
> squadron who was still wearing his flight lieutenant's stripes,
> not having had time to get his new rank stripe sewn on. We
> were asked if we were prepared to fly early the next day and
> were at once detailed for a sortie at 4.30 am. It was to be the
> squadron's last Dunkirk patrol. The 54 Squadron Spitfires were
> fitted with the new VHF radio and the Rotol variable pitch
> propellers as contrasted to the fine and coarse settings of 609's
> aircraft. I was then given cursory instructions on how to use the
> new equipment.

The squadron, consisting of nine aircraft, took off and headed off across the
Channel towards Dunkirk, and at 5.15 am 54 sighted an enemy bomber
flying at an altitude of 6,000 feet. Deere's combat report states:

> I sighted an enemy aircraft to the north of Dunkirk and led two
> sections of the squadron in pursuit. I identified the enemy
> aircraft as a Dornier 215 and when I was about 500 yards
> astern, I encountered fire from its rear-gunner – one shot at
> least entering my engine. I closed to about 200 yards, firing
> half my ammunition before I was forced to land on the beach
> between Nieuport and Dunkirk. After I had force landed I saw
> the Dornier (which had been attacked by others of the
> squadron) crash.

Pilot Officer John Kemp:

> We passed a lone Lysander aircraft on the way and later saw a
> single Dornier 17. Al Deere who was leading the squadron
> ordered the section of three aircraft that I was in and which was
> led by Colin Gray, to stay on guard at high level whilst the
> others dived down to attack. As Al turned in behind the
> Dornier, I saw a trail of white glycol vapour coming from his
> aircraft where the rear gunner had hit him. Al was forced to

crash land in France. 'Red' Garton was lucky enough to have been detailed to one of the other sections and was able to fire his guns and claim a fifth share of the destruction of the Dornier.

Fifty years later, Alan Deere reflected on that day:

At Dunkirk, I regret to say I was shot down by the rear-gunner of a Dornier, which eventually came down itself. It was fairly cloudy and this Dornier had just appeared out of the clouds over the bridgehead; I had my flight with me and we chased him. I got onto his tail and fired a burst at him. I could see return fire from the rear-gunner and suddenly I felt a juddering sort of thing. I think I was fairly lucky; a bullet from the gunner went into my glycol tank, which meant my coolant system was gone.

I had to come down and I crash-landed on the beach between Nieuport and Ostend. The smoking Dornier came down over the top of me, and glided away inland. I think he must have landed somewhere further inland.

I wasn't injured until I landed. Then I hit my head on the front of the cockpit and cut it, which knocked me out momentarily; it cut a gash on my forehead. I had landed wheels-up of course, right on the edge of the water, and the tide happened to be coming in when I came to. I scrambled out of the thing, got my parachute out and walked up the beach towards a cafe I could see further up the beach. By that time the tide was gradually coming up over the Spitfire and it was never recovered, so I imagine it sank into the sand.

Anyway, I had this bad cut on my forehead and at this small cafe on the coast, a young woman said that I was bleeding rather badly. She stuck it together with plaster and put a bandage around it. I knew they were evacuating from Dunkirk, so I set off for there. I expect it took me around two or three hours because there was a lot of refugee traffic. Eventually I found a bicycle, which I saw lying unattended and got onto it and rode off. I was originally going to go to Ostend, but I met a couple of British Army Tommies inland. I said to them, 'Where are you going?' They said, 'You tell us.' I said, 'Aren't you evacuating?' They replied that they were staying put until they had met up with some of their particular company, but they were eventually heading for Dunkirk. So that's where I went with the soldiers.

When I arrived there it was pretty hectic, with the strafing and the bombing; we were on the beach taking cover. There was an organisation run by the Army to get off the beach; you got into a sort of line. At the time I got out, they were still able to get the ships alongside the jetty at Dunkirk; a destroyer had come in and I'd been able to get on it. But there were other people swimming out to the boats and other things.

The conditions aboard the destroyer were very cramped; we were crowded out with soldiers, 'stuffed to the gills' in fact. We were bombed near to pulling off, but fortunately the cloud was fairly low, which made the Germans' accuracy poor and we didn't get hit.

The soldiers aboard gave me a very rough time; they were very anti-RAF. They said where the hell had we been, and I who had been flying ten days non-stop until the time I was shot down, flying two or three sorties a day, was feeling pretty tired.

I answered in no mean manner and said, 'We were there, and perhaps you didn't see us.' They weren't very pleased with me; I was the only airman on board of course. They were pretty unpleasant I suppose, but one couldn't blame them really, they were rather worn out, you know.

After Dunkirk, the squadron was moved up to Catterick in Yorkshire for re-equipping and rest. We had lost quite a few pilots. I think there were about eight of us left; some were shot down and didn't come back, some were badly injured and we had lost both of our flight commanders. In fact our casualties for the amount of flying we did and in the timespan was greater at Dunkirk than during the Battle of Britain.

On 4th June 54 Squadron returned to take up its role at Hornchurch, re-equipped with replacement Spitfires and some new pilots, and prepared themselves for the battle that they knew must shortly be coming. The *London Gazette* dated 14th June 1940 carried the official announcement of Alan Deere's award of the Distinguished Flying Cross. The recommendation stated:

During the period 21st May to 28th May 1940 inclusive, Pilot Officer Deere has, in company with his squadron (No.54), taken part in a large number of offensive patrols over Northern France, and has been engaged in seven combats, in some of which his squadron was outnumbered by as many as six to one. In the course of these combats he shot down two Me110s, two Me109s and one Ju88 himself, and one Me109 and one Ju88 in conjunction with other members of his section, all of which are confirmed. In addition he has to his credit one Me109, which is not confirmed, and a further unconfirmed Me109 and Ju88 in conjunction with other pilots.

On one occasion, in company with one other pilot, he acted as escort to a Miles Master which was proceeding to Calais to rescue a squadron commander who had been shot down there. When taking off from Calais, the Master was attacked by 12

Me109s and Pilot Officer Deere, in company with the other pilot, unhesitatingly engaged these much superior forces, successfully driving them off, and between them shooting down three of the enemy and badly damaging a further three.

Throughout these engagements this officer has shown great courage and determination in pressing home his attacks in the face of great odds, and his skill and offensive spirit has enabled him to destroy or damage seven enemy aircraft.

Pilot Officer Deere was reported as 'Missing' after taking part in an offensive patrol on the morning of 28th May 1940, when his aircraft was shot down in the neighbourhood of Dunkirk. He was uninjured and reported by R/T that he had landed safely.

On 17th June, the whole squadron was ordered to patrol German-occupied French airfields in the Abbeville area. Eleven aircraft took off at 8.33 pm and were diverted to investigate X-Raids over Boulogne. Red Section encountered three Junkers Ju88s operating independently. During the encounter both Squadron Leader Leathart and Al Deere severely damaged one of the Ju88s. They both claimed a half share on the bomber as an unconfirmed kill.

On 20th June 1940, *Flight* published the RAF announcement of awards that James Leathart, Johnny Allen and Al Deere were to receive in recognition of their gallantry displayed in flying operations against the enemy. Deere's announcement read:

During May, this officer has in company with his squadron, taken part in numerous offensive patrols over northern France, and has been engaged in seven combats often against superior numbers. In these engagements, he has personally shot down five enemy aircraft and assisted in the destruction of others. On one occasion, in company with a second aircraft, he attacked 12 Messerschmitt 109s with the result that three enemy aircraft were shot down and a further three severely damaged.

Seven days later, on 27th June, the telephone rang at 54 Squadron's dispersal hut down at Hornchurch's satellite airfield, Rochford. Alan Deere had just returned from a routine training flight with some replacement pilots, when he was greeted by Johnny Allen, who informed him that their immediate presence was required back at RAF Hornchurch. The only information that they could manage to extract from the squadron adjutant was that an important dignitary was going to arrive that morning. Both Deere and Allen tidied themselves up and jumped into the squadron's Miles Magister and flew back to Hornchurch. The station seemed to be a hive of activity, with airmen and ground staff preparing for the arrival of the VIP. Presenting themselves to the Station Commander, Group Captain Bouchier, they were told to prepare to receive a visit by His Majesty King George VI, and the Commander-in-

Chief of Fighter Command, Air Chief Marshal Sir Hugh Dowding. The King was to present Deere, Allen and Leathart with their awards for bravery during the Calais-Marck rescue, together with those to other Hornchurch notables Robert Stanford Tuck and 'Sailor' Malan.

Various ranks were drawn up in columns to form a small square between two of the hangars. On arrival the King, with Dowding and his aides, walked to where the awards were to be presented. After an opening address, Squadron Leader Ronald Adam, the station operations controller, read aloud the citations for the individual recipients as they stepped forward to receive their decorations. Alan Deere stepped forward and saluted, while the King pinned the Distinguished Flying Cross on to his tunic. Deere would later recall that it was one of the greatest moments of his life. After the ceremony was completed, all the pilots who had been decorated joined the King for refreshments back at the officers' mess. Deere was able to talk briefly with the King and found him to be well informed and genuinely interested in what the pilots had to say. As His Majesty left to go back to London, all the officers lined up outside the officers' mess for his departure and cheered. The following day, Deere and the rest of Hornchurch resumed their operational status and prepared for Hitler's next move.

CHAPTER 3

THE BATTLE FOR BRITAIN

With the Luftwaffe now occupying the French airfields nearest to Britain, Germany now prepared for the next phase of its European conquest. On 22nd June France signed its armistice with Germany; the invasion of Britain would be next on the agenda. Their first objective would be to destroy the Royal Air Force's Fighter Command in order to gain air superiority before the seaborne invasion could sweep across the Channel to land on the south coast of England. Alan Deere remembers this crucial time waiting for the Luftwaffe to make its move against Britain:

> The Battle of Britain was a gradual build-up. In July, we were doing convoy patrols again, because by that time the Germans had occupied the Channel coast and the convoys had to be protected. We had the odd engagements; I had one engagement with a Dornier for example and managed to shoot it down.
>
> Then we went from convoy patrols to a more defensive role in that the Germans started to send formations of fighters across with the intention of drawing us up into combat and of course hoping to destroy the fighter force before they launched an invasion. So gradually through July, the tempo was being built up and we were doing three or four sorties a day, not always getting into combat, but mostly. The Germans were getting more and more aggressive as they built up their forces on the other side of the Channel. Their penetration at the time was only twenty to thirty miles inland in to England, but their intention was to get our squadrons up and knock us out. Fortunately Dowding and his Group Commander, Park, realised this would probably be their aim and therefore the number of RAF fighter squadrons committed to battle at any one time was fairly restricted, so we always had a reserve.
>
> Eventually of course, the German bombers came over and their first targets were the coastal airfields such as Manston, Hawkinge and Tangmere. Then the real fighting started in that we were not only coping with fighter escorts, but with bombers as well. Gradually they moved their penetration further and

further until they were bombing the London airfields, where all
the sector controls were based.

During the late afternoon of 9th July, two sections of 54 were patrolling over
the area between Deal and Dover. Deere was leading Red Section, while
Johnny Allen led Yellow. Within the next few minutes Deere's skill and luck
would see him survive another close brush with death. His combat report
details what happened next:

> I was leading 'A' Flight on a patrol over Deal at 6,000 feet,
> when I sighted a silver seaplane approaching Deal at 100 feet.
> Four Me109s were flying above and in front. I ordered Yellow
> Leader to attack the seaplane with his section. I led my section
> towards the Me109s, but on doing so saw about another 12
> 109s flying in loose formation close to the water.
>
> I ordered my section into line astern, but apparently the
> order was not received as pilots broke away to engage the
> enemy. I attacked the tail end aircraft of the original four from
> above and behind. It dived straight into the sea after I had given
> two bursts of fire. I then pulled up, climbing for height, and
> reported to home station that the seaplane had landed in the
> water, ten miles east of Deal.
>
> I then dived down to attack the seaplane, but saw an Me109
> endeavouring to position itself on my tail. I turned towards him
> and opened fire at about 1,000 yards head-on. He was also
> firing and I could hear his bullets striking my fuselage. We both
> held our fire and apparently my propeller hit some of his
> fuselage as he passed, because two tips were bent right back
> and my hood had been pushed in. The engine vibrated
> tremendously and then stopped dead; smoke then began to
> come out.
>
> I was heading landwards at the time of collision and carried
> on for an open field. Flames then appeared at 1,000 feet and I
> was unable to see ahead, eventually crash-landing in a field.
> The aircraft was burning fiercely, but I managed to break the
> hood open and get out with slight injury.

Deere had crash-landed his Spitfire at Gunstan Farm, Ash, five miles from
Manston. What he does not mention in his combat report was the terrific
struggle he had to fight his way out of his aircraft once he had landed. While
still airborne and with smoke pouring into his cockpit, he had tried to release
his cockpit hood, but this would not budge. He tried this several times but
to no avail. He had had no choice but to try to land the aircraft by gliding it
down in open countryside. Once he had survived the landing, which was not
without its dangers, such as crashing through the anti-invasion posts, which
had been erected in the field, he still had to struggle to open the perspex
hood. Through a combination of strength and fear, he managed to punch his

THE BATTLE FOR BRITAIN

way through the perspex and free himself from the burning wreck. He staggered to a safe distance and fell to the ground exhausted from his efforts. A few minutes later he watched as his Spitfire succumbed to the flames. The aircraft had ploughed through three fields, which were covered with its debris.

Taking stock of himself, he found he had cut his hands badly in the effort to break free, both of his knees were bruised and the fire had singed his eyebrows; he had also a slight cut to his lip.

As he sat contemplating his situation, a woman approached him, from a nearby farmhouse, having witnessed his landing. She informed Al that she had already telephoned the airfield at Manston and that an ambulance and fire engine had been despatched. She then invited him to her farmhouse for a cup of tea. Al asked her if he could partake of something a little stronger and she said she thought there might be a bottle of whisky in the house. As they walked to the woman's abode, a small gathering of people arrived at the crash-site. Al warned them not to get too close, as there was still the danger of exploding ammunition and fuel. His announcement had the desired effect and they all began to move back. A short while later the ambulance and fire engine arrived and with them a medical officer who gave Deere a quick examination before driving him back to Manston to have his wounds dressed. He remained at the airfield overnight and was returned back to his home base the following morning by Flying Officer Ben Bowring in a Tiger Moth trainer.

Many years later in 1987, the collision incident was brought back to life, when historian David Smith, together with American aviation artist Jerry Crandall embarked on a project to portray a painting showing the dramatic collision that Deere had survived on 9th July 1940. During the research for the painting, Dave Smith uncovered that there was some confusion as to which aircraft Deere had been flying that day. It had always been thought that he had been flying Spitfire P9390, but this aircraft had been lost on 7th July 1940, after being force-landed by Pilot Officer Jack Coleman. The salvage reports from 49 Maintenance Unit confirm that Spitfire N3183 was salvaged at Ash. Another thing Smith and Crandall discovered was the name of the pilot with whose aircraft Deere had collided on that day. Deere's opponent had been Oberfeldwebel Johann Illner of 4 Staffel JG 51. His aircraft was Messerschmitt Bf 109E-4, Work No. 1160 and coded 'White 2'. After colliding with Deere, Illner had managed to nurse his badly damaged aircraft back across the Channel to land in France. He claimed Deere's Spitfire as a victory. Johann Illner claimed seven victories before he was himself shot down on 7th November 1940. He spent the rest of the war in a prisoner of war camp.

Another point of interest regarding the day's actions concerned the German seaplane that 54 Squadron had attacked prior to Deere's head-on collision. The aircraft, a Heinkel He59B-2 with code letters D-ASUO of Seenotflug-kommando, had been attacked by Johnny Allen and forced to land in the sea on the Goodwin Sands, where it became stranded. The crew, which comprised three Unteroffiziers (Corporals) Helmut Bartmann, Walter Anders and Erich Schiele and Unterfeldwebel Gunther Maywald, were all captured. The Heinkel was eventually towed by the Walmer lifeboat and beached at Deal, but the aircraft was later destroyed by German bombing. Sadly, 54 Squadron suffered two pilots killed during the engagement with the seaplane and its Messerschmitt fighter escort; Pilot Officer Tony Evershed was killed south of Dover at 7.15 pm, and Pilot Officer Garton was shot down 15 minutes later near Manston.

On 24th July 54 Squadron was ordered off at midday to patrol over Deal. At 12.25 pm, while at a height of 7,000 feet, the squadron sighted a large formation of around 40 enemy bombers with their escort fighters, which were layered above, and some partially hidden by, cloud. The formation was heading up the Thames estuary.

Deere, who was flying that day in Spitfire R6895, relates in his combat report:

> There were three Me109s and a further 12 above and in cloud. I told Blue Leader to go for the first three and I would take my section above after the other nine. At that moment nine He113s (109s) came from behind and I saw them in time to avoid being shot at. I managed to stall turn into their tails and fire a burst into the centre of the formation, which then broke up. Other 109s then came down and a dogfight ensued.
>
> I had general wild bursts at various aircraft, but was unable to get a decent bead on any of them, because of constant attacks from behind. I managed however one decent long burst of fire at a 109 at close range and he went down with glycol pouring from his machine.

Years later Deere recalled his first victory in what was to become famous as the Battle of Britain:

> My flight was ordered off to intercept, in the words of the Controller Ronnie Adam, '50+ enemy aircraft approaching from the east at 17,000 feet'. And they were at this height, a force of at least 50 Heinkels escorted by Me109s. It was a black spotted mass, which forged its way across the sky intent on reaching its target – a convoy of some 20 merchant ships, which puffed and smoked a passage through the troubled English Channel.
>
> 'Tally Ho' Red Leader, the sighting report came excitedly over the R/T from my number two. I replied, 'Yes I've seen them. We'll climb up behind the fighters and try and draw them off.' So I issued my orders to my flight of six aircraft against 50+. We were to become accustomed to such odds. On sighting an overwhelmingly large enemy formation, there was a sort of hysterical humour at the hopelessness of the task, erased

almost immediately by the onset of quick stabbing shafts of fear as the enemy drew closer, and finally, before joining combat, a consciousness of thudding heart and moist brow, accompanied by a breathless panicky fear.

The enemy fighter escort was not drawn off; indeed, it was we who were diverted from our task of getting at the bombers by a frontal assault by a small detachment of 109s, which had broken formation to ward off the Spitfires.

'Attack individually,' I ordered. I barely had time to issue the order before the 109s were among us. My experience over Dunkirk had taught me that when attacked the best counter was to go into a right turn. In this manoeuvre, the Spitfire was infinitely superior to the Messerschmitt, and so long as one remained in the turn, the enemy pilot could not bring his guns to bear. And this I did, as the German pilot flashed past, turning as he did so, to get behind me. But it was I who finished astern of him.

The rest was easy. He could not escape the lethal burst of fire from my eight Browning guns, which poured incendiary and armour-piercing bullets into the Messerschmitt. For a time it seemed to absorb them without any apparent damage, but then a small yellow flame began to appear from behind the Germans' cockpit. Black smoke spouted from the engine and then, as if a time bomb had ignited, the fighter exploded in a shower of hot flaming metal, which I avoided by breaking away and up.

My first victory in the Battle of Britain hurtled towards the ground, its pilot undoubtedly dead in the cockpit.

In fact for almost an hour 54 battled with the enemy formation whose target had been a convoy in the estuary. On returning to base, the squadron claimed 16 Me109s despatched with the following claims by the pilots:

2 Destroyed confirmed (P/O Gray & Sgt Collett)

4 Destroyed unconfirmed (F/Lt Deere – leading the squadron – F/O McMullen, P/O Coleman, P/O Turley-George)

8 Probably destroyed (F/O McMullen, F/Lt Way (two) P/O Gray, P/O Gribble (two) F/Sgt Tew, P/O Turley-George)

2 Damaged (P/O Coleman and P/O Matthews)

Unfortunately the success of the claims was soured for Deere by the tragic loss of his friend, the popular Johnny Allen. His aircraft had been damaged by an enemy fighter, which had caused the Spitfire's engine to stop. He was making for land to undertake a forced landing, when his engine appeared to come to life again. On hearing this Allen must have decided to head for the airfield at Manston, but the engine cut out again causing the aircraft to stall and spin straight into the ground at Cliftonville, Kent. Pilot Officer Allen was killed instantly.

The only other casualty was Sergeant Collett who had to force-land his Spitfire at Sizewell near Orfordness after running out of petrol during a prolonged chase after a Me109. He suffered slight injuries on landing. That same day, Deere was given the rank of acting flight lieutenant to lead A Flight.

On 31st July, Deere and the rest of 54 received the signal to take them north to Catterick to take a well-earned rest, regroup, and to take on new pilots. During its eight-day break the squadron continued to fly non-operational training to help the new pilots accustom themselves to their aircraft and tactics. At midday on 8th August, the squadron arrived back down south at Hornchurch with 22 pilots and aircraft, and by 3.30 pm had proceeded to carry out a patrol over Manston for nearly an hour without sighting the enemy.

On 11th August, RAF Hornchurch laid on entertainment for the pilots and ground staff, with the famous Windmill Girls arriving from London to do a performance. Ricky Richardson remembers this particular show:

> On the occasion when the Windmill Girls arrived, Al Deere came into land and he had something wrong with his aircraft. I think it was something to do with the spark plugs and the engine was running red-hot. But there was not much I could do about it till the engine had cooled. Al wanted the plugs changed immediately and I complained bitterly that I had got myself a seat to see the Windmill Girls. I thought that was that, I won't see them now. Anyhow, I changed the plugs and arrived later during the performance and went in, and Al had saved me a seat right beside him, right up the front, which I thought was quite nice of him.

During August, Vickers Supermarine sent their test pilot Jeffrey Quill to Hornchurch to find out first hand about the Spitfire's capabilities in combat. He was sent to fly with 65 Squadron, but recalls meeting Al Deere in the Hornchurch Mess and talking with him about his experiences in air combat. Deere obviously passed on his own rules and advice, which Quill later quoted in his own book *Spitfire*:

> I learned much, which I have no doubt contributed towards my own subsequent survival. From this and other sources I acquired that evening, many nuggets of sound advice such as: 'Get in close as you can, you're usually further away than you think.' 'You get shot down yourself by the man you don't see.' 'If you hit a 109 don't follow him down to see him crash – another will get you while you're doing it.' 'You need eyes in the back of your head.' 'Scan the sky constantly – it's essential you see them before they see you.' 'Never get separated if you

can help it – and don't hang about on your own.'

On 12th August, the squadron undertook two patrols and both resulted in combat with the Luftwaffe. During the morning at 11.34 Pilot Officer Colin Gray claimed two Me109s destroyed, while Pilot Officer Henry Matthews claimed one 109 destroyed and one probable. Later that day Al Deere added further to his own score by claiming an Me109 and 110 both destroyed during an engagement 10 miles out to sea off North Foreland. He recalls in his general report for that day the combat that took place:

> I was leading 54 Squadron (11 aircraft – two sections of four and one section of three) on a patrol inland of Dover at 21,000 feet, when a raid was reported over Manston aerodrome. I saw 50 bombers over North Foreland turning from west to east. At this moment Blue Leader gave a Tally-Ho of aircraft over Dover. I instructed him to remain with me and we would attack the raid over Manston, which at a distance appeared unescorted.
>
> Blue Leader did not hear this order and together with Yellow Section engaged the bombers over Dover. I did not realise that Blue Leader had left me until I came within striking distance of the enemy bombers, which were now flying east, 10 miles off North Foreland; he then said he was engaged over Dover. Messerschmitt 109s appeared from the left as I closed in on the bombers, so I gave the order for my section to break and engage the fighters. After a quick turn I saw a Me109 shoot a Spitfire down in flames, and I got on the Me109's tail and dived from 17,000 to 11,000 feet firing short bursts at 250 yards. The enemy aircraft burst into flames and continued in a vertical dive towards the sea.
>
> On the return journey I ran into about 12 Me110s in mid-Channel and was able to surprise them as I was approaching from the direction of the French coast. I fired a long burst at about 150 yards and the enemy turned for France. I fired two more long bursts using deflection and the enemy aircraft prepared to pancake on to the sea. I followed him down and saw a man climbing into a rubber dinghy. I then had a front gun exercise [sic] at him, but unfortunately a 109 came from out of the blue and shot the hell out of me. I quickly retired and headed for home using 12 boost.

With the German raids increasing in strength and size as the intensity of the battle developed, how did Deere and his fellow squadron members decide what tactics to use against the overwhelming numbers of enemy aircraft? In his own words:

> It so happened that by that time my squadron had Spitfires with constant speed propellers. The original Spitfire MkIa had a

two-speed airscrew, either fully fine or fully course. No.54 was experimenting with the new Rotol constant speed airscrew which was very quickly coming into use, and as a result we were sent up to operate at high altitude to draw off the German fighter escorts, normally at 30-35,000 feet. We would climb straight out from Hornchurch. Originally we moved down to the forward base at Manston, which was hell as we were getting strafed and bombed there; it was the first airfield the Germans would sight and the last one they would sight, so they got it both ways. At Manston we would take off and climb back inland to get height; but at Hornchurch we would climb flat out to height, because the raids were becoming so big, and once they were committed, you could see them for miles once you were up there. As for tactics, we just hoped we had got in the best position to attack. Our job was to deal with the fighters and draw them off, which we did fairly successfully, and which helped the Hurricane pilots deal with the bombers.

The German air armadas were frightening; you would see this great mass of aircraft in the distance, just black spots. You'd see the bombers first obviously, because they were in close formation and as they got closer you would see little black specs weaving all around them. You knew these would be the 109s and there seemed to be no way of stopping them. We were operating in squadrons and flights depending on the time you had to scramble and get airborne. It was probably the best way we could have operated anyway as it gave us some flexibility as we were always outnumbered.

As the battle for the skies over southern England intensified, the squadrons at Hornchurch were on a state of constant readiness. During the morning of 15th August, the pilots of 54 Squadron were sent scrambling for their aircraft, when the Operations Room picked up information of an incoming raid at 11.00 am. Once in the air, the 12 aircraft of 54 were ordered to intercept the Germans over the Dover and Hawkinge area. The Spitfires were at 16,000 and still climbing, when they met about 40 Me109s. Surprisingly, as soon as the 109s sighted 54, they half-rolled and streaked back towards Calais, losing all formation. In the ensuing chase, Deere latched on to a couple of fleeting 109s:

I shot at two of these and succeeded (with a long burst from astern – range 300-250 yards) in bringing one down in flames. I saw it dive from 17,000 feet down to 1,000 feet, before I had to break away.

I then understood that Hawkinge was being bombed and proceeded there, climbing to 18,000 feet, where I encountered a number of He113s. [In fact He113 never actually saw service but was constantly and incorrectly misidentified. All the

German single-engine fighters during the battle were 109s.]
These were circling above and obviously staying to protect
bombers.

I managed to get on the tail of one and had no difficulty in
overtaking it. I got in a number of rounds from astern and must
have damaged him badly as glycol was streaming out. I
followed the enemy aircraft back to Calais at 18,000 feet
before returning.

Landing at Hornchurch's forward base at Manston, Deere claimed one
Messerschmitt 109 destroyed and the other damaged.

During early evening at around 6.00 pm, 54 was again sent aloft to
investigate and engage an enemy formation over the Maidstone area. At
6.26 over Maidstone the 12 aircraft sighted a formation of Dornier bombers
at 18-19,000 feet together with their fighter escort of some 50-strong 109s,
whose altitude ranged from 23-25,000 feet, all heading towards London.
The Spitfires climbed to engage the fighters and battle commenced at
19,000 feet. Deere managed to get in a short burst of machine-gun fire at
200 yards on one of the fighters before he was forced to break away. He then
followed two Me109s who had broken away from the main combat and
were now heading back across the Channel. After a long chase, he
eventually caught up with them. Now at 17,000 feet, he fired at the first one
from a range of 300 yards. There seemed to be no response whatsoever from
the German pilot, who took no evasive action. Deere later recalled that his
machine-gun fire must have killed the pilot, because the German's machine
went straight down into the sea with glycol and smoke pouring from it.

With one of the Messerschmitts downed, Deere concentrated on the other.
He once again attacked the surviving German in the same way and again
glycol and smoke began to appear. This time however, he did not see the
German aircraft crash. Deere had become aware of how far he had now
travelled inland from the French coast. Coming out of cloud, he found
himself over Calais-Marck Aerodrome. Within an instant, he was suddenly
confronted by the appearance of five Me109s who appeared from nowhere
and began to attack. Deere's report of the encounter makes harrowing
reading and shows how lucky he was to escape against such odds, while
caught on the wrong side of the Channel:

Five Messerschmitts appeared from nowhere and chased me
back over the Channel. They were very fast and must have been
within range most of the time. My instrument panel and hood
were shot about and the machine sustained heavy damage. I
was at only 800 feet above the sea, when the enemy aircraft left
me at Folkestone. I continued inland, but my engine stopped
and the aircraft began to catch fire. I managed to gain a little
height (up to 1,500 feet) when I baled out.

I just felt the jerk of my parachute opening, when some tall
trees broke my fall. My machine crashed 50 yards from me.

My only injury was a sprained wrist. The 109s, which had
attacked, not only had yellow on the wing tips, but also on the
top of the tail.

In fact, his departure from his Spitfire R6981 had also been somewhat
dramatic and was not mentioned in his report. While he was leaving the
stricken aircraft, his parachute had become caught within the cockpit. He
struggled to free himself and the parachute, but with the substantial airflow
it forced him backwards and pinned him against the fuselage. The Spitfire
was now almost at the vertical when at last he somehow broke free, but he
was hurled backwards and struck his right wrist a glancing blow against the
tail plane. He pulled the ripcord immediately with just seconds to spare. Just
after the parachute opened, he touched the ground with a heavy thud.
Somewhat dazed and surprised at how little injury he had sustained in the
fall, he began to try and release his parachute.

It was while still trying to unravel himself from this predicament that
Deere was surprised when two men suddenly appeared from nowhere. They
were both RAF airmen who had seen his aircraft fall from the sky. Both had
been on their way to Kenley. One introduced himself to Deere as an
ambulance driver while the other was a nursing orderly. They helped him
carefully into their vehicle and began the long and uncomfortable journey to
Kenley. It was at this point that the orderly pointed out that Deere's
wristwatch looked as if it had taken a severe bashing. All that appeared to
be left was the strap and the outer casing. On further investigation, he
noticed that on the top of his hand was a short red graze mark, and came to
the conclusion that during combat an enemy bullet had shot the main
mechanism of the watch completely away.

During the early part of the journey Deere had managed to fall asleep in
the back of the ambulance, but he awoke sometime later to find that the
airmen had lost their way. By this time, the injury to his wrist was beginning
to cause extreme pain, and he suspected it might be broken. After much
debate, the airmen finally realised that they had taken the wrong road,
although they were certain they were near East Grinstead, which in fact
turned out to be the case.

Arriving there, they drove to the Queen Victoria Hospital, where Deere
was at once admitted and attended to by a nursing sister. She examined his
wrist and noted that it looked in bad shape due to the swelling and purple
bruising around the joint. She gave him a couple of sleeping tablets and told
him that an X-ray would have to be taken the following morning. He then
asked the nurse if she could contact Hornchurch to tell them he was safe.
Deere was then taken into one of the small wards at the hospital and in no
time the sleeping tablets took their effect.

On awaking next morning he asked one of the nursing staff whether
Hornchurch had been informed, but was told that she had not been able to
get a message through. The consequence of this was that his parents in New
Zealand were informed the following day, that their son was listed as

'Missing in Action'. That morning an X-ray was taken, but fortunately it showed no breakage in the wrist, although it was encased in plaster as a precaution. By this time Deere was eager to get back to Hornchurch, but was held up from leaving the hospital awaiting his final release, which could only be obtained from the medical superintendent. It was while he was waiting that the air-raid siren suddenly sounded and pandemonium erupted as patients and nursing staff began to make their hasty way to the shelters. During this alarm Alan Deere quietly slipped away out of the hospital and to the railway station to catch a train back to Hornchurch.

When interviewed years later, Deere recalled his hospital stay and also meeting fellow New Zealander Archibald McIndoe:

> If my recollection serves me it was at East Grinstead Hospital where I met Archie McIndoe, the famous plastic surgeon. He came to see me; it was getting late in the evening by then. I wasn't burnt, but I was in great pain from this injury to my wrist. They gave me an X-ray and found nothing was broken, but it was badly sprained. He said I'd have to have it in a sling and taped up. He said, 'You could stay here and have a rest for two to three days.' Well the next morning there was an air raid, and everybody evacuated to the shelters; I evacuated myself to the railway station, and got a train back to Hornchurch. McIndoe was furious with me; he'd apparently rung the station commander at Hornchurch earlier and said he had got me there at the hospital. The station commander's reply to what Archie had said was, 'Keep the little bugger there for a day or two.' When I arrived back at the airfield, much to the surprise of the station commander, he didn't say anything; just, 'You got back rather quickly.' I was flying again the next day.

In one of his letters to his parents in New Zealand, Al told them about his experiences during the battle:

Hornchurch 18.8.40

Dear Mum and Dad,

I received your first lot of letters for about two months, so I expect half yours, like mine, are at the bottom of the sea or stranded. I also received a letter from Henry Burroughs for which you might thank him, as I really have no time to answer it. Your letters were dated in the middle of June, as it has taken about two months for them to arrive. As for getting a photo taken to send to you, I just haven't the bally time.

The last two weeks have been one hell of a fight and we are beating the stuffing out of the Huns. My squadron has now reached a century, we are claimed as the crack Spitfire squadron and I myself have now sixteen, being top scorer in Home Defence squadrons. We have had some grand fights and it makes a great difference being over one's own territory. I have been shot down again and had my narrowest escape.

I became mixed up with five of Germany's newest fighters – Heinkel 113 – and managed to get two before they got me. My machine caught on fire at 1,500 feet and I baled out. Unfortunately I got caught halfway out and could not free myself. Somehow or other I came free and the parachute had no sooner opened than I hit the ground – talk about a delayed drop – Phew!!

Most of our fighting these days is done between 20,000 and 30,000 feet and it makes me very tired. I have just returned from twenty-four hour's leave, having been shot up again. I had my watch shot off my wrist, the bullet making a sort of groove across the back of my wrist. Another bullet came through the hood and clipped my left eye sufficiently to make it bleed and then went out through the other side of the hood. Some shooting. They wanted me to take seven day's leave, but I wouldn't go.

Colin Gray, the other New Zealander, has just been awarded the DFC; he is second to me in total with 11. The counties of Essex and Kent are an amazing sight these days, just strewn with the wreckage of German bombers from which the swastikas are collected. They dragged German bodies out of the wreckage and I'll bet they were sorry they came our way.

The RAF is tremendously popular over here now and it seems rather embarrassing. I went to a big theatre in London with Mary the other night and there was a newsreel showing dogfights and German bombers coming down in flames, everybody clapped and cheered. Unfortunately for me, when the news was over and the lights went up, somebody saw me sitting in front wearing a DFC ribbon and my hand in a bandage and immediately everybody began to clap. I wish the ground could have opened up and swallowed me.

I am enclosing a clipping where I appear in the *Daily Sketch* Roll of Honour (not of the dead, thank God!)

I was talking to a New Zealander today who had seen Terry Deere at Aldershot. I have not seen or heard from him and if he hasn't the energy to write or ring me, I can't be bothered chasing him.

Well, there is nothing much else to write, much is on the same lines. The Huns are expected to come over again in hordes and we expect to shoot them down in hordes.

Love
Alan

One incident, which took place at Hornchurch, and which is worth recalling, was when a captured German Luftwaffe officer was brought under guard into the station in August. Wing Commander Frank Dowling OBE, who was then Pilot Officer Dowling, and the assistant station adjutant, remembers that Al Deere was none too pleased:

We had heard that one German aircraft had been shot down near the airfield, and that the surviving crew had been rounded up. They were brought to the station and led into the station adjutant's office; they consisted of a German major and two NCOs. They were marched into the presence of Flight Lieutenant George Kerr and myself. The Germans clicked their heels and bowed; they were quite smart-looking chaps. I knew that Flying Officer Tubby Markwick, whom I had succeeded as assistant adjutant, spoke German. So he was sent for to look after the major and take him over to the officers' mess. The station warrant officer dealt with the two NCOs, taking them to the sergeants' mess.

It was whilst in the officers' mess, that one of our chaps reminded the German major that a German delegation had visited Hornchurch earlier, in 1938. With that the German replied, 'We will all be here soon' or words to that effect. Later that evening Al Deere strolled in and seeing the German officer, walked over to him, feeling like belting him one. Al said, 'Why do you buggers always run away, and shout "Achtung Spitfeur" as soon as you see us?' Al couldn't stand them.

Deere like many other pilots at this time was increasingly having to deal with the disadvantage of attacking the enemy while on the climb to gain height and be above the enemy to gain superiority during battle. It was while climbing to engage that pilots felt vulnerable to being bounced by the Messerschmitt 109. Deere gave his own assessment on the German fighter:

The Messerschmitt 109 was the most feared; the Me110, which was a twin-engine fighter-bomber was very easy to combat against. It was slower, they had a rear-gun, but that was pretty useless and the Germans eventually withdrew the aircraft from escort because of its vulnerability. The 109 was a tough customer; they were well flown and they had a .5 cannon in the nose which was pretty lethal. [A misconception. It had a 20mm cannon in each wing and two rifle-calibre machine guns in the nose.] We always tried to get above the 109s if possible and come down on them from out of the sun if we could, but it didn't always work that way. Sometimes they engaged you; you didn't see them and we were bounced.

People ask 'Were you frightened?' Yes, we were frightened. On taking off, you'd have a gut fear and the adrenaline would be pumping and there's no time to be frightened, but clearly you are.

With the squadron losing pilots either killed or wounded every day or two, new young fresh-faced, but inexperienced men would arrive to make up the losses. One of these was Sergeant Pilot Leslie Walter Harvey. Les was given his first operational posting and joined 54 Squadron at RAF Hornchurch on 22nd August 1940. He recalls:

> I arrived at Hornchurch with another young fresh-faced pilot by the name of Ronnie Stillwell; in fact we drove down in his car, an old Singer 9. He went into 65 Squadron, I didn't see him again as 65 shortly afterwards went up to RAF Turnhouse in Scotland. I remember the sergeants' mess was really swish, marvellous, the rooms were big and it was still up to peacetime standards in immaculate order.
>
> When I first walked in I spoke to a sergeant pilot named Angus Norwell who was sitting quietly on a bed in one corner. I asked him what the 'chopping rate' was like on this squadron. 'Oh', he said, 'if you're here next Friday you'll be doing alright.' So that was my initiation. Al Deere said to me, 'What time have you got on Spitfires?' I said, 'About 4 hours and 20 minutes and 4 hours on the Hurricane.' 'Oh', he said, 'That's useless, I don't know why they bothered to send you here, we haven't got time to train you, and we are very busy.' So he arranged to have me sent back to the OTU at Aston Down for another week.

Les was extremely lucky to have had the chance to get a few more precious flying hours on Spitfires. Many of the young inexperienced pilots who had been sent to front-line squadrons at that time were ill-prepared to fight the experienced men of the Luftwaffe and lasted only weeks, indeed in some cases only days or hours, after arriving at their squadrons. During the month of August the attrition rate of pilot losses was an extreme worry to Air Chief Marshal Sir Hugh Dowding, Commander in Chief of Fighter Command. The loss of an aircraft could be replaced, with the steady stream of supply from the aircraft factories, under the supervision and encouragement of Lord Beaverbrook. But the loss of a pilot was a worse problem, for training new fighter pilots could take up to six months. Just before leaving Aston Down to return to Hornchurch, Les remembers:

> I always remember just before leaving, the commanding officer there, who a chap by the name of Hallahan, who had been with 1 Squadron, said to us all: 'I'm sorry gentlemen you have had such a short time here, but I would say to you don't worry too much when you get to an operational squadron. Having survived this place, you'll survive any operational squadron.' This was indeed true, because the amount of crashes and that sort of thing was unbelievable; people were going through stonewalls, undershooting and overshooting the runway.

On his return to Hornchurch, he found that 54 Squadron had been in the thick of the fighting and the airfield had been bombed:

> I suppose I had just missed all the serious stuff, fortunately for me I suspect. Looking back on it, I was rather regretful that it had happened like that, because when I hear the stories of what happened it was like missing a party. But that's the way the dice falls.

Many new pilots like Les Harvey were now being thrown into action with little or no combat experience, Alan Deere received two new replacements to his flight who lasted only hours before falling victim to the German fighters. Deere remembers:

> At that stage of the Battle of Britain, between August and the beginning of September, the aircraft had started to be available again. But we were still short of pilots, and we were getting pilots who had not even flown Spitfires, because there were no conversion units at that time. They came straight to us from their training establishments. Some of them did have a few hours on Hurricanes, but not on the Spitfire. For example, two young New Zealanders, Mick Shand and Charlie Stewart, were sent to my flight, and chatting to them I found out that they had been six weeks at sea coming over to Britain, and they had been trained on some outdated aeroplane called a Wapiti back in NZ. They had been given two trips in a Hurricane, and then sent here to the squadron. We were pretty busy, so we gave them what was known as a cockpit check. We had a Miles Master monoplane; we'd give them one trip in that, then one of the pilots would take them up to see how they handled it. Then we'd brief them on the Spitfire and send them up for one solo flight and circuit; then we'd send them off into battle.
>
> Of course they didn't last long. I think it was two trips before they were shot down, and both of them ended up in Dover Hospital, strangely enough. One of them was fished out of the Channel, while the other managed to parachute down. All I could say to the new boys was, 'Don't do anything by yourself, stick with your leader and just watch; unless you are attacked yourself, stay out of trouble until you get a feel of the things.' Well it was pretty hard for a young chap to follow that dictum. In fact what generally happened was that they would follow their leader, and then the next thing they'd be on their parachute, shot down by an unseen Me109 who had got up behind them.

Les Harvey was soon involved in his first combat patrol and a few days later on another occasion accompanied Alan Deere as his No.2:

> On seeing so many enemy aircraft I was frightened to death, or

should I say very apprehensive. I looked around and there were only six of us and looking up there were 60 to 70 of them coming towards us. But looking back on it, it was a good thing, because there was so few of us and so many of them that when you did get tangled up, they didn't know who was who. It was so easy to get confused, with so few Spitfires and so many 109s; you had to be careful when you did get the chance to let off a burst of fire in case it was the odd Spitfire.

I remember one particular day, when I was flying with Alan Deere. Deere had said to me, 'You better stick with me, be my No.2 and stick to me like glue,' which I did.

Then we ran into the enemy over the Thames estuary; I remember we were up at about 25,000 to 26,000 feet when we hit them out of the sun. Al Deere went down straight through the middle of them and I followed him. I thought, he's the kingpin, I can't go wrong, I must stick with him, create a good impression being a new boy and that sort of thing. On the way down he hit a 109 and so did I. I don't know what happened to it, but I remember we kept on going down and down. I looked at the clock and it was showing 400 mph and the altimeter was unwinding. I was fascinated by this, the speed was incredible. Then of course I could feel it in the controls; they were getting very hard to operate.

When you get into what is known as a terminal velocity dive, the ailerons, you can hardly move them, you can move the control stick back and forwards, but the ailerons lock almost solid. While coming down I was watching Deere waiting for the pull-out, and as I looked across, I couldn't get my head up because the G forces were terrific; my head was way down in the cockpit. I thought Deere would give me some sort of signal, but obviously he was suffering the same problem as I was. Suddenly he pulled up and I spotted him and did the same, having to use both hands and all my strength on the control column to achieve this.

After pulling out of the dive, which seemed like forever, I suddenly noticed two buildings very close to us as we flashed by. These later, I found out to be the flak towers in the Thames estuary. When we arrived back over Hornchurch, I glanced down at the speedometer and it was just starting to lose speed as we arrived over base. We later learnt that during our dive we had been followed down by two enemy 109s, and both had flown straight into the drink, being unable to pull out of their dive while trying to shoot us down, quite amazing.

The constant German raids were beginning to take their toll on the pilots of 54 Squadron, as probably with every hard pushed squadron in Fighter

Command. On 28th August, the Luftwaffe began its first raid of the day at 8.30 am, when a 100-plus formation was picked up by radar massing over Cap Gris Nez. This consisted of some bombers, but the majority of the aircraft were fighters. A second large raid was plotted at around 12.20 pm and the alert was sounded. 54 Squadron was scrambled and as the battle-weary pilots became airborne, they received instructions to head for the North Foreland area. As they approached the area to which they had been vectored, they sighted a large formation of Dorniers escorted by Me109s. The bombers were in a Vic formation at around 20,000 feet, while the fighters circled over them at 28,000 feet in formations of five and six. Ronald Adam, the senior controller at Hornchurch's Operations Room, remembers hearing Deere's reaction on seeing such a formidable enemy force over the radio:

> I heard his voice in my ear as he sighted the enemy 'Christ Almighty, Tally Ho, whole fucking hoards of them.'

James Leathart (Rabbit Leader) then led his section in to attack seven of the Me109s. He fired one long burst at 250 yards' range until he was only 100 yards from the enemy fighter, then pulled away to his left. The Me109 seemed out of control and smoke began to appear from it. From that moment Deere was subsequently engaged in a series of dogfights, twisting and turning either to get on to an enemy aircraft's tail or avoiding it. He did manage to fire a close burst at one 109 at close range, but did not observe any positive results.

It was while at 23,000 feet, during the mêlée all around, that Deere's aircraft was hit. In his combat report he states:

> When at 23,000 feet, I was shot down by a Spitfire (no markings observed). My control wires to the rudder were shot away and I had to bale out.

With no control over his aircraft (Spitfire R6832), he had no option. After trimming the aircraft to stay on a level and even course, Al unstrapped his Sutton harness and climbed out of the cockpit. He abandoned his Spitfire with no trouble and the parachute opened, leaving him gradually descending from a height of 10,000 feet with a splendid view of the fields and vales of Kent below. It took a good ten minutes for him to come down not far from Detling airfield. This caused him slight injuries since he landed astride a small plum tree in an orchard, although they only amounted to a few scratches here and there. Whilst checking himself over, Al was suddenly confronted by an angry and red-faced farmer who owned the land, on which he had so unexpectedly dropped in.

He found himself looking down the barrel of a shotgun as the farmer shouted: 'Stay where you are, I've got you covered.' Al hastily replied; ' I'm British.' The farmer, once convinced that Al was not a German, lowered his gun, but remarked angrily, 'Why did you have to land on my prize plum tree?'

Al followed the farmer back to his home where he was allowed to use the telephone to contact Detling airfield to arrange for transport to pick him up. Having thanked and said his farewell to the farmer, Al arrived at Detling and here he met another Hornchurch-based pilot, Squadron Leader Desmond Garvin, who commanded 264 Squadron, which flew the Boulton-Paul Defiant aircraft. Garvin had also been shot down that day, the victim of German ace Adolf Galland. Unfortunately Garvin's gunner, Flight Lieutenant R.C.V. Ash, was not so lucky; he had baled out, but was killed.

Al and Garvin were flown back to Hornchurch in an Avro Anson aircraft, arriving back there three hours after Al had taken off to engage the enemy.

Spitfire R6832 crashed at Pond Field, Vinson Farm, Oad Street, Boreham near Sittingbourne. In 1973 the Kent Battle of Britain Museum undertook an excavation of the crash site, recovering the remains of the Rolls-Royce Merlin engine, tail wheel strut, windscreen frame and gun-firing button amongst other items.

On 30th August, the squadron had a quiet day compared to the previous few days. Two patrols took place and the morning patrol at 9.27 am was uneventful. During the afternoon however, Red Section took off to patrol over the Billericay area and at 4.50 pm sighted and attacked a formation of 50 Dorniers with their escort of Messerschmitt 110s at a height of 18,000 feet.

With the advantage of height, 54 dived down from 25,000 feet and although unable to inflict serious damage on the enemy formation, they continued to harass them considerably. One Dornier 17 was destroyed, this being shared by Flying Officer McMullen and Pilot Officer Edsall. Al Deere claimed a probable on a Dornier 17, which he attacked near Thameshaven. His report claims:

> I intercepted a Dornier 17 at 18,000 feet going southeast. Enemy aircraft were in pairs taking considerable evasive action. No escort of fighters was visible at this time. I led my section to attack but lost both of them. I got on to the tail of the enemy aircraft and had great difficulty in getting in a decent burst owing to the manoeuvres of the second aircraft. I fired all my ammunition. I last saw it flying east just north of Thameshaven losing height.

Amazingly, at Rochford airfield, Squadron Leader James Leathart witnessed this engagement from the ground and stated that he last saw the Dornier bomber losing height rapidly with engines smoking.

For many who served at RAF Hornchurch and 54 Squadron, 31st August was a day they would never forget. By 8.00 am that morning, British radar had picked up and reported that four large enemy formations were building up over the French coast.

One raid was headed for Dover, while the other three formations were heading towards targets up the Thames estuary. The RAF airfields were again the Luftwaffe's main targets, with heavy raids on Biggin Hill, Manston, West Malling, Lympne, Hawkinge, Debden – and Hornchurch. It was a crisis point in the battle.

At 1.00 pm, the air raid sirens at Hornchurch began to wail, after a formation of German raiders had turned their course at Dungeness and were now heading for Hornchurch. It had been caught unprepared and 54 Squadron still had its aircraft on the ground. Over the Tannoy radio system came the frantic call from the operations controller for all pilots to get airborne immediately and for ground personnel to take cover in the air-raid shelters. As 54 Squadron began to taxi its aircraft out to take off, the German bombers began their bombing run over the aerodrome. Leading the squadron in its desperate attempt to get airborne was Squadron Leader James Leathart who remembered:

> We were all at standby at our dispersal point, expecting to be scrambled at any moment, when suddenly I saw German bombers appearing over the horizon, coming closer and closer, and still we weren't scrambled. I did the most unspeakable thing, I decided to take off without permission, alas ten seconds too late. I got away with it, but Eric Edsall, Al Deere and Sergeant Davis were caught as the bombs began to drop.

Alan Deere, leading his section of three Spitfires, was now caught in the middle of the flightpath as they prepared to take off. Deere now recounts that harrowing event:

> I was caught taking off by the German raid on the airfield. We were ordered to take off and then ordered to cancel the order. You must remember that the radar, which was the reporting chain, only worked effectively up to the coast; then inland it was up to the Observer Corps, and there was a bit of an overlap. If they couldn't visually see the enemy aircraft, there was a bit of indecision and they'd get raids mixed up. This was no criticism, it was just the system ironing itself out; one minute there would be an X-Raid, then the next minute it would have disappeared from the plotting board.
>
> However, we were told to get to readiness, which we did, then to standby, which meant in your cockpits, all ready and strapped in; we were then told to go back to readiness. As we got out and were walking back to dispersal, the phone rang and dispersal said, 'Scramble as quickly as possible.' So we had to run back to the aircraft, and that's when we were caught taking off; the Germans were already overhead and dropping their bombs. I was leading the section on the right, and I was held up from taking off by a new pilot who'd got himself stuck in the take-off lane, and didn't know where to go. He delayed me and, by the time I'd got him sorted out, I was the last one off and caught the bombs. I was blown sky high, the three of us were, but we all got away with it. I was pretty badly concussed

and my Spitfire was blown up. I finished up on the airfield in a
heap, and my No.2 had his wing blown off. No.3 was not seen
for two hours, until he re-appeared at dispersal with his
parachute. He had been blown in his aircraft about a mile away,
into what we called 'Shit Creek'. He landed the right way up
and got out, and had to walk all the way around the airfield to
get back in.

I was pretty well shaken, and I'd had the top of my scalp
badly torn from my head scraping the ground, when the aircraft
had careered upside down along the ground. The doctor
plastered and bandaged me up and said, 'Forty-eight hours'
rest, then report back.' Well, 24-hours and I felt all right, so I
just went back. We were under tremendous stress at the time,
so I took just the night off and went back flying the next day
all bandaged up.

Ronald Adam recalls the chaos that took place:

I remember getting the depleted squadrons off the ground to
meet the oncoming raid, and they were all off except the last
section of three, when the bombs fell. All three aircraft had
opened up their throttles to take off; the first was blown upside
down and slid about two-hundred yards on its cockpit, the
second was blown into the air and one of its wings fell off, and
the third was blown clean out of the aerodrome into a nearby
brook. In the middle of the smoke and confusion, a pitch battle
raged in the centre of the aerodrome; the undamaged pilot of
the second aircraft had run to the first one, and had managed to
pull the pilot out of it and was trying to carry him. Eric was a
little fellow, he had great admiration for the big husky pilot he
was trying to save, but the husky pilot had no wish to be saved
by Eric and the protests he made ended in a furious battle. This
raid drove the Operation's Room away from its aerodrome to
retire to an emergency pitch some four miles away in a small
unoccupied grocer's shop, where we almost sat on one
another's laps to control. We were bombed there within a few
days of setting up.

One of 54 Squadron's ground crewman was Jack Shenfield, who was a B
Flight mechanic. And after making sure that the Spitfires had got away, he
raced for the shelter, and as the all clear sounded, he emerged to witness the
aftermath of the bombing. Today, he remembers the raid as if it had
happened only yesterday:

At the time, we had just got the aircraft away when the bombs
started falling, and I ran towards the air-raid shelter. What I
also remember was that there was an ack-ack unit or gun
emplacement near to the Sutton's end of where our dispersal

point was. There was so much dust from the bombs and the guns going off, it made me wonder how these soldiers could see what they were shooting at. Once I got into the shelter, we were all packed in there, and the sergeant closed the door. We had been only in there a minute or so when there was a banging at the door. He opened the door and it was the driver of the Bowser; this was the vehicle that carried all the high-octane petrol for the aircraft. He'd parked the thing outside the shelter with all the bombs falling all around. The sergeant said, 'Sod off, and take that bloody thing with you and park it somewhere else before you blow us all to pieces.'

The driver had to go back and park it before they'd let him into the shelter. After the raid was over and we came out, some of the lads got on top of the shelter and started shouting, 'Oh look they've shot a German down, I can see the crosses on the back.' What they didn't realise was that it was the three kites from our squadron, Al Deere and the others, the crosses were the victory scores on the side of the aircraft. Poor old Sergeant Davis appeared hours later, asking for a cup of tea after being blown up. The whole fuselage went; the wings were left on the aerodrome and the fuselage blown into the river, which was quite a distance. How they all survived was a miracle.

No.54 Squadron's Operations Book enlarged further on the day's unexpected attack:

A really amazing day. Hornchurch bombed. The miraculous escape of three of our pilots who were bombed out of their planes. The station bombed a second time.

At 13.15 a large formation of enemy bombers – a most impressive sight in Vic formation at 15,000 feet – reached the aerodrome and dropped their bombs (probably 60 in all) in a line from the other side of our original dispersal pens to the petrol dump and beyond into Elm Park. Perimeter track, dispersal pens and barrack block windows suffered, but no damage to buildings was caused and the aerodrome in spite of its ploughed condition remained serviceable. The squadron was ordered off just as the first bombs were beginning to fall and eight of our machines safely cleared the ground; the remaining section, however, just became airborne as the bombs exploded. All three machines were wholly wrecked in the air. The survival of the pilots is a complete miracle. Sergeant Davis, taking off towards the hangars, was thrown back across the River Ingrebourne two fields away, scrambling out of his machine unharmed. Flight Lieutenant Deere had one wing and his prop torn off; climbing to about one hundred feet he turned over and coming down slid along the aerodrome for a hundred yards upside down. He was rescued from this unenvious position by Pilot Officer Edsall, the third member of the section, who had suffered a similar fate except he had landed the right way up. Dashing across the aerodrome with bombs still dropping, he extricated Deere from his machine. 'The first and last time, I hope' was the verdict of these truly amazing pilots – all of whom were ready for battle again the next morning.

The remainder of the squadron, at low altitude, engaged what oddments they could find and succeeded in accounting for one Me109 destroyed, shared by Flight Lieutenant George Gribble and Sergeant 'Jock'Norwell, and one Dornier 17 was claimed probably destroyed which was a shared claim by Flying Officer McMullen and a Hurricane pilot from another squadron.

Later that same afternoon at 5.04 pm, nine of the squadron's aircraft went into combat over Manston during the second big raid of the day, where they encountered 20-30 Dorniers with a heavy escort of Me109s. Pilot Officer Colin Gray destroyed an Me109 in the combat, while Sergeant Gibbons probably destroyed another. Gibbons' Spitfire was hit during this engagement and he was forced to bale out, but landed safely. Whilst this engagement was in progress Hornchurch was bombed again, when a formation dropped a stick of bombs next to the earlier raid's efforts, but it caused little additional damage.

The explosions awakened Al Deere who had earlier been seen by the station doctor, and ordered to bed. He was half asleep due to the medication that the doctor had given him to take, but managed to lift himself from his bed and make his way, staggering to the nearest air-raid shelter, which was situated just behind the officers' mess and used by officers, WAAFs and the civilian staff alike. Deere mentions in his own book *Nine Lives* that at this point he was pleasantly amused when a woman scantly clad in an untied dressing gown, suddenly found herself showing her female assets to all and sundry as she entered the shelter, taking people's minds off the immediate danger of the falling bombs for a few brief moments. After the all-clear had sounded for the last time that day, Deere returned to his bed. That night he suffered with nightmares and woke up sweating. He finally managed to sleep and did not wake till mid-morning. After being giving an examination by the station medical officer, Deere was told that he could return to operations on 2nd September but he went back a day earlier.

On 3rd September 1940, 54 Squadron received orders to move back up to Catterick for a well-earned rest period, its place being taken by 41 Squadron. 54 would not operate again from Hornchurch during the Battle of Britain, which reached its turning point on 15th September. Two days later Hitler postponed the invasion of Britain indefinitely. The RAF Hornchurch Station Diary records the squadron's departure:

In the late afternoon, 54 Squadron left us for a period of rest and recuperation at Catterick. During the previous fortnight they have been bearing the brunt of the work in the Sector, for they had to hold the fort, while various new squadrons arrived and settled down into Sector routine. With the exception of two very short breaks, they had been with us continuously during the first year of the war, and in this period had destroyed 92 enemy aircraft.

54 Squadron would return to Hornchurch in early 1941, when Fighter Command operations were then on the offensive rather than defensive.

As the squadron arrived at Catterick, Al Deere must have reflected on his time at Hornchurch and the many colleagues whose faces were now permanently missing from the squadron. His friends Johnny Allen and Basil 'Wonky' Way were dead, together with others who had only been with the squadron for a few weeks, while many others had been badly wounded. The squadron was then categorised as a 'C' class training squadron, as new pilots and aircraft arrived. One new pilot who arrived during this time was Air Commodore Sir Archie Winskill, then a pilot officer, who remembers meeting Al Deere for the first time:

> I first met him up at Catterick; this would have been about the middle of the Battle of Britain. He had been through a tough time since Dunkirk with his squadron, and I was sent to 54 en route to be a replacement for a front-line squadron, which had suffered heavy losses. I was only there for two weeks before I was posted to 72 Squadron at Biggin Hill. We became friends immediately we met; our personalities seemed to click and we remained good friends until his death. It was from people like Al and Colin Gray who had been through the battle up to that moment with 54 at Hornchurch that we got all our information about what was going on, the tactics, the dog fighting and improving one's skill on the Spitfire. I had had only one week's course on conversion at the operational training unit at Hawarden.

Good news arrived for Deere while at Catterick, when on 6th September the *London Gazette* announced a second DFC award. This recommendation stated:

> *Flight Lieutenant Deere was awarded the DFC on 14th June 1940 for the conspicuous gallantry he displayed in the Dunkirk operation. Since then he has been promoted to the command of a Flight, and his gallantry and determination, coupled with his skilful leadership, have contributed largely to the outstanding success achieved by this squadron.*
>
> *From the date of award of the DFC on 14th June 1940, this officer has shot down a further four Me109s, one He113 and one Me110, and in conjunction with another pilot, probably destroyed a Ju88. Since the beginning of the war, Flight*

Lieutenant Deere has, himself, destroyed 11 enemy aircraft and
a further four in conjunction with other pilots. In addition, he
has probably destroyed a further one enemy aircraft himself
and shared with other pilots in the destruction of two more.

In addition to the skill and gallantry he has shown in leading
his Flight, and in many cases, his squadron, into attack, Flight
Lieutenant Deere has displayed conspicuous bravery and
determination in pressing home his attacks against superior
numbers, in many instances pursuing the enemy across the
Channel to France in order to shoot them down.

Group Captain Edward 'Hawkeye' Wells first met Alan Deere when he
joined 41 Squadron in early October 1940. Then a pilot officer, Wells
remembers:

> I knew he was quite an experienced pilot at the time I first met
> him. Al being in 54 Squadron and myself in 41 Squadron, we
> often used to meet up together in the officers' mess up at
> Catterick. As both of us were New Zealanders we both had a
> common bond and a friendship developed which would
> continue throughout the war and afterwards. He was a quiet
> chap, but very determined.

54 Squadron remained at Catterick throughout the remainder of 1940.
During this time, Deere spent most of his flying time either air-testing new
Spitfires that had been brought into service on the squadron or giving new
pilots practice flights and passing on his experience of combat procedure
and tactics. On 28th December 1940, Deere took off from Catterick with
Sergeant Pilot Howard Squire on a dogfight practice flight. Deere recalled
the following sequence of events that took place that morning:

> The job of putting Sergeant Squire through his paces had in
> fact been allotted to my deputy in the morning's training
> programme, but when he woke up with flu, I stood in and took
> Squire up instead. I might have known what such a change of
> plan could mean!
>
> After the first encounter, which began at 10,000 feet, we
> found ourselves down to 3,000 feet, 'OK Red 2,' I said, 'I'll
> climb up to 10,000 feet again and we'll have another go.' After
> a series of hectic manoeuvres, I saw the nose of Squire's
> aircraft right on top of me. The next second he had flown into
> me and chewed clean through my tail. The Spitfire whipped
> into a vicious spin, completely out of control. The centrifugal
> force kept me anchored to my seat. I was stuck fast.
>
> At some point the force must have lessened. After twisting
> and turning, kicking and fighting, I was released for a couple
> of seconds from the cockpit, only to be blown on to the
> remnants of my tail plane where, again, I stuck fast. I reached

for my ripcord handle, only to realise that my parachute had been partly ripped from my back, and the handle was out of my reach.

'Fancy,' I remember saying out loud, 'after all that fighting, being killed this way.'

Then, suddenly, and miraculously, with the ground now uncomfortably close, my parachute opened, only partially, but just enough and just in time. Almost at the same moment came the impact. I was submerged horizontally in a thick, foul, stinking farmyard cesspool. I nearly drowned in the muck, as my back was agony and I could barely move. A passing motorist and his wife came running to my aid. Despite the stench and filth, they put me on the back seat of their car and drove me seven miles back to Catterick from where I was rushed to hospital.

The 'soft' landing in the farmer's cesspool – a million to one shot – had undoubtedly saved my life.

Deere's aircraft, X4276, came down at Town End Farm, Kirk Leavington, North Yorkshire. Sergeant Squire had also managed to escape from his doomed Spitfire, which had caught fire on impact with Deere's aircraft. He too had baled out, and was uninjured. In the meantime, Deere had arrived back at Catterick and he was at once taken by the station's ambulance to the nearest hospital. He was immediately taken for X-ray, which revealed a chipped coccyx at the base of his spine. His body ached all over, especially his back, which had been badly strained by the fall. He was then told he would not be hospitalised, but would need to rest in bed for several days to recover properly.

Howard Squire had joined the RAF Volunteer Reserve and was called up at the outbreak of war and selected for pilot training. In December 1939, he underwent initial training at Bexhill and by June 1940 he was at 10 Elementary Flying Training School at Yatesbury. He passed out as 'above the average' in July and was sent to 5 SFTS Sealand, where he passed top of ground studies and was above average in flying. He declined an invitation to go to the Central Flying School for instructor training and this probably cost him a commission, because he had been selected at FTS as a cadet officer. In October, he went to the Operational Training Unit at Hawarden and was sent to 54 Squadron at Catterick in November. Howard Squire recalls his time with the squadron and the collision with Deere:

I chose to go to 54, because Flight Sergeant Phil Tew who was my instructor at OTU, had also served with them during the Battle of Britain.

I joined A Flight 54 Squadron at Catterick on 1st December 1940, with a total of 150 hours flying; 10 hours and 15 minutes on Spitfires at 7 OTU Hawarden. Up to 28th December my log records I had 22 hours' flying time on Spitfires. I had flown three patrols, the rest being taken up with formation flying, aerobatics and three sessions of practice air-fighting, one of these with Alan Deere who was my flight commander. Most of us were newly in from OTUs including Jack Charles. The old sweats in A were Flying Officer Colin Gray, Flying Officer Coleman and Pilot Officer N. A. Lawrence who was formerly a sergeant. B Flight commander was George Gribble. The atmosphere was great. Other than a morning salute on entering the hut, formalities were forgotten and officers and NCO pilots played cards and generally mucked in together. Alan Deere was very much part of the company and certainly had everyone's confidence as a leader. On 28th December, I took off with Deere for the second time for air-fighting practice. It was a cold winter day, sunny with little or no cloud. We climbed to 10,000 feet over the aerobatic area of north-east Catterick. I was instructed to start the exercise by trying to hang on to his tail, while he took evasive action with the object of throwing me off.

After a strenuous bout during which I hung on and was very pleased with my efforts, I suddenly found I was closing very rapidly. I have always believed that he turned up-sun and slowed to check I was still with him, climbing slightly. To avoid him I closed the throttle and pushed the stick forward to dive under him. There was a resounding crash as I caught his tail, passing under him. He vanished and I found myself with a vibrating engine still in balanced flight, but with no hood and the rear fuselage and part of the tailplane and fin flattened, I assume from both the impact and his prop.

I decided the damage was such that I might not be able to get back and that I should get out. I undid my Sutton harness, stood up on the seat and as the aircraft was still stable, I stood on the flattened rear of the cockpit and dived clear.

I knew I was high, so I delayed opening the chute until I had fallen well clear and had turned over a few times. When the ground came into view, I pulled the ripcord. The aircraft I had been allocated had had someone else's parachute on board, we must have taken off in a hurry, anyway it was not mine and he was bigger than me.

The parachute opened with a bang and gave me a moment or two of acute discomfort until I could grasp the shroud lines and wiggle the leg straps into an easier position.

I spotted a big ploughed field and aimed for this, looking for a more comfortable landing. I drifted however and I gave up slipping the lines as I saw the ground coming up. At the end of the field was a small ravine with a stream and it looked for a bit as if I would land on this. I yanked on the cords to make the impact softer and was lucky to miss a substantial wooden fence, landing on the top slope of the ravine, having fallen straight through the branches of some light timber. I collected the chute with little difficulty and bundled it up and climbed the fence into the field.

There was a substantial house at the other side of the field and I made for this, knocked on the door and asked for help. I was received hospitably by the occupants and allowed to telephone Catterick. They despatched transport for me from Thornaby, then a Coastal Command Station. While I waited the lady of the house provided tea and fruitcake and a large double whisky. The house no longer exists; its land having become a small estate on the edge of the village of Hilton.

A short while later an ambulance arrived, I got in and directed them to search for Flight Lieutenant Deere, whom I had been told had landed a mile or two away. We located his crash-site – a smoking hole in a ploughed field by the Kirk Leavington road. He had, it turned out, grabbed a lift back to Catterick. I was taken to Thornaby, where I had lunch. I was picked up by the squadron Miles Master in the afternoon and flown back to the station.

I was more than a little apprehensive of the consequences of my action. Alan Deere was after all a well-known Battle of Britain ace and I had been within feet of killing him. After supper in the sergeants' mess, Pilot Officer Lawrence – a recently promoted sergeant pilot – came over from the officers' mess to ask me to go over and see Flight Lieutenant Deere, who I found in his room with a few other officers, including Flight Lieutenant Gribble, B Flight commander. To my surprise, though I might have suspected a lynching party, they had gathered at Deere's instigation to help concoct a plausible story to be presented to the CO the next day.

I had asked Lawrence on the way over what was likely to happen to me. His cheerful reply was that I was likely to find myself on target towing – a fate to any budding fighter pilot worse than death. I reflected that I had passed up an instructor's course at Central Flying School to get on to Spitfires, after I had finished flying school. So an agreed version of the incident was plotted there and then, and the next day I imagine we wrote out our crash reports.

Squadron Leader Robert Finlay-Boyd sussed out the deception when I saw him in ten seconds flat. I was not however put on a charge and my reprimand was tempered by a short dissertation on how difficult it was to shed speed in a Spitfire. The same day I was back on duty, counting myself a very lucky fellow.

It was certainly Al Deere's influence that prevented me from getting the chop over the crash and enabled me to stay with the squadron. I was very pleased when I got back into the Volunteer Reserve after the war, to learn that he had survived and had such a distinguished service along with Colin Gray and Jack Charles.

Howard Squire continued to fly with 54 Squadron until on 26th February 1941, while on their first offensive sweep over France, he was shot down and made a prisoner of war. (See Appendix J.)

On his first flight after being given the OK to return to flying duties, Alan Deere realized things were not quite right. He immediately felt uneasy in the air and the anxiety made him break out into a cold sweat, which was completely unnerving and alien to him. After suffering the same reaction on a couple more flights, Deere decided to seek advice from squadron commander Squadron Leader Pat Dunworth, who in turn told Deere to have a word with Station Commander Guy Carter. Carter had already been informed earlier that Deere was to be promoted to squadron leader rank and told him that from hence-forth his new role would be as an operations controller at Catterick. He also instructed Deere to take a week's leave pending the start of his new duties, and Alan spent that following week down in Cornwall with the Dumas family.

CHAPTER 4

602 'CITY OF GLASGOW' SQUADRON
1941

After his leave, Deere returned to his duties at Catterick on 11th January 1941. The winter of 1940-41 was one of the most severe for many years and flying during January was nearly non-existent at Catterick. Most mornings, the main activity on the airfield would be the ground crews hurrying about with brooms and brushes trying to clear the snow and ice that had built up on the aircraft overnight.

It was during this period that Deere was learning the rights and wrongs of being an operations controller, and getting to know ground to air procedure. Working with him at this time was another Battle of Britain veteran, George Bennions.

Bennions had joined the RAF in 1929 as an apprentice at Halton to become an engine fitter. He decided that he wanted to fly and attended Cranwell College as an officer cadet, where he undertook basic flying training. He finally completed his training at Grantham in 1935 and joined 41 Squadron in the Middle East at Kharmaksar, Aden. He was commissioned in 1940 and was in the thick of the action during the Battle of Britain, so much so that he suffered a wound to his foot, and on 1st October, he was grievously wounded when attacked by Me109s. A cannon shell came through the canopy and wounded him in the head and right hand.

He somehow managed to bale out and landed before losing consciousness. After receiving emergency treatment at Horsham Hospital, despite which he lost his left eye, he would spend many months in Queen Victoria Hospital, East Grinstead, undergoing plastic surgery. After making a good recovery, he was posted to Catterick as a controller.

On 23rd February, 54 Squadron bade farewell to Catterick and returned south to Hornchurch to start offensive operations. Fighter Command was planning sweeps across France, which were given the name Rhubarbs. In 54's place came 41 Squadron for their rest period. Deere was no doubt delighted to meet some old friends who were still in 41, the squadron commander Don Finlay, Flight Lieutenant Tony Lovell and fellow 'Kiwi' John Mackenzie; another was Flying Officer Edward Darling, who had the nickname of 'Mitzi'. Alan Deere would become a good and close friend.

During the following month, Deere would occasionally fly with 41, and on one night flight patrolled over the city of Hull to witness the results of German night bombing.

On the social side of his time at Catterick, Deere and his friends frequented some of the delightful village pubs around that area and it was while on one night out that he met a person that would change his life: Joan Fenton.

Al's first meeting with Joan had come about when an army officer friend had invited him to dine with him and friends at the Morritt Arms Hotel at nearby Barnard Castle. Accompanying Al that evening was Flight Lieutenant John 'Mac' Mackenzie. On arrival at the hotel, Deere was introduced to an attractive blond and told this was Joan. They talked and obviously got on very well. In *Nine Lives* he records the meeting: 'The usual formalities were exchanged and that was that. Certainly, I thought to myself, my friend was not exaggerating when he said she was pretty.' They met again soon afterwards at a party held at the officers' mess and soon began seeing each other regularly when time allowed.

Born on 12th June 1921, Joan Fenton came from Harrowgate, Darlington, and lived at home with her parents, George and Polly. Her father had been responsible for the opening of the first cinema at Catterick. He had always been in the world of entertainment and in the early part of the century had been involved with circuses and the 'Wild West Show' that William Cody alias 'Buffalo Bill' had brought to Britain during its tour of Europe.

As their relationship developed, Al would spend more of his spare time with Joan, which included going to dances, parties, and such like. Pat Bishden became a good friend of Joan Fenton's when they served together as drivers for the American Ambulance, Great Britain. She recalls:

> I first met her just after I had completed the training course in Leeds, when we were at the depot in Birmingham. The Americans financed the unit and we worked in conjunction with the hospitals. We had a very smart uniform to wear as well.
>
> She had a very brief marriage before meeting Alan, just literally in and out of marriage, an absolute disaster from the word go. She had gone to live back with her parents in Darlington. She told me that when she met Alan, that she was very impressed from the word go, in every way. She was absolutely taken with him; she wouldn't look at anybody else. I think he was delighted to meet somebody with a bit of life.

Deere's role as a controller was becoming tedious to him and he was itching to get back on to operational flying, so towards the end of March 1941, he applied to return to it. The weeks dragged by with no news, until finally on 6th May he received the communication he had waited and hoped for, the notification of his next posting – to 602 'City of Glasgow' Squadron to take up the position of flight commander. This meant he had to revert back to the rank of a flight lieutenant. The squadron was based at Ayr on the east coast of Scotland.

The young, as well as seasoned, pilots of 602 heralded his arrival at the squadron with much welcome anticipation. One of the pilots that Deere would now lead was Pilot Officer Hugh Glen Niven; he had joined 602 Squadron before the war at Abbotsinch, Scotland in May 1939 to undertake flying training on Avro Tutors. When war did finally break out, he then undertook further training at 11 Elementary Flying Training School at Perth; he then went on to 15 FTS before completing his final training as a fighter pilot at the 5 Operational Training Unit at Aston Down in August 1940. Niven then rejoined 602 Squadron during the Battle of Britain on 1st September 1940. While in action during this period, his Spitfire suffered damage, when Me109s shot the wing tip to pieces over Maidstone on 29th October. Niven remained with 602 into 1941 and recalls Al Deere's arrival at the squadron:

> The squadron commander up until Al arrived was 'Killy' Kilmartin; he had been given the job in the April, and he was there for a short spell until he was posted away to West Africa. A chap called Pat Meagher then took Killy's position.
>
> When Al arrived at the squadron he was a well-known chap and as soon as somebody said, 'Oh there's Al Deere' we practically got down on our knees. Everybody knew about Al Deere. He'd been shot down so many times and had shot up so many Germans, that he was terribly well known. Everybody was chuffed that he'd come to 602. He was very easygoing and so good at flying that everybody respected him tremendously.

On 10th May 1941, the Deputy Fuhrer of the Third Reich, Rudolf Hess boarded his Messerschmitt Me110 aircraft and began his flight into history. Hess had taken it upon himself to try and persuade the British to negotiate a peace treaty with Germany.

In Alan Deere's book *Nine Lives* he refers to Hess's flight to Britain and his subsequent baling out and capture in Scotland, but he also relates to the reader the fact that he missed the opportunity of shooting down Hess's aircraft. Unfortunately, this does not seem to be the case. Deere was indeed airborne that day in Spitfire P9510, taking off at 4.35 pm and landing at 5.25 pm, but Hess's aircraft was not picked up on radar until late evening, and the author has found no further evidence that Deere was in the air again that day.* Hector MacLean was the sector controller that night and he recalls:

> 602 Squadron were not called upon to play any role in Hess's arrival. I was the Sector Controller on duty at Rosemount at the time, during the 6.00 pm till midnight watch. To my surprise at

---

*This new information also contradicts the report of the incident as published in *Lions Rampant* by Douglas McRoberts.

10.30 pm, a 'hostile' appeared on our plotting table in the vicinity of Selkirk and flying west. Fortunately we had two Boulton-Paul Defiant night-fighter aircraft fully armed and airborne from 141 Squadron. I contacted them over the R/T and told them to orbit the area around Kilmarnock, which seemed to lie in the path of the intruder. I then phoned the Controller of the Royal Observer Corps at Ayr. He had already had positive identification that the hostile aircraft was an Me110. I thought to myself, 'If it is, it hasn't enough fuel to get back home.' One hour later, the telephone rang and a police sergeant informed me that they had a German officer under guard at the police station at Eaglesham, who had just parachuted from an aircraft.

By all accounts, Hess had somehow seen the Defiants and mistaken them for Hurricanes and had decided to bale out before they could have opened fire.

Rudolf Hess spent the rest of the war in captivity, and after his trial at Nuremberg, spent the rest of his life in Spandau Prison. A few days after the Me110 episode, Deere learnt of Hess's astounding capture from a newspaper report.

On 6th June, 602 Squadron took off on a local practice flight, and while flying at 10,000 feet about 10 miles out from the Scottish coast, Deere noticed that his aircraft was beginning to handle oddly. First of all, the Rolls-Royce engine was vibrating badly, secondly, the oil pressure gauge reading had completely dropped. Suddenly, there was an incredibly loud bang followed by a large stream of oil, which covered the cowling of the Spitfire and some of the front windscreen. He immediately switched off the engine and quickly weighed up the situation. Was it better to try and glide back to the mainland or bale out into the choppy cold waters of the North Sea? He decided within a few seconds that it was better to make for land as he still had sufficient height.

A few minutes later as he sighted the coast, he looked for the most likely place to force-land his aircraft. The nearest landfall was the cliff tops at the Heads of Ayr. As his Spitfire approached, however, it became apparent that he would only clear the cliff top with a few feet to spare. Fortunately he managed this, but was then confronted with the reverse side of the cliff falling away steeply and being dotted with small fields separated by stonework fences. He had to act fast now or face being torn apart by the fences.

He pushed the control column hard forward and the Spitfire's propeller buckled as the aircraft slammed down at 90 mph into a field full of potato crops. The aircraft ploughed its way across part of the field before nosing in, causing the tail to rear up and turn the Spitfire on to its back, leaving Deere strapped upside down inside his cockpit. This was fortunate, for if his Sutton harness strap had failed, he would have probably broken his neck or suffered serious head injuries.

Aware of his predicament, the next problem was how to get out of the stricken aircraft. Stranded in the middle of nowhere and with no one within sight to help, he found that the soft earth around the Spitfire's cockpit side door panel allowed just enough passage to pull his body through. On rising from the ground he surveyed the situation while brushing off the dust and dirt, then began walking. He soon came upon a building, which was in fact the clubhouse for the local golf course at Girvan. On entering, he startled a woman whose first words were: 'Good gracious, where did you spring from?' Deere was offered a cup of tea, but probably would have preferred something a little stronger after yet another of his escapades. Soon afterwards the familiar face of the Station Commander, Group Captain Loel Guinness, appeared through the clubhouse door to collect Deere and drive him back to the aerodrome.

After the aircraft maintenance crew had recovered the aircraft and examined the engine, it was found that one of the connecting rods had pushed its way through the engine block. The engine was then sent away for further investigation by Rolls-Royce engineers, but a conclusion was never reached on how the problem had occurred.

On his return to the aerodrome, he was greeted by his fellow pilots who ribbed him about his latest misfortune with Al taking it all in good heart. One of his old 54 Squadron comrades, Flying Officer John Hopkins commented, 'Just like old times,' obviously referring back to Al's escape when Hornchurch was bombed.

Glen Niven can remember another accident, which befell Deere one day, although it was not connected to flying:

> I can remember Al and the incident with a motorbike. I had been lent a small motorcycle by an uncle when the squadron was at Prestwick in early 1941. It had a very small horsepower engine and did incredible mileage on petrol. Al asked if he could borrow it (and if Al asked for something, he got it!). He leapt aboard and set off at a rate of knots and immediately ran straight into a thick hedge. End of trip, the motorcycle was damaged, but the squadron's mechanics were excellent at fixing it so that my uncle wouldn't find out! While at Prestwick, Al and I used to crawl through a gap in the hedge of the airfield to visit the Orangefield Hotel to get to the bar. Al was much senior to me, but there was no 'side' to him at all and we became good friends.

One operational role that 602 was given was that of the air cover and protection for the Royal Navy battleship HMS *Prince of Wales*, which was returning from the North Atlantic to Scotland after the sinking of the German battleship *Bismarck*. The squadron flew and operated from Limavady in Northern Ireland, from where they would send one flight of four aircraft to cover the battleship and its destroyer escort as it made its way up the coast to Scotland. Again Flying Officer Glen Niven remembers the operation:

> We all went up and did about half-an-hour trip, four of us flying in pairs. The one thing we objected to strongly, was that if you went too close, it bloody well opened fire on you. We thought 'you stupid buggers' how on earth could German single-engine fighters be over the Clyde? The Navy did fire off once or twice, then, somebody got on to them and said, 'Don't be so damn silly.' We did beat them up a little bit though, flying in fairly low.

Niven also remembers the fun times in the squadron, when they would all go to the local pub to relax and let off steam. When Deere and Darling came along, there was always a good laugh to be had between them, especially when ordering drinks at the bar. Niven explains:

> 'Mitzi' Darling was a very pleasant guy and a big pal of Al Deere's, both having been at Hornchurch during the Battle. We were always amused when they talked over the radio when flying, calling each other 'Deere' and 'Darling'. When we went for a drink at night in the local pubs we would roll up with laughter when you would here at the bar, 'Are you going to have another drink, Darling' 'Yes, Deere, thank you.' Everybody would look around wondering what the bloody hell was going on. Al wasn't a great drinker, but like all of us, he enjoyed a pint.

On 10th July 1941 the squadron received its marching orders and was sent down south to operate from RAF Kenley. Here they would join two other squadrons, 452 (Australian) Squadron and 485 (New Zealand). On landing, the squadron was met by the Wing Commander Flying, Wing Commander John Peel. The very next day, the squadron pilots entered the station's operational briefing room for an introduction to the type of operations they would take part in. They were amazed to find two legendary figures of Fighter Command standing before them, 'Sailor' Malan and Douglas Bader. Wing Commander Peel opened the briefing by telling the pilots of the various different types of missions and what these would entail. Rhubarb offensive sweeps would be fighters only. Circuses would be fighters and bomber sorties. Ramrods were bomber forces escorted by fighters. Their aims were the destruction of military targets and of enemy fighters, and generally to concentrate the Luftwaffe's attention on northern France, so that Bomber Command would be freer to launch raids on Germany.

For the next few days the squadron familiarized themselves with the local area and practised formation battle tactics. Six days later on 16th July, Air Vice-Marshal Trafford Leigh-Mallory visited Kenley and met the commanding officer and pilots of 602, to find out how they were all settling in.

On 27th July, Deere was asked to undertake a visit to London to speak about the role that Fighter Command was playing at this time in its fight against the enemy. The venue for this was the HMV factory at Hayes in Middlesex. Unbeknown to him and his friend Pilot Officer Darling, who came along as support, was that they would have to stand before 2,000 women and girls. Taking the platform he was somewhat nervous, but he enthralled the audience with his stories and facts. His talk was hailed a great success. Always the modest quiet type, he was bemused by all the attention he received after the reception, when the press took numerous photographs of him with the women workers. Because the visit had been such a success, the management of HMV promised to send a new radiogram to the squadron as a present; it eventually turned up some years later!

On 1st August, Deere was delighted when he was instructed to take over command of 602 from Squadron Leader Pat Meagher who had been hospitalised.

Deere states in his own autobiography that during that day he led the squadron over the Channel, and he claimed to have shot down a Messerschmitt 109 during an engagement near Gravelines, when they bounced a formation of German fighters on the climb. The identity of this aircraft has been challenged and one recent publication has claimed that Deere had actually shot down a RAF Hurricane fighter of 242 Squadron in what now would be called a friendly fire incident. During the research for this book, the author found that the 602 Squadron Operations Book clearly stated that the squadron did not undertake any operations that day and only a little practice flying was done. Further research showed that indeed a Hurricane aircraft was shot down, the unfortunate occupant being a Canadian Sergeant Pilot, M.G.A.C. Casgrain of 242 Squadron who had taken off from Manston aerodrome at 11.15 am on a bomber-escort mission and had encountered heavy flak. Sergeant Casgrain, flying Hurricane Z2986, was listed as missing after the squadron's return at 12.10 pm. Did Deere fly with one of the other two squadrons based at Kenley that day, 452 or 485 Squadron, the latter operating from Redhill, the satellite airfield for Kenley? Again operational records for both squadrons show that they did not fly operations that day and Deere's name is absent. Unfortunately with the loss of Deere's flying logbook and no combat report available to confirm Deere's claim, the author concludes that there is no firm evidence to support his claim for the Me109 or his shooting down of a fellow RAF pilot.

In early August, Glen 'Nuts' Niven who was the longest serving pilot with 602 Squadron, was asked to go and see Al Deere. He recalls:

> I went and stood before Al, who was now commanding officer
> of the squadron, and he informed me that my name had been
> drawn out of the hat to be posted to another squadron. He said,

'Sorry, Nuts that's it,' and I said, 'You can't send me I'm the last original.' Al then said, 'Well you'll have to go. I'll see what I can do.' I was sent to No.603 Squadron and I was with them for a very short time down at Hornchurch. Their new commanding officer had been posted in and had never flown a Spitfire. He asked me to go up with him so he could formate on me and I could show him around the place. I thought it was a hell of a thing to be thrown in as a CO of a Spitfire squadron, and never having flown one.

Glen Niven returned to 602 a couple of weeks later and stayed with the squadron until 23rd September 1941. Unfortunately he contracted tuberculosis and was immediately admitted to Horton Emergency Hospital on 24th September. After many months of treatment, he was finally invalided out of the Royal Air Force on 12th March 1942 as a flying officer. After the war, in June 1946, he rejoined his beloved 602 Squadron, which had been reformed, working as a civilian clerk.

Another fellow 602 Squadron pilot was Pilot Officer Stuart Nigel Rose, who had served with the squadron since June 1939, and he remembers the squadron's offensive operations during this phase of the air war:

The sweeps were a mixed bag altogether. In a way it was a bit unsatisfactory because we were put up chiefly as Aunt Sallys, to draw the Luftwaffe up. Germany had attacked Russia in June and had taken quite a bit of their fighter strength away from the Pas de Calais area, but it was the Air Ministry's reckoning that we ought to keep them busy, so we were sent across to escort three Stirlings or six Blenheims or a few Hampdens or something and our furthest target was Lille. It got rather nasty, because after a while the Germans got used to this, they used to sit up in the sun and as we came over, they came down on us; there wasn't much we could do but grin and bare it. The Germans would just whistle through the formation. I would say that the operations weren't terribly successful at that time.

Deere led 602 on a sweep over Béthune on 9th August, flying at 22,000 feet with another squadron, 452, which was positioned below and to the left. At 11.25 am, Deere saw enemy 109Fs streaming down to attack 452. He ordered his Blue Section down to help:

I then noticed four Me109Fs to my left and slightly above. I turned into them and got behind one, which dived almost vertically for cloud some 7,000 feet below. I opened fire at about 300 yards with slight deflection. A biggish piece fell off from the right side of the enemy aircraft, which then disappeared into cloud.

At 15,000 feet, on pulling up from the above attack, I saw one Me109F below and to port. I attacked from above to starboard, and at a range of 250-200 yards I fired short bursts of cannon. The enemy fighter then entered cloud, but I noticed black smoke coming from the starboard side of its fuselage. I was then at 7,000 feet.

Suddenly another Me109 came across my nose flying north. He dived through a thin layer of cloud on seeing me and headed for ground level. I followed him, but could not close up. I fired the remainder of my ammunition from one gun only.

On landing, Deere claimed the two Messerschmitt 109Fs as damaged. Glen Niven recalls Alan Deere's attitude towards claiming enemy victories:

Al asked me: 'Did you see that one go down?', because he wanted confirmation and I had to say, 'Sorry Al, I was somewhere else at the time.' He never pressed it and never claimed I think because he didn't get confirmation. That's one of the reasons he didn't get his Distinguished Service Order for some time. He'd shot down 17 enemy aircraft by then and the automatic thing was at 18, you got a DSO. I said to him, 'I'll say I saw it go down if you want.' But he said, 'No way.' Al had tremendous integrity and would have never falsified a claim.

Deere led 602 on another close escort mission on 12th August, this time escorting six Hampden light bombers to attack a target at Gosnay, near Lille, as part of a wing operation with 452 and 485 Squadrons. While 602 squadron was at 25,000 feet and just 10 miles short of the target area, they were totally surprised by a large formation of Messerschmitt 109Fs, who had dived down through broken cloud above to attack the bombers. Over the R/T the Wing Leader, Johnny Kent, yelled a warning of fighters coming down. Deere ordered his section into the attack and immediately engaged the 109s, but they dived through and away, but not before they had shot down Deere's No.2, Bell-Walker. There were no further attacks by the enemy fighters over the target, but on the way back the bombers would have to run the gauntlet yet again.

Suddenly Deere's attention was alerted, when Red 4 of his section shouted a warning of fighters coming in. He managed to latch on to a 109 as it dived down past him and fired a short burst into it. At that moment, his aircraft shuddered, as cannon shells and machine-gun bullets penetrated into it, from a German he hadn't seen. He broke away and found his aircraft had been badly hit. A cannon shell had hit one wing and his cockpit instruments showed that his glycol tank had been damaged as well. As his engine began to overheat, he flew into cloud to seek cover from the enemy fighters. He turned and headed for the French coast, keeping a constant eye on the engine's coolant temperature gauge and checking his altitude. Deere was still at a fair height, so his chances of making it back across the Channel were quite good. He sent out a 'Mayday' signal, which was picked up, and the air rescue service was put on alert.

Soon Deere saw the coast of Kent ahead in the distance and his spirits were lifted. He was now within gliding distance of the airfield at Manston. As he safely touched down and shut off the aircraft's engine, he must have given a terrific sigh of relief as yet another harrowing adventure in action over France came to a successful conclusion. On inspection of his battered aircraft, he counted 37 bullet holes through the fuselage together with the large hole in the wing caused by a cannon shell; his top petrol tank had also received hits as well as the glycol tank. After some refreshments, he returned to Kenley in a Miles Magister aircraft later that day. Glen Niven had been flying that day in Blue Section, and remembers:

> We were at this time on mostly operational sweeps and when you entered into the fray of combat, you usually lost sight of everybody in your own section. I can remember we were at 25,000 feet and there was something going on down below. We were close escort at that time. I was leading a section and Al said, 'Blue Section go down there and see what the hell's going on.' When I got down there, the other three chaps in my section had been shot down. One of them was picked up by the Resistance and they got him safely through Paris, over the Pyrenees and finally back to England.

The Kenley Wing was once again busy providing escort cover to Circus operations on 13th October. It was briefed and given its role for Circus 108A, which was to take it over the St Omer area of northern France. Al Deere was again leading 602 Squadron with 452 in support. The squadrons met up with and supplied close support to four Bristol Blenheim light bombers.

Deere was leading his section of four aircraft on the port side and slightly above the bombers. At around 1.20 pm, 15 miles north-west of St Omer, they were attacked by enemy fighters ranging up to 100 in strength. In his combat report, he states the seriousness of the situation he was confronted with:

> We were attacked repeatedly by pairs of Me109Fs and had no alternative but to fight back. I was unable to warn Sergeant Brayley (Red 2) as my transmitter was useless. I saw him being attacked and saw him go down with smoke and glycol coming from his machine. I also saw another Spitfire; I think it was Sergeant Ford, my Yellow 4, going down in a similar manner. I also saw a 109 spinning out of control.
>
> I was by now alone and had to ward off repeated attacks on my return. I managed a short burst at two 109Fs, the second from about 150 yards and above. I feel sure his canopy disintegrated and caved in, as if hit by a cannon shell. I cannot definitely confirm this. He then went on to his back and then down vertically from 13,000 feet.

Back at Kenley, he notified the Intelligence officer of the claim and pronounced it as a damaged.

It was in November 1941, that another keen New Zealander arrived at Kenley to take up his position with 485 Squadron; his name was John Milne Checketts. He had joined the Royal New Zealand Air Force just three days before war was declared on 3rd September 1939, but he did not start his initial training until October 1940. He then sailed for Britain in July 1941. Here he continued his flying training and was then sent to 56 Operational Training School at Sutton Bridge before being posted as a pilot officer to 485. On arriving at Kenley, Johnny Checketts found he was having a problem when trying to land his aircraft and this is when he first bumped into Alan Deere. When interviewed in February 2003, Johnny remembered:

> I found that the Spitfire was very light to fly compared to the Hurricane, which I had flown during training. At Kenley, they had short runways and I was coming into land at the recommended speed, but I seemed to run on and on and misjudged my landings. I got very depressed with this and I thought, 'Hell, I'll get the sack over this lot,' because I'd never flown a Spitfire before. I was sitting in the Mess bar room cogitating about this and my CO and Al and somebody else were talking away and drinking, when Al came up to me and sat beside me and said, 'What's wrong?' and I said, 'I couldn't get the bloody thing to land properly and I thought I might get the boot.' He said, 'Don't be silly come on.' Bill Wells had just been made the commanding officer and he came over and he said, 'No that's alright.' So that's how I first met Alan Deere.
>
> I found Al to be a very cheerful bloke and we seemed to get on very well together right from the kick off. I was still an acting pilot officer at that time; Al was a squadron leader, which was a great differential. You must remember, he was commanding 602 Squadron at this time and it was odd that a pilot officer from one squadron should be a friend with the CO from another, but we got along famously.
>
> We used to play a bit of squash together if we had any spare time and he was a very good player.

Deere's close friend 'Mitzi' Darling left the squadron on 13th November, to take up his new role as an instructor at 53 Operational Training Unit based at Llandow in Wales. Darling had flown 292 operational flying hours while with 602 Squadron.

On 18th November 1941, 602 took off at 10.45 am on a Ramrod mission to attack the Hesdin Alcohol Distillery. They rendezvoused with other squadrons over Dungeness and proceeded across the Channel. They were then given instructions to patrol between Hardelot and Dungeness, when suddenly they were bounced by about 20 Me109s and FW190s. The squadron broke in all directions and individual combats took place. Pilot

Officer Glen Niven had his starboard aileron shot away, but successfully managed to fly his damaged aircraft, AB848, back to Kenley. Sergeant Willis flying AD189 had his wing peppered with bullet holes, but he too survived and claimed one German probable and one damaged. Al Deere, flying in Spitfire AD251, also claimed one Me109 enemy fighter damaged on his return to base, the action taking place 10 miles north of Le Touquet. It was after landing that Al inspected his aircraft and found that he had sustained damage from enemy machine-gun fire from the ground, whilst heading low back across the Channel. During his exit, he had also been targeted by the heavier German coastal defences and was suddenly alerted to the situation, when a salvo exploded extremely close in front of his Spitfire. Luckily, he was soon out of German range.

Deere's luck was still holding, for his flight sergeant after giving his aircraft a thorough inspection, walked up to Al holding a fragment of German shell which he had found imbedded within the Spitfire's glycol header tank. Had it gone clean through Al's aircraft's engine, it would have seized within minutes and he would have had to bale out or been forced to ditch into the sea. He decided to keep the shell fragment as a good luck charm. It was this action bringing with it his eighteenth victory that ensured Deere would get a DSO.

CHAPTER 5

PROMOTION AND TRAGEDY
1942

On 26th January Alan Deere was posted from Redhill back to Kenley pending a further posting to an operational training unit. On arrival back at Kenley, he presented himself before the station commander, Group Captain Victor Beamish, who told him that his squadron would now be led by the famous Irish ace Squadron Leader Brendan 'Paddy' Finucane DSO, DFC and two bars. Beamish also informed Deere that he was to make his way to 11 Group Headquarters as the Air Officer Commanding, Air Vice-Marshal Trafford Leigh-Mallory, wished to see him regarding an assignment in the United States, which had entered the war in December 1941.

Although Al was pleased at the news of a tour to the United States, his concern was whether on his return, he would be able to go back to operational flying or would have to see the rest of the war from behind a desk or at an OTU. The next day he walked into Leigh-Mallory's office and was given his assignment. He was to travel to the US as part of an RAF delegation to Washington to share some of his experience on air combat. The tour would start on 4th March. Leigh-Mallory also stated that he wanted Deere fit and ready for his planned offensive against the Germans in the summer of 1943. He also pushed up Al's hopes of leading his own wing, once he returned from across the Atlantic.

After relinquishing his command and leaving the squadron in the capable hands of Brendan Finucane, Deere spent the next several days sorting out various necessities for his trip to the United States as well as meeting his girlfriend Joan Fenton. Joan travelled down from her unit in Birmingham to meet Alan, whose ship was departing from Cardiff docks. Edward 'Mitzi' Darling also came to see him before he left. The following morning (the 28th), he joined other fellow RAF and Naval officers chosen for the delegation.

The RAF was represented by three pilots. As well as Deere, there was Group Captain Alexander Hess, a Czechoslovakian who had fought the Germans during their advance through his country in 1939. He escaped capture when France was overrun in May 1940, and reached Britain in June

1940. By the beginning of the Battle of Britain, he was squadron leader of 310 Czech Squadron based at Duxford. Flying with Bader's Big Wing on 15th September, he was shot down over the Thames estuary, but baled out successfully, without injury. His position for the trip to America was as Czech Air Attaché. The other officer was Gregory 'Gus' Daymond, an American flyer from Montana who had joined the RAF before America had entered the fray. He had served with 71 Eagle Squadron – made up of American airmen who had decided to fight for Britain in 1940, while America remained neutral – in 1941, and had been awarded the DFC in October that year for destroying five enemy aircraft.

As the ship weighed anchor and left port, what might Al's thoughts have been on leaving not only the bombed and battered island that had survived the threat of Nazi invasion, but also the friends with whom he had fought? He was heading for America, where there were no air-raid warnings or fear of being bombed night after night and no rationing of food. The land slowly disappeared from the horizon, and the ship set its course for Halifax, Canada. The trip across the Atlantic was fortunately uneventful probably due to the bad weather, which caused mountainous waves to toss the vessel about for most of the trip. But this also slowed the ship's progress and as a result they arrived late into port.

On arrival at Halifax, the passengers' first immediate reaction was at the bright lighting of the streets and buildings. After spending nearly three years with blackout in Britain, it must have been like entering a fairy world or fantasyland. From Halifax, the three RAF officers travelled by train to the city of Montreal, and then proceeded to Washington DC by aeroplane. For the next two days, they relaxed and spent time visiting the sites of interest around the capital. Following this, they reported to the Royal Air Force Delegation offices for their itinerary. Much to Deere's surprise and joy, he found that his orders had been changed and instead of visiting units of the United States Navy, he was now given the task of visiting various American Army Air Force squadrons. His task was to lecture them on the fighter tactics employed over Europe, and while doing this he would also get the chance to fly some of their latest aircraft.

After travelling and lecturing for nearly six weeks, Deere began to tire of this type of work and he felt that he would serve better if he was sent back to Britain to return to operational flying. However, he still had more lectures scheduled over in California. He then sent a telegram to the Air Ministry who were disappointed with his request, but again Deere's luck was in. It just so happened that the First Sea Lord of the Admiralty, Admiral Sir Dudley Pound had arrived in Washington while en route to Montreal, where he would board an aircraft bound for England. With such an important figure as the Admiral, it was operational procedure that an aide accompany him to ensure that any needs he might have during the flight would be taken care of. Alan Deere stepped forward and offered his services for the flight and was accepted immediately. He had found his ticket home. They boarded the Liberator aircraft and set off across the Atlantic for Prestwick, Scotland.

Once landed, both Sir Dudley and Deere were transferred to another aircraft for the trip down to London.

The following morning he presented himself to the Air Ministry to report on his tour of the United States and to find out what his next appointment was to be. He found to his astonishment that in his absence he had been given a staff position in the Far East. Somewhere, the signal of his posting had been late in arriving and as he had returned home early with Admiral Pound, the message had not been received.

It was a posting that he did not relish, as he desperately wanted to get back into the air war in Europe, so Deere asked the officer in charge of personnel at the Air Ministry whether another officer could fill this position. He was told that there were plenty of other chaps who would jump immediately at the chance.

This answer made him feel a lot more comfortable and his thoughts then returned to how to get back to flying. He remembered what AVM Trafford Leigh-Mallory had said to him about leading a wing on his return, and arranged a meeting with him through his personal assistant. The response was immediate and that same afternoon, he walked into Leigh-Mallory's office and was greeted warmly by the AOC of 11 Group. Leigh-Mallory asked how he had fared over in the USA, and then Deere put to him the question of his returning to operations and leading a wing. Leigh-Mallory was somewhat hesitant with his answer. He could not offer him a wing to lead at the present time, but could possibly offer him a squadron in 11 Group. Leigh-Mallory told him that one of the Canadian squadrons, 403, based at North Weald had recently taken a beating. They needed a new leader to raise their morale. Al accepted the job there and then; he also asked about the position of a new flight commander, immediately thinking of his old friend 'Mitzi' Darling. Leigh-Mallory surrendered to this question as well and told him to see the personnel officer on his way out to organise all relevant paperwork.

Leaving 11 Group Headquarters, Deere must have felt over the moon. At last he was returning to what he knew best.

Just before his appointment to take over 403 'Wolf' Squadron, he met his New Zealand friend and colleague 'Hawkeye' Wells. Wells had been given the position of Wing Leader at Kenley. He recalls:

> We both met up at a place called the Kemul Club near the Regent's Palace Hotel in London. This was owned by a guy named Bobby Page who was a bit of a character, but very hospitable; he would encourage all the flying chaps to come to his club. It was here that I chatted with Al and brought him up to date on the air war and the Germans' new fighter, the Focke-Wulf FW190. I told Al of the terrible time we'd been having at Kenley and at Redhill. We were flying our clapped-out Spitfire Vbs and had a very hard time when the Focke-Wulf appeared. We were taking a lot of pilot losses during this period because

we couldn't compete with the new German fighters.

Back at the family home in Wanganui, Al's father received a letter from Mr W. Nash of the New Zealand Legation based in Washington DC. Dated 26th March 1942, it read:

Dear Mr Deere,

I have just had the pleasure of meeting your son, Squadron Leader A.C. Deere, DFC, who has been sent to the United States on a special mission by the Air Ministry.

Your son was spending some few days at an airfield near Washington and I need hardly say how welcome a visitor he was to the Legation. I understand that his mission will take him to a number of airfields and production centres in different parts of the United States, before he returns to England which, incidentally, he seems very anxious to do, once his work here has been completed.

You will be glad to know that he is in the best of health and in the best of spirits.

We had the most interesting talk with him and feel rather proud of his magnificent record of service with the RAF; as indeed you and your family must do also.

I know that your son is very highly thought of by his superior officers and believe that on his return to England, will be promoted to the rank of Wing Commander. I hope it will not be too long before you have him back with you in New Zealand, safe and sound – he is the type of young New Zealander whose service the Dominion will need in peace no less than in war.

In the meantime, I am sure you must be pleased to know that he is doing a splendid job with credit to his country and to himself.

On 30th April 1942, Alan Deere took up his new posting with 403 RCAF 'Wolf' Squadron at North Weald aerodrome in Essex. The squadron had suffered badly in pilot losses over the previous weeks and on 27th April whilst carrying out a sweep over northern France, had lost its commanding officer and a flight lieutenant. The other squadrons, which with 403 made up the North Weald Wing during this period were 121, 222 and 331 'Norwegian' Squadron. The Wing Leader at North Weald was another old friend of Al Deere's, David Scott-Malden. He was also an experienced Battle of Britain pilot who had served with 603 Squadron at Hornchurch and also Al's old squadron 54, which he had commanded in 1941. The station commander was Group Captain Tom Pike. On his arrival at North Weald, Al was introduced and told of the previous week's events that had taken their toll on the squadron.

On 27th April 403 Squadron had been tasked with carrying out a Rodeo operation (a fighter sweep without bombers) with 12 Group Wing. During its briefing it was instructed that it would rendezvous at 10,000 feet off Southend with the other wing, then climb until both wings were stepped up from 20,000 to 25,000 feet. They would then proceed to sweep the area over Mardyke, St Omer and out between Hardelot and Le Touquet. Unfortunately things did not go according to plan and cloud prevented the North Weald Wing from climbing to the altitude intended. Another squadron, 121, was positioned just below cloud at 22,000 feet, 403 was at 21,000 and 222 Squadron was at 20,000 with the 12 Group Wing below. No enemy aircraft were seen or encountered, but heavy German anti-aircraft fire was experienced over the Dunkirk, Mardyck area.

Suddenly tragedy struck. At 6.50 pm Flight Lieutenant Duval, RCAF, who was leading Yellow Section and flying on the port side of 403, was seen to turn sharply to the right and collide violently with the Spitfire of 403's commanding officer, Squadron Leader Campbell, who was leading Red Section. Campbell's aircraft lost a great part of its right wing and was seen to roll over on to its back and go down out of control just inland of the coast. Flight Lieutenant Duval's machine was streaming glycol and crashed about half-a-mile offshore without Duval baling out. Pilot Officer Smith of 121 Squadron reported seeing a parachute at 5,000 feet inland from Le Touquet and this could have been Campbell.

When the collision occurred it was reported that a squadron of Spitfires was seen heading straight for the wing at the same height, causing some of 403's pilots to dive down to avoid hitting them. The remaining nine aircraft of 403 landed back at base at 8.05 pm. The squadron's operations book read; 'This completes another bad show for 403 and a very great loss to us all.'

Alan Deere was now given the task of getting the squadron back up to operational status within one week. The squadron would operate from RAF Southend aerodrome (also known as Rochford) during this period, while he got to know his men and worked on new fighter tactics. During the first four days of May, the pilots worked hard together on air tactical exercises, flying three or four times each day until they got their formations and tactics up to par.

The next day, the 5th, was an important one for the unit, as it was declared operational and would be flying that day with the rest of the North Weald Wing. That morning the wing was ordered to sweep the area over the Belgian coast. 403's 12 aircraft took off from Southend. Red Section, led by Deere, consisted of Pilot Officer Doug Hurst, Warrant Officer D.G. Campbell and Sergeant Johnson. Yellow Section, led by Flight Lieutenant Walker, had Flight Sergeant Walker, Pilot Officer L.J. Somers and Pilot Officer Magwood, while Blue Section, with Pilot Officer Rainville leading, had Sergeant A. Monchier, Pilot Officer J.F. Parr and Flight Sergeant G.D. Aitken. The squadron reached its rendezvous over Malden, Essex, to join the rest of the wing, but owing to a fault in Al Deere's watch, the rendezvous was made a minute or so late and after orbiting the area for three minutes and not sighting the other squadrons, 403 proceeded to Felixstowe.

When they were about halfway there, they received a signal from the Operations Room to proceed directly to the target. 403 climbed steadily up until it was positioned at 23,000 feet, 10 miles north of Zeebrugge. Al then called up Squadron Leader 'Dickie' Milne who was leading the wing and told him he had seen the bombers already turning for home. 403 then turned on to a reciprocal course to the bombers at the same height and maintained this height until halfway across the Channel, where it reduced height and headed for home. It did not encounter or sight any enemy aircraft during the whole trip and landed back at midday.

During the rest of May the squadron was involved with further sweeps over St Omer, Zeebrugge, Dieppe and Abbeville, but it was not until June that it was to be heavily involved in combat with the Germans.

On 1st June 403 carried out two operational sweeps. During the morning, it carried out an operation to Gravelines, acting as withdrawal support to the Kenley Wing, and returning intact to North Weald at 11.35 am. In the afternoon it took off for Martlesham Heath at 3.05 pm and on landing there, the squadron was refuelled and given the operational briefing for its role as target support to 12 Boston bomber aircraft on an anti-shipping attack at Flushing.

Alan Deere led the squadron off at 5.50 pm and was followed by 222 Squadron as bottom cover with the two other squadrons from the wing, 121 and 331. Flying across at zero feet they then climbed to 18,000 feet when over Haamstede. They turned south and then west, coming out over Flushing, where they observed smoke rising from the docks that had just been bombed. It was when they were north of Ostend at a height of 18,000 feet that Deere and the others saw 15 Focke-Wulf 190s heading towards them from the south at 25,000 feet, and another seven or eight coming in from the north. The enemy fighters from the north attacked the Norwegians of 331, while the FW190s from the south hurtled down on to 403. Deere managed to keep the squadron together with the exception of Yellow 3, Pilot Officer Somers, and Yellow 4, Sergeant Johnson, who both turned to meet the attack. Somers got in a three-second burst of fire at a range of 400 yards, but made no claim. He then set course for home, but was attacked from astern. He turned to attack and managed to get in another burst of fire and observed a piece of engine cowling drop off from the FW190. At the same time his own aircraft was hit in the port wing by a cannon shell, which tore a large hole through it. Spiralling down to 10,000 feet, Somers headed for home and landed without further damage at 7.35 pm. Sergeant Johnson had also fired at one of the FW190s, but did not claim any damage.

The following day was to be even more hectic. At 9.30 am on 2nd June, Deere briefed the squadron about its next mission. Taking off from Southend it would form up with the rest of the North Weald boys over Chatham and set course for Hastings. 331 Squadron would lead followed by 403 and 222. Over Hastings they would rendezvous with the Hornchurch Wing and head for Cap Gris Nez flying at zero feet. On reaching the French coast they would climb to 20-25,000 feet with the Hornchurch Wing stationed below. They would turn east to sweep over St Omer and come out at Le Touquet and then home.

Everything that Deere had briefed his men about went according to plan, until 403 turned for home over Le Touquet as the last squadron out. They were then confronted by 15 to 20 FW190s, which came in at them from the south. He turned 403 to meet the incoming attack when a further 15 plus FW190s attacked from above and behind. At this point the squadron split into pairs and was committed to fighting its way out. While this action was taking place, the pilots of 403 noticed more enemy fighters entering the battle area from the south. The enemy opposition now engaging the squadron was somewhere in the region of 40-50 fighters; the Canadians were totally outnumbered.

Deere found himself under heavy attack from all sides. He had exhausted all his cannon and machine-gun ammunition by using short bursts at close range and engaging the enemy in head-on, astern and deflection attacks. Being continually attacked he had no time to observe the results from his gunfire. He did however see two aircraft hit the sea about 10 miles west of Le Touquet. One was definitely a Spitfire, which broke in half in mid air, but the pilot managed to bale out. He also saw another parachute in the vicinity, but was unable to give a fix, as he was chased by a FW190 into mid Channel. Fortunately the enemy fighter broke away and when 20 miles south-east of Dungeness, Deere sighted another pilot bale out from his Spitfire. He flew over the area and orbited while sending out a 'Mayday' message. Three other Spitfires arrived over the scene and also patrolled the area, and shortly afterwards rescue boats appeared.

Al then decided to set course for home, but when 15 miles south-west of Dungeness he saw yet another Spitfire crash into the sea. The pilot of this aircraft managed to get into his dinghy and signal to the Spitfire above. Deere gave the pilot's position and directed two rescue boats, which were 15 miles west of the downed pilot. He was eventually rescued, and turned out to be Flight Sergeant Aitken. Al then set course for Southend, landing at 12.10 pm. He reported to the intelligence officer that he had seen a FW190 go down, pouring black smoke and definitely out of control, during the combat over Le Touquet.

Other members of the squadron also gave their reports of the action. Flight Lieutenant Walker who was flying as Yellow 1 reported he had seen 20 plus enemy fighters come in from the south. He turned left to meet the attack, when four FW190s came down out of cloud astern of Red and Blue Sections. He then turned right to head them off, followed by his No.2, but Yellow 3 and 4 continued turning left. Walker managed to fire a short burst at the enemy as they came down on the other two sections, and one of the German fighters broke away and dived into cloud.

Sergeant Murphy, an American who had left his hometown of Turkey Point, Michigan to join the Canadian Air Force when war was declared, was flying as Red 2. He reported:

> I was attacked at the same time as Squadron Leader Deere; I
> saw a FW190 come up dead in front and gave him a two
> second burst of cannon and machine gun as the enemy machine

climbed past me. The FW190 stalled turned over on his back and spun away. I thought I had him, until later I saw another do the same manoeuvre in combat without being fired upon. I managed to get on the tail of a FW190 and opened fire from a range of 200 yards from dead astern with machine guns only as my cannons had both jammed. The German rolled on his back and spun away. I was then myself attacked and took violent evasive action and found myself upside down hanging on my straps. When I pulled out I was at 3,000 feet and in coming out headed for France instead of home. I passed many small villages which all seemed to have ack-ack batteries which opened fire at me. I flew low at 1,500 feet, opened the throttle and got on to the right bearing for home, never expecting to get there. I saw an enemy aircraft crash in the sea, three miles off Le Touquet on the way out. After crossing the English coast, I landed at Manston and refuelled, then took off for Southend.

After being picked up by a rescue launch, Flight Sergeant Aitken reported how he had come to be shot down during the battle against overwhelming odds:

I was Blue 4 and heard Pilot Officer Hurst (Red 3) shouting over the R/T that there were six enemy fighters behind. I looked back, following Blue 3 (Pilot Officer Parr), and heard the CO say, 'Break.' We broke left and I saw a German, which I think was a 109F, attacking Pilot Officer Parr from quarter port astern. I turned slightly to port and gave the German a long burst sweeping him along the fuselage as he crossed my sight with cannon and machine gun. I then felt bullets hit the armour plate at my back and bullets perforate my cockpit hood. My aircraft gave a lurch and the radio was suddenly useless. I went into a steep turn and levelled out and started weaving, I saw nothing more of the aircraft in my section.

Then an enemy aircraft appeared on my starboard side, some 500 feet above and approximately 400 yards away. I took a hasty look around and saw another on my port above and about 500 yards away. The enemy fighter on my starboard side dropped his port wing slightly, so I figured he was coming in to attack. I turned towards him and opened fire from a range of 200 yards. He fired as he came down and I saw his tracer pass underneath me. He then broke away; I continued a steep turn right and levelled out at 10,000 feet and headed for home.

I then saw tracer pass on both sides and saw cannon hits on both my wings. I went into a steep dive, but levelled out again at 5,000 feet. I throttled back and reduced boost and then looked around to see what damage had been done and whether I could make it to Hawkinge airfield. The nose of the aircraft wanted to go up, so I trimmed fully forward, which took most of the pressure off the control column. The engine then started to sputter, puffs of white smoke and flames started to come from the exhausts and gasoline was leaking out into the cockpit as the aircraft began to lose height.

I then decided it was about time I got out. Holding the stick with my left hand, I undid the straps and slid the hood back. I then changed hands and removed my helmet with my left hand, opened the door and throttled back and pulled the nose up then held onto the stick and put my left leg on to the wing. I then pulled the ripcord and fell backwards out of the aircraft. My parachute opened and almost got entangled on the tail. This all happened at 1,000 feet. As I went down, I saw my aircraft hit the deck with a hell of a bang and sink immediately. I inflated my Mae West and turned the quick release as I hit the water. I had hold of my dinghy strap as I could not swim, and gave the strap a hard jerk to free the dinghy from the parachute. It inflated and I climbed in, found the paddles and looked for the shore. I saw a Spitfire circling and this was Squadron Leader Deere; later several more aircraft arrived and one I recognised as David Scott-Malden's, the Wing Leader. I was picked up 25 to 30 minutes later by a rescue launch, given a big drink of scotch, rubbed down and put to bed and eventually landed at Dover.

Alan Deere had landed at Lympne and had made it just in time, having almost run out of fuel. He had been airborne for two hours and ten minutes. While waiting for his aircraft to be turned round by the ground crew, he contacted the other airfields for any news of his men. He felt sure that the occupant of one of the dinghies he had flown over was his good friend Mitzi. As he walked back to his aircraft, he was delighted to see Flight Lieutenant 'Brad' Walker walking towards him. His face however told a different story; Walker told him that most of the squadron hadn't made it back, and this included Flight Lieutenant Darling. There was little they could do but wait. Both Deere and Walker decided to go to the Mess for something to eat and drink while they waited for further news. It was an hour later that they received the good news that Flight Sergeant Aitken had been rescued. But what of the others?

The weather over the Channel was now deteriorating with the haze and visibility getting worse. Deere decided he would take off again and try and locate his comrades who might have ditched their aircraft. He was accompanied by Walker, but their flight was fruitless. The rescue search continued throughout the rest of the day, but no one else was found. The loss of the pilots in his squadron, especially that of his friend, whom he had known more or less since the outbreak of war, played on his mind heavily, as he confessed to friends later. Had he done enough to ensure that the rescue boats could locate the downed pilots?

The 403 Squadron report for that day stated that of the 12 aircraft that took off, only six of the pilots returned home. The squadron was so greatly outnumbered and the fight so furious that no accurate assessment of damage done to the enemy could be made. There was however little doubt that the two enemy aircraft seen out of control by Alan Deere and Sergeant Murphy were shot down by 403, as there were no other Spitfire squadrons in the area at the time of combat.

The losses in 403 that day were Flight Lieutenant Darling, Pilot Officer Parr, Pilot Officer L. Somers, Warrant Officer D. Campbell and Sergeant Hunt.

The following morning after a sleepless night, Al Deere was asked to report to the station commander at North Weald. On his arrival, he presented himself to Tom Pike, who was most understanding and sympathetic regarding the losses the squadron had suffered the previous day. Pike told him that the squadron would temporarily move to Martlesham Heath, while they awaited replacement pilots; it would be employed on convoy protection patrols while this was happening. Al Deere led the squadron off from Southend at 6.00 pm that evening, and they arrived at Martlesham Heath at 6.25 pm. For the next few days Al felt unwell and spent time in bed suffering from a mild attack of quinsy, an inflammation of the throat.

On 16th June, he received a signal that the squadron was to get ready to move up to Catterick for a rest period, which was scheduled for 18th June. The Norwegian Squadron, 332, would replace 403 Squadron. Deere felt that although the squadron had suffered grievously, the amount of hard work that he and the pilots had put in to get it back up to operational strength did not warrant this, and that the pilots' morale at this time was still high.

That same day, he telephoned the station commander at North Weald and asked him if he could arrange for him to meet Leigh-Mallory to talk about the squadron's predicament. He immediately received a return telephone call telling him to fly up to RAF Northolt that afternoon, where a car would take him to see Leigh-Mallory at 11 Group Headquarters at Uxbridge. As he entered, he was met warmly by the AOC, but when Deere asked him about the future of 403 in 11 Group, Leigh-Mallory's mood soured somewhat. He told Deere that as the squadron for the second time in a month had sustained serious losses, he had decided it should be taken off operational duties for a rest. At that point Leigh-Mallory pointed out that he thought Deere's leadership was not totally without fault, stating, 'You are rather too fond of getting into a fight and taking unnecessary risks.'

One can imagine Deere's initial reaction to such criticism. Here was a man who had no real grasp of fighter combat as it was being waged at this time, now accusing and attributing the blame to him for something which no fighter pilot could have avoided; being suddenly bounced from above by a superior enemy force. Deere held his composure and replied that he was sorry, but they had had no other option in the situation they were presented with than to fight. Leigh-Mallory seemed to turn a deaf ear to Deere's reply and told him that the decision was final as far as he was concerned.

It seemed the meeting was at a close, but before leaving Deere decided to press Leigh-Mallory on the promise he had made prior to the United States trip. Would it be possible for him to stay in 11 Group and would he get the wing he had been promised? The reaction was cold and abrupt. 'No, I'm afraid not. You must stay with 403 at this time and go with them to Catterick.' At this point Deere saluted and left the room.

A week later, after arriving at Catterick with the squadron, Deere received a letter from Leigh-Mallory asking him to pass on his thanks to the pilots for their faithful service. The letter read:

> I would like to thank No.403 Squadron for all the very excellent work they have done while they have been in No.11 Group.
>
> I hope they will have a successful time in the north, and come back to the Group again later on, all the better for a period of rest. I wish the squadron the best of luck
>
> Yours sincerely,
>
> Leigh-Mallory

During the squadron's time at Catterick they were visited by Air Marshal H. Edwards, who was shown around the aircraft and introduced to various members of 403. On 22nd July, Deere received the following letter from the air marshal:

> Dear Deere,
>
> I would like to thank you for all that you did for my party and me, during our visit to your squadron. I was very much impressed with what I saw and I wish to offer my warmest congratulations on the keenness and efficiency of your personnel, who seemed to be in the very highest spirits and this reflects no little upon yourself as their leader. You will appreciate that it is difficult for me to get down to see you as often as I would like to, but I hope that time will permit me to visit your squadron more often in the future than I have in the past.

The following day, on 23rd July more good news arrived, when word was received that Pilot Officer Douglas Hurst, who had been shot down on 2nd June, was alive as a prisoner of war. This news bucked up the squadron, and much cheering was heard around the dispersal areas.

On the 24th the squadron intelligence officer, Flying Officer T.S Mackay, left to take up a new appointment with 401 Squadron. He had been responsible for keeping the 403 daily diary and on his last day wrote:

> My stay with the boys of this squadron has been both interesting and enjoyable and although I am attached now to 401, I will follow with interest the progress of the squadron and the individual exploits of its excellent fighter pilots.

The scrapbook contains all newspaper clippings of their

endeavours and to the new intelligence officer who takes over, I trust he will ensure that all the individual exploits of merit are suitably recognized in the press for the reason that this is the one source we can assure will gladden the hearts of the folks at home, and is the only channel in which they can follow the outstanding achievements of their sons. It has meant a great deal to this squadron to have as its leader the ace fighter pilot of New Zealand. His leadership has been an inspiration to all the pilots who with confidence would follow him into any combat.

On the 26th Al Deere left the squadron on a week's leave, and spent the following seven days relaxing, and meeting Joan in the south of England. He returned to Catterick on 3rd August looking tanned and fit. The squadron continued to build up to strength while carrying out formation practices and carrying out local patrols. Some excitement was aroused on 12th August, when, five miles from Whitby, Pilot Officer C.R. Olmsted, flying with Sergeant A.D. Dow of Green Section, sighted what appeared to be a Dornier 217. They tried to intercept, but the enemy disappeared into cloud and was not sighted again.

The following day, Al Deere received a communiqué from 11 Group informing him of his immediate posting for staff duties at 13 Group Headquarters; he would leave Catterick on 16th August. The squadron diary read:

> Word received today that Squadron Leader A.C. Deere, DFC and Bar has been posted. It is bad news for the squadron as his ability and leadership have been an inspiration since he joined the unit. Flight Lieutenant L.S. Ford will assume command.

It was in the autumn of 1942 that Lieutenant General Baron Michael Donnet first met Alan Deere. He remembers their first meeting:

> At this time 64 Squadron had a new commanding officer, Colin Gray, an outstanding New Zealand fighter pilot and a great friend of Al Deere's. We first met at Shepherd's, a London pub where the 11 Group fighter pilots used to gather together when off duty on Saturday evenings. Joan Fenton was with Alan and I got to know them both and appreciate Al's quiet and unassuming personality.

After only a short period at 13 Group, Deere suddenly received his marching orders once again, when on 26th October 1942 he was posted to attend an officers' staff training course at the RAF Staff College, Gerrards Cross, in Buckinghamshire. At the college, he undertook various paperwork exercises and exams and found the work very taxing. One of the more interesting highlights of this time occured when officers from the Dominion's three military services were invited to attend a tea party given by King George VI and his wife, Queen Elizabeth at Buckingham Palace.

During the event, Deere was reintroduced to the King and Queen and related his recent flying exploits. He was also introduced to the two princesses, Elizabeth and Margaret. The younger princess, Margaret, was greatly impressed when told that Deere was a fighter pilot. Perhaps this was the initial interest that sparked her fascination later with another RAF fighter pilot, Peter Townsend?

CHAPTER 6

THE BIGGIN HILL WING

1943

During most of January 1943, immersed in study continually, Deere was trying to keep up with the mass of paper work he had to undertake. After the three-month-long course, he passed his exams successfully. Deere was posted back to 13 Group Headquarters on 25th January to carry on his duties as an air staff officer. His hopes of returning to operational flying seemed to have been thwarted yet again; it looked like he would never climb back into the cockpit of a fighter aircraft again and would see out the rest of the war from behind a desk.

Fortunately for Deere, an old friend was about to give him a helping hand. At the beginning of February 1943, Air Commodore Cecil Bouchier, former station commander of RAF Hornchurch, arrived at 13 Group to take up his new position as Senior Air Staff Officer. He had known Deere since 1938 and through the Battle of Britain and they were friends. Deere pleaded with Bouchier to allow him to return to operational flying as a supernumerary with one of 11 Group's squadrons. After a few telephone calls, Bouchier managed to arrange for Deere to go on a two-week attachment to Biggin Hill as a supernumerary squadron leader flying. Here he would be under the command and watchful eye of another of his old Hornchurch comrades, 'Sailor' Malan, who was now station commander.

Arriving at Biggin on 11th February, Deere was introduced to the Wing Leader, Squadron Leader Richard Maxwell 'Dickie' Milne who in turn introduced Deere to the commanding officer of 611 Squadron, Squadron Leader Charlton 'Wag' Haw, a Battle of Britain pilot who had flown with 504 Squadron in 1940 and had fought in Russia in 1941, when the squadron operated as 81 Squadron from Vaenga airfield, near Murmansk. Deere would fly with this squadron for the next two weeks. The other squadron based at Biggin was the Free French squadron, 341.

On 16th February, Deere was given leadership of a section in the wing during a sweep over France. When the wing was over St Omer at 37,000 feet, 12 Focke-Wulf 190s were sighted 10,000 feet below. Deere called to his Wing Leader over the R/T to get his permission to attack. Milne gave the

OK and Deere led his section down accordingly. The Spitfires did not go unnoticed and the Germans split in all directions to evade the RAF fighters. Deere was now in pursuit of one of the FW190s and with cool determination gave the German no quarter. He had been off operations for quite a while: did he still have the same reactions and skill needed to compete in air-to-air combat? The answer was yes! Pressing the gun button on the control column, the Spitfire's cannons burst into life; the resulting fire meant the destruction of the enemy was only seconds away as pieces of airframe began to fall away from the doomed aircraft.

Alan Deere was once again a fighter pilot.

Two days later his time had run out and he had to return to 13 Group. Feeling that the last two weeks had been all in vain, he was summoned before 'Daddy' Bouchier on 21st February and on entering his office, he was congratulated with an outstretched hand by the Air Commodore and told of his appointment as Wing Leader at RAF Kenley. Deere was overjoyed with the news for which he had waited for so long. He was told to report to Air Vice-Marshal Saunders of 11 Group on the Monday, but on arriving was completely bemused (but no less happy) to find that his posting had been changed. The change of command was due to the loss of Biggin Hill's Wing Leader 'Dickie' Milne. He had been shot down on 18th March during an engagement with FW190s near Hardelot and had been forced to bale out over the Channel. Fortunately, Milne was rescued by a German patrol vessel and spent the remainder of the war as a prisoner.

Wing Commander J.E. 'Johnnie' Johnson would take over Kenley, while Deere would now become Wing Leader at Biggin Hill. Posted to Biggin Hill on 14th March 1943, it was here that Alan Deere would put some of his own theories of fighter tactics into practice.

Deere was obviously excited with his new appointment and one other thing that delighted him was to be working with his friend 'Sailor' Malan, who was still the station commander. Each had great respect for the other's abilities both as a pilot and leader. On arriving at Biggin Hill, Malan gave Deere his complete confidence and the freedom to adopt the tactics he would use while leading the wing in action. Alan Deere presented his new tactical ideas to Malan and all the squadron commanders, who listened attentively to his more flexible approach for squadron operations:

> 1. That all squadrons and sections in the wing formation would be independent, but also remain interdependent when the need arose.

> 2. He would lead the wing and would have total control over the formation, routes and critical timings on operations; the squadron and section leaders could use their own judgement in event of enemy attacks, but they must inform him before going into action.

> 3. He felt that all squadrons should be relied upon to take

equal responsibility when the wing was undertaking escort for a raid. And if the event arose, they might be called upon to take over the lead, if the other squadrons were engaged with dealing with enemy attacks.

4. He also underlined the need for their fighters not to be restricted by the bombers they were to escort. The German High Command had tried this procedure during the Battle of Britain with disastrous results. The Spitfires would always be in sight of the bomber formations, but would not be tied to their speed.

One pilot who flew from Biggin Hill during this time was Frenchman Pierre Clostermann. He had joined the Free French Air Force on 18th March 1942. He remembers:

> I had learned to fly in Brazil in November 1937, where I had obtained my private pilot's licence and then I travelled to America to continue flying. When I arrived in England after the war had broken out, I had about 340-350 hours flying hours which was quite capital at the time. I then had to go through all the flying tests again to find out whether I would be selected for fighters or bombers. I joined 341 Alsace Squadron at the end of 1942, but it was then sent to Biggin Hill at the beginning of 1943. At that time Biggin Hill had been going through a series of bad luck. On the 14th March for example, the Biggin Wing was jumped by the second squadron of Jagdgeschwader 26, which was commanded by Wutz Galland, the younger brother of ace Adolf Galland. Wing Commander 'Dickie' Milne, the Wing Commander Flying was shot down, as was the commander of 341 Squadron on that day. Alan Deere was brought in to replace Milne. The first time I saw Alan Deere was at the briefing. He gave us the usual talk and instructions and his code-name in the air was 'Brutus'.
>
> I was very surprised when I first saw him getting into his Spitfire; he was wearing a white flying suit like the old prewar times. He was an experienced leader and we were very lucky to have him because he helped to reduce considerably the losses and also increase considerably the victories at the time. There was never any communication problem with language in the air. You couldn't fly an operation without speaking decent English; any pilot could understand 'Break' or 'Bandits'.
>
> Deere was a decent chap and got on easily with the French pilots. One of these was René Mouchette. Commandant Mouchette was one of the old hands and had joined the air force practically at the time of the Battle of Britain and he could speak good English. He was in a sense very British, he was always very smart, he always wore French uniform, I

never saw him with an RAF uniform or flying kit, except at the beginning of his career. He was an excellent flyer and I was his favourite No.2; he even wrote this in a letter to his mother, which was received after the war. It also stated that on 17th May I had saved him from a couple of Focke-Wulf 190s.

Another of Deere's good friends arrived at Biggin Hill on 3rd April, to take up his new position as a flight commander with 611 Squadron. This was Flight Lieutenant Edward 'Jack' Charles, a Canadian and a former veteran of 54 Squadron, who had served during the Battle of Britain.

On 4th April, Deere led the wing on an operational raid for the first time. The squadrons had been at readiness by 6.30 am that morning, but due to delays they were not needed until 1.00 pm. Accompanied by Group Captain Malan, Deere and the wing set off on Ramrod 51. They rendezvoused with the bombers at 27,000 feet over Beachy Head and then set course for Le Tréport, from where they would then go on to the target at Abbeville. No enemy fighters were encountered, but on the way out Deere's aircraft began to develop engine problems and he was forced to hand over his leadership to Malan. He successfully reached Manston and returned to Biggin once his aircraft had been checked over. He continued to lead the squadrons on escort missions during the early part of April, but the Germans would not be drawn up into combat and the sky seemed somewhat lacking in enemy activity.

Deere was again leading the wing on 21st April on a raid on Abbeville aerodrome, when on the way over the Channel, his auxiliary fuel tank refused to jettison as he was changing over to his aircraft's main fuel tank. His No.4 also suffered the same problem and so Deere and Red Section, with whom he was flying, were forced to return to base. This was unfortunate, for that day German fighters were sighted.

Malan had taken over command as Deere was forced to return and had led the wing to Abbeville. On their approach, while at 16,000 feet, eight Focke-Wulf 190s were seen at 10 o'clock below. But when the squadrons went down to attack, the Germans half-rolled and flew inland. Another 10 FW190s were seen crossing from port to starboard, but they again refused to be drawn into combat. As the bombers left the target area, operations control passed a message that the bombers wanted the squadrons in a lower position. Several formations of 190s appeared and tried to attack the squadrons from behind, but these attempts were foiled when the Spitfires turned towards the enemy fighters, who dived down out of range.

On the 22nd, 'Jack' Charles was appointed squadron commander of 611 Squadron. Another pilot who flew with 611 during this period was Johnny Checketts, the fellow New Zealander hailing from Invercargill. He was a flight commander and remembers Deere's calibre at briefings and as a fighter leader:

> He was just a natural; he had everything planned before he started the briefing, what the target was, what we had to escort, their numbers, the timings, routes and everything meticulously

planned. He didn't leave anything to doubt and made sure
everybody knew what he was talking about. He came over very
strongly.

His leadership in the air was very good and he didn't make
any stupid mistakes. He had a very steadying influence if we
got tangled up with the enemy. He didn't go in bald-headed
like he had been accused of doing. But when he was having a
go himself that was a different matter.

On 15th May 1943, Biggin Hill aerodrome was buzzing with anticipation:
would that day bring the 1,000th victory over an enemy aircraft to be
claimed by one of the station's pilots? There was so much excitement
and media attention that some leading newspapers had sent their
correspondents down to capture the event first hand. One such journalist
followed Al Deere around the station and wrote the following story of that
day:

The pilots' thoughts are not only on the next raid that they will
undertake, but also of that one thousandth plane. Who is going
to shoot it down for the station? The pilots are thinking too of
the sweepstake. Many tickets have been taken on the station
and in London. There are prizes for first, second and third – the
pilots will receive a percentage, so will the ground crews. One
of the pilots asks Wing Commander Alan Deere DFC and Bar:
'Have they drawn the sweep, yet Sir?' 'No, all the tickets aren't
in yet, Bill,' he replies. The Wing Commander is sitting with a
famous South African, Group Captain A.G. Malan. They have
been working on last-minute details for this afternoon's flight.
Now they are ready to slip on their lifejackets and climb into
their Spitfires. The Group Captain tugs his yellow and black
scarf to ease it. Deere's scarf is deep blue with white spots.
Deere looks up at the sky and stretches comfortably. 'Isn't that
sun marvellous?' he says. 'You wouldn't think there was a war
on, would you? Except for the Spitfires.'

There is an atmosphere of tense excitement around the
dispersal hut. You sense it in many different ways. There is
much good-natured competition. 'You needn't think you're
going to get that Hun, I am' . . . 'We'll all line up and watch the
Wing Co shoot it down' . . . 'Groupie says if Wing Co gets in
the way of the Hun, he'll scare him off by firing his cannons.'
The Station Intelligence Officer, 'the Spy', Squadron Leader
de la Torre said, 'It will have to be good shooting before I allow
claims today.'

I follow Deere through a concrete doorway and out into the
protected bay to his Spitfire, and while he climbs into the
cockpit, I clamber up the side of the bay and join the
squadron's intelligence officer, Pilot Officer 'Tommy'

The family home in Westport, 1925. Young Alan on left, his mother standing and father sitting on right; the woman seated centre is unknown. *(Erin Englert)*

Top: The old family house at 43 Plymouth Street, Wanganui. *(Brendon Deere)*

Bottom: Alan visiting his uncle's (mother's brother) farm in Wairarapa, helping with the horse-drawn dray. *(Erin Englert)*

Top: Alan Deere, seated front row on extreme left, a member of the Wanganui Technical College 5th Grade Rugby Team in 1932. *(Brendon Deere)*

Middle left: Alan pictured in 1935 after playing a round of golf. *(Erin Englert)*

Middle right: The adventure begins! Sailing to Britain to join the RAF aboard the SS *Rangitane* are back row: Ken Tait and Jack McKay, front: Steve Esson and Al. *(The Deere Collection)*

Left: Formal photo taken just before Alan left Wanganui to join the Royal Air Force in 1937. *(Brendon Deere)*

Top left: Still at sea, Al Deere poses for the camera of one of his shipmates. *(The Deere Collection)*

Top right: Solo at last! Deere after completing his first solo flight at 13 Elementary Flying Training School,

White Waltham, November 1937. *(The Deere Collection)*

Bottom: Group photograph of 6 Course Flying Training School at Netheravon 1938. Deere is second right, back row. *(The Deere Collection)*

Top left: Proud to be wearing the RAF blue uniform, Al Deere photographed just before he received his Wings. *(The Deere Collection)*

Top right: Early days at Hornchurch. A Gloster Gladiator of 54 Squadron stands in front of the main hangar and watch office. *(The Deere Collection)*

Bottom: Rosslyn Park Rugby Club for which Deere (pictured standing third from right) played several times at inside centre. *(The Deere Collection)*

Top left: Deere's Spitfire Mk I 'Kiwi I'. Although published in Deere's own book *Nine Lives* the photograph was cropped and did not show the dispersal pen and buildings at the top, which have been drawn through with ink pen. *(The Deere Collection)*

Top right: Enjoying a spot of leave down at the Dumas's home, with friend Bob Blake of 54 Squadron. *(The Deere Collection)*

Middle: Deere's burnt-out Spitfire N3180 lies wrecked on the beach near Dunkirk surrounded by inquisitive German soldiers, May 1940. *(Brendon Deere)*

Bottom: Squadron Leader John Leslie Kemp flew with 54 Squadron during 1940 as a flying officer during Dunkirk and the Battle of Britain. *(Author's Collection)*

Alan Deere (signature)

Top: Deere being awarded his DFC from His Majesty King George VI at RAF Hornchurch on 27th June 1940. To the King's left is Air Chief Marshal Sir Hugh Dowding, Commander-in-Chief of Fighter Command; extreme left is Station Commander Cecil Bouchier. The photo is signed by Al Deere. *(Author's Collection)*

Middle: Deere pictured with his Spitfire 'Kiwi II'. Note that the pilot's rear view mirror is inside the front windscreen not outside and above. *(The Deere Collection)*

Bottom: The Heinkel He59b-2 Red Cross seaplane that was forced down by 54 Squadron on the Goodwin Sands and beached at Deal on 9th July 1940. *(The Deere Collection)*

Top left: Pilots of 54 Squadron line up for a casual photograph. Taken at Rochford airfield in July 1940. Standing left to right: P/O McMullen, P/O Deere, F/Sgt Tew, F/O 'Wonky' Way, P/O Gribble. Sitting: P/O Hopkins, P/O Coleman, P/O Matthews. *(The Deere Collection)*

Top right: George Gribble was one of 54 Squadron's most likeable characters. Seen here looking not unlike the cartoon character of 'Tin Tin'. Gribble lost his life over the Channel on 4th June 1941, when he was seen to bale out of his aircraft after developing engine trouble on being bounced by Me109s. His body was never found. *(Author's Collection)*

Middle: Two German crewmen of the Heinkel He59 downed on 9th July 1940 paddle their way to shore, to be made prisoners of war. *(The Deere Collection)*

Bottom: Don't let the flight engineer see you doing that! The pilots of 54 pose on one of the squadron's Spitfires down at Rochford airfield. *(The Deere Collection)*

Top: An unusual photograph showing Hornchurch aerodrome being bombed on 31st August 1940. Centre of photograph shows a Spitfire trying to take off. *(The Deere Collection)*

Middle left: Howard Squire seen standing next to his German captors and his damaged Spitfire P7743, after making a forced-landing in Calais on being shot down by German ace Herbert Ihlefeld on 26th February 1941. *(Howard Squire)*

Middle right: Sergeant Pilot Howard Squire joined 54 Squadron in November 1940 and was to escape along with Al Deere from a mid-air collision during a dogfight practice on 28th December 1940. *(Howard Squire)*

Bottom: Seen in the cockpit of his Spitfire, Les Harvey flew with Al Deere as his No.2, when he was a sergeant pilot with 54 Squadron in 1940. *(Author's Collection)*

Top left: The girl of his dreams! Joan Fenton in the uniform of the American Ambulance, Great Britain, of which she was a driver. This unit was financed by donations from the United States. Joan met Al Deere at Catterick in early 1941. *(The Deere Collection)*

Top right: Al Deere pictured here when flight commander with 602 'City of Glasgow' Squadron in 1941. *(Author's Collection)*

Middle left: Edward 'Mitzi' Darling, who became a great friend of Deere's and flew with him in 602 and 403 Squadrons. *(Author's Collection)*

Middle right: Deere listens attentively to a 602 Squadron pilot's account of an air combat. *(The Deere Collection)*

Bottom: Flying Officer Hugh Glen Niven of 602 Squadron. *(Glen Niven Collection)*

Top: A group photograph of 602 Squadron taken at Ayr, Scotland in 1941. *(The Deere Collection)*

Above: Deere takes centre stage during a visit to the HMV factory in July 1941, to talk to the workers, the majority being women. *(The Deere Collection)*

Middle right: With the Czechoslovakian Delegation during his tour of America in 1942, seen pictured on left. *(The Deere Collection)*

Bottom right: Al and his fiancée Joan spend time together during a brief respite from flying. *(The Deere Collection)*

Top: Discussing the 1,000th enemy aircraft shot down by Biggin Hill pilots, May 1943. Left to right: G/Capt Malan, S/Ldr Charles and W/Cdr Deere. *(The Deere Collection)*

Middle left: Lining up for the Press! The two pilots who shared the claim of shooting down the 1,000th enemy aircraft destroyed by Biggin Hill squadrons with their commanding officers. Left to right – Jack Charles, René Mouchette, 'Sailor' Malan and Al Deere. *(The Deere Collection)*

Middle right: Seated in his Mk IX Spitfire. Al sent this photograph to Johnny Checketts' sister Peggy in 1943. *(Johnny Checketts)*

Bottom: The French fighter ace Pierre Clostermann who flew with 341 'Alsace' Squadron as part of the Biggin Hill Wing, seen seated in his Spitfire in 1943. *(Pierre Clostermann Collection)*

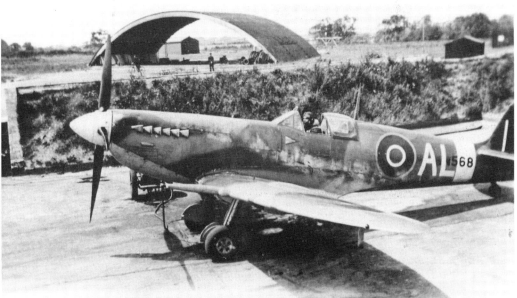

Three excellent photographs showing Deere's Spitfire Mk IX EN568 at Biggin Hill during 1943 with his own code letters of AL painted on the aircraft's fuselage. *(Peter Arnold Collection)*

Top left: At Biggin Hill with friend and fellow New Zealander Johnny Checketts DFC. *(Johnny Checketts)*

Top right: Three of New Zealand's finest meet up at the Grosvenor Hotel, London, June 1943, at the party held for Biggin Hill's 1,000th; W/Cdr Pat Jameson DSO, DFC; Deere and W/Cdr Edward Wells DSO, DFC.

Middle: Douglas Brown flew with 485 New Zealand Squadron under Deere's leadership as wing commander, flying on many sweeps over northern France. *(Douglas Brown)*

Bottom: A group photo of pilots of the Free French 341 'Alsace' Squadron with RAF officers also present. This photograph was taken after René Mouchette had been killed on 27th August 1943. Left to right: Christian Martel, ?, Guy Le Torre, Johnny Checketts, 'Sailor' Malan, Bernard Duperier, Pat Jameson, Deere, ?, Bill Crawford-Compton, General Valin, Michel Boudier, others unknown. *(The Deere Collection)*

Top left: Deere pictured with another New Zealand ace Jack Rae (middle) at Biggin Hill in July 1943.
(Sport and General)

Top right: Congratulations! Al and Joan cut their wedding cake after becoming husband and wife on 18th September 1945.
(The Deere Collection)

Middle: Deere relaxes after a flight, during his tour in Malta 1947.
(The Deere Collection)

Bottom: Leading the March Past at North Weald during the AOC 11 Group's Inspection in May 1952.
(The Deere Collection)

Top: Chatting with Air Marshal the Earl of Bandon and John Cunningham (in civilian clothes) at North Weald on 19th June 1952. Behind second from left is Air Marshal Sir Basil Embry. *(The Deere Collection)*

Middle: Escorting Princess Astrid of Norway during her visit to North Weald on 19th June 1952, to unveil the memorial to the Norwegian aircrews who served there during WW2. *(The Deere Collection)*

Bottom: Group of 72 Squadron aircrew that served under Al Deere when he commanded North Weald in 1952. American pilots Major Jack Brown, back row centre and Bob 'Chuck' Breeze extreme right. *(Jim Barton)*

Top: North Weald, September 1952. A De Havilland Vampire jet aircraft of 72 Squadron B Flight stands at dispersal after arriving at the aerodrome. *(Jim Barton)*

Bottom left: Jim Barton (left), whose memories of Deere are included within this book, at North Weald at 72 Squadron's old dispersal, 1952. He is pictured with Jock Elliott. *(Jim Barton)*

Bottom right: A shop window advertising the release of Al Deere's *Nine Lives* autobiography in 1959. *(The Deere Collection)*

Top: Deere is shown a sports trophy on which his name is engraved, during a reception held in his honour on a visit back to Wanganui, New Zealand in 1959. *(The Deere Collection)*

Bottom left: Al relaxes with his son John and daughter Jacqueline. *(The Deere Collection)*

Bottom right: An official portrait photograph taken when Deere was appointed as Aide-de-Camp to Her Majesty Queen Elizabeth II in 1962. *(Air Ministry)*

Top: 'Churchill's Few'. Air Commodore Al Deere with RAF group captains who took part in Winston Churchill's funeral procession to St Paul's Cathedral in January 1965. Standing left to right are: L.H. Bartlett, R. Berry, E.W. Wootten, R. Haine, D. Sheen and G.H. Westlake. Seated left to right are: J.L.W. Ellacombe, G.C. Brunner, P.M. Brothers, R.Dutton and E.W. Wright. *(Air Ministry)*

Bottom: The Warriors Return! Lord Dowding visits location filming of the Battle of Britain movie at Duxford with some of his fighter boys in 1968. Left to right: Tom Gleave, Bob Stanford Tuck, Ludwik Martel, Johnny Kent, Boleslaw Drobinski and Al Deere. *(The Deere Collection)*

Top left: Al Deere and ex-test pilot Jeffrey Quill take a break during a round of golf in the 1970s. *(The Deere Collection)*

Top right: The Mitchell's School Spitfire Trophy and model of Alan Deere's aircraft, which is still awarded every year to the best achieving school 'House'. *(Fox Photos Ltd)*

Bottom: Pictured at the opening ceremony of the Battle of Britain monument at Capel le Ferne near Folkestone in July 1993, Deere is photographed with ex-Hornchurch veteran John Cox. *(Author's Collection)*

Thompson. From the top of the bay you can see the ground crews fussing around their pilots and aircraft. Deere's Spitfire shatters the silence and a great gust of blue exhaust is wiped away by the wind. It is the signal for the other Spitfires to bellow into life. I wave to Deere and Jack Charles, their faces hidden by their masks and radiotelephone transmitters. The Spitfires trudge their way out of the bays and make their way across the grass to the far side of the aerodrome. There is a dip in the airfield and the Spitfires disappear beyond it. It is silent except for the wind. One of Deere's ground crew climbs to where I'm standing, LAC 'Bill' Potts from Liverpool. You can now hear a deep humming and Potts says, 'Here they come,' and cups his cigarette in his hand to shield it from the wind. Then a line of aircraft came streaming over the rim of the airfield. It is a magnificent sight as the 12 aircraft rise above you.

I look at the letters on the leading aircraft, they read 'AL' and you know that it's Deere. While following the Spitfires, now climbing steadily and closing in to take up formation, there is another roaring behind. The Fighting French Squadron is taking off. The first squadron is now four miles away, small dark neat forms. The Fighting French are taking a shorter turn to link up with them. Suddenly, 'Let's go' says Tommy Thompson. We clamber down from the top of the bay and find his car and drive to the Intelligence Office to watch the progress of the raid on the plotting board. It is quiet and cool in here. A WAAF in neat dark blue uniform is standing by a circular board on which southern England and northern France are outlined. The walls are covered in large maps with different coloured tapes. They indicate the routes taken by the Spitfires and the bombers. It is a diversionary raid. The main attack is on Poix. The plots are over the target now. No enemy aircraft have appeared. 'The boys from Abbeville should be up. What's the matter with them?' the Spy remarks. The boys from Abbeville are German Focke-Wulfs.

The squadrons had taken off at 4.21 pm to undertake Circus Operation 297 which detailed the Biggin Hill Wing along with the Northolt Wing to escort six North-American Mitchell bombers of 2 Group to bomb the airfield at Caen-Carpiquet; this was occupied by the German fighter squadron 'Richthofen Jagdeschwader'. The attack against the Germans would be carried out in two waves; after dropping their bombs on the target, the Mitchell bombers would be followed in by a second wave of 12 Hawker Typhoon fighter-bomber aircraft of 181 Squadron, which would continue to wreak havoc on the ground after the initial assault. While this was all taking place another enemy aerodrome at Poix would also come under attack by a

formation of Douglas Boston bombers from 2 Group, who were supported
by a larger fighter escort of five Spitfire wings.

Al Deere was leading Red Section, which included Malan flying as Red
3. They crossed the French coast at Trouville at 5.00 pm flying at 21,000
feet and then carried on to 10 miles south-east of Caen. It was here that
Deere sighted aircraft in combat below. Just after the bombers had dropped
their load over the target, nine FW190s of I/JG2 had attacked the two Polish
squadrons, 315 and 316 of the Northolt Wing, which had been caught out of
position after the bombers had turned for home. During the Germans' diving
attack they claimed two Spitfires shot down, that of Group Captain
Pawlikowski and Sergeant Lewandowski of 315.

Deere ordered Blue Section down to investigate and they became
embroiled with FW190s. Jack Charles claimed two of the 190s in quick
succession and at about the same time the commanding officer of 341
French Squadron, René Mouchette, also claimed an enemy fighter
destroyed. The wing reformed and returned to Biggin, landing at 5.54 pm.
On landing, Jack Charles was surrounded by a small crowd of pilots and
journalists. With Malan and Deere on hand, Charles relayed the following
information regarding the action that had taken place and the press reported
it:

> 'I was just about to break away when you sang out,' Charles
> tells Deere. 'It looked as if the Huns were going down under
> the bombers with the idea of coming up and catching them
> from underneath. They were in line astern, and I chased them,
> and I don't think they saw me. They turned right into my
> sights. I could see bits of stuff flying off the first FW190 in all
> directions. Then the pilot baled out. I just flew straight on and
> got the other one. He didn't even turn. He blew clean up and
> went straight down.'

Johnny Checketts was also flying on the day of the 1,000th victory. He was
No.3 in Charles's section and when interviewed remembered:

> It was a lovely clear day and we seemed to be behind the
> bomber crowd. Jack Charles was leading and I was leading the
> sub-section. There were two Huns flying along below us and
> Jack went and shot them down for which he got three hundred
> quid. But he had to share the money with the Frenchman,
> Mouchette, who had claimed a German around the same time.

The two unfortunate German pilots that Jack Charles had triumphed over
were Oberleutnant Horst Hannig and his No.2, Unteroffizier Ernst Godde.
Hannig was an ace pilot in the Luftwaffe with a score of 98 enemy aircraft
destroyed, the majority of these being claimed when he was flying against
the Russians on the Eastern Front with JG54. After his aircraft had been
badly damaged by Charles, Hannig had baled out wounded, his parachute
failed to deploy and he was killed.

As the news of the enemy engagement and of the squadrons' victories spread throughout the station, both Charles and Mouchette were quickly surrounded by fellow pilots, newspapermen and photographers, who eagerly wanted to know the details of the action. Many photographs were taken of them both that day, the most notable being that of Charles chalking up a propeller blade with 1,000th written on it.

Johnny Checketts again:

> The atmosphere on the station when we got back was pretty buoyant to say the least. The French had already organised a big party at the Hyde Park Hotel for that night, so we all went along there and they seemed to be able get lots of beautiful women to attend. Alan came along with Joan who had recently moved down to Highgate with the ambulance unit she was with.

Pierre Clostermann also relates his memories on Biggin Hill's incredible day:

> It was one of those days when we met a lot of German aircraft; it was a little bit funny that we in fact shot five down. Mouchette and Charles practically shot theirs down at the same time and the thing to do was to share. It was the gentlemanly way to settle the problem. There was a large party supposed to take place up at Hyde Park and everybody wanted to participate including representatives from Supermarine and Rolls-Royce. The Yanks, they sent us a couple of cooks to prepare the chickens and food in a thousand ways.

Michael Donnet:

> In 1943, as commanding officer of 64 Squadron, we were attached to the Biggin Hill Wing. Alan Deere was the Wing Commander Flying, a post he filled with great distinction. We all in Fighter Command were full of the admiration at the news of the wonderful achievement by the Biggin Hill Wing on the 1,000th kill.
>
> Al had been the architect of the success, having brought in his experience and his know how, with new tactics, which he imposed on the wing and which turned out to be the answer when engaged in offensive operations against the Luftwaffe.

At the beginning of June, the weather deteriorated and no operations were carried out. It was not until 7th that the Biggin Hill Wing would be operating again. Good news arrived at the aerodrome, however, on 4th June, when Deere received a telegram telling him that he was to be awarded the Distinguished Service Order. He received many letters and telegrams of congratulations from his many friends and RAF colleagues including Cecil Bouchier, who wrote:

My Dear Al,

A line to send my heartiest congratulations to you on your well-earned DSO. Well done, Al. I'm so glad. You're right back now, old boy, on the top of the world. Your renewed successes must make you as happy as it does your close friends when they read about it. Just take care of yourself and the best of luck attend you.

Another RAF friend, the then Squadron Leader J.E. 'Johnnie' Johnson, also contacted Deere on the day he heard of the award. Johnson recalled:

Al Deere and I were awarded the DSO on the same day, and I telephoned him at Biggin and suggested that we rendezvous at the Kemul Club in Burleigh Street for a small celebration. This convenient and hospitable little place was run by an ex-captain of the Royal Flying Corps, Bobbie Page. Later that evening a fair number of the Biggin and Kenley pilots were packed together in the crowded bar. We were all having a marvellous time, when I noticed an officer chap sitting alone in one corner. He asked what were we celebrating and I explained about the awards we had been given. He then offered me a drink and I found out later that evening the chap was none other than Guy Gibson VC, who had led the raid on the German dams.

A few days later, on 9th June 1943, the official celebration for the destruction of Biggin Hill's 1,000th German aircraft destroyed was held at the Grosvenor Hotel in London. At midday the station was released for 24 hours in order that the pilots could attend. Johnny Checketts who went along to the lavish celebration remembers:

We went to the official party at the Grosvenor Hotel. You'd never seen a party like it. They organised such a big party that it made half the Messes in Fighter Command bankrupt. They had three RAF bands playing along with the Windmill Girls. They sent out invitations for 1,000 couples; the Commander-in-Chiefs of Fighter, Bomber and Coastal Command and so on. It was great! I'd never been to a party like it or been to one since.

After the evening's entertainment had finished the pilots, wives or girlfriends were driven free of charge back to Biggin Hill or to their homes, courtesy of the London taxi-drivers.

The next morning, Deere and the rest of the Biggin Hill pilots were awoken at dawn, back to reality. They were to give escort to a formation of Ventura bombers targeted to attack the Morlaix airfield in the Cherbourg Peninsula. The trip took over four hours and luckily they did not encounter any enemy fighters.

Three days later, Al Deere was back on the score sheet again, when he claimed a Focke-Wulf 190 as damaged. During the late afternoon, Deere with 611 Squadron took off with the rest of the wing on Ramrod 86. They flew across to the Belgian coast and crossed south of Knocke at 19,000 feet at 6.34 pm. Deere and the squadrons saw no sign of the bombers they were supposed to escort, so he led them to the target area. With still no sign of the bombers the wing was about to set course for Dunkirk, when suddenly the bombers appeared. Deere gave his instructions and positioned his squadrons behind the formation. With 15 miles to go before reaching the target, a formation of around 50 German fighters was sighted coming in to attack. Deere ordered the squadrons to split into sections as the enemy fighters approached and they set off to repel the attack. Deere himself managed to fire a burst at one of the enemy aircraft as his combat report states:

> When between Ghent and the coast, I closed to 350 yards and fired a short burst at 10 degrees at an FW190. I saw cannon strikes on the starboard wing and then had to break off. I claim the FW190 damaged from this combat.

The very next day, the wing was again heavily involved in action when again protecting the bombers. Over St Pol, they encountered 13 FW190s in line abreast, each aircraft at 50 yards apart. Johnny Checketts was the only pilot who managed to fire on one of the enemy fighters and he claimed it destroyed. Al Deere and the others were about to open fire, when suddenly a Spitfire appeared from nowhere and dived through the section, causing everybody to break and upsetting the attack. It was lucky that none of the aircraft collided. Slightly shaken, the pilots reformed and crossed the Channel, landing at base at 5.17 pm. The pilot who had caused so much disruption was later identified. Unfortunately the wing lost one pilot that day, Flying Officer Gordon Lindsey, who was last seen going down with eight FW190s on his tail.

On 15th June, Deere was notified that he had been awarded the French Brevet Militaire de Pilote d'Avion by General Valin of the Free French Air Force.

Deere increased his score yet again on 23rd June, when he claimed an FW190 destroyed three miles north of Rue in the Pas de Calais without having to fire a single round. His report of the action states:

> I was leading Green Section of 611 Squadron on Ramrod 100. When at 11,000 feet just north of Berck, I saw two FW190s coming in behind and I made a sharp turn to port to engage. The enemy aircraft broke violently up and to port and the No. 2 went into a high-speed stall and spun violently to starboard. He did not recover from the spin and hit the ground about three miles north of Rue.

On 1st July, 485 New Zealand Squadron arrived at Biggin after spending the last few months operating from Merston. On arriving, it exchanged its Spitfire Vs with 611's Mk IXs. The latter unit moved up to Matlask in Norfolk, which was the satellite airfield for Coltishall. Johnny Checketts remembers the changeover:

> As a flight commander of 611, we were told that we were to
> move out and we were told that 485 were coming in. We had
> to take their Spitfire Vbs and they took over our IXbs. My stuff
> was all packed up on the truck and ready to go, when Jack
> Charles walked up with a signal in his hand and said, 'You're
> not coming with us, Checks, You're going to command this lot
> who are coming in.' I thought he was having me on and I was
> very annoyed about it. I said that it was a bloody poor joke;
> 'I'm going up to see the CO about this.' When I got up there, I
> got ticked off. Both Sailor and Al were there together and I said
> I didn't want to command the squadron. That's how I got to
> know that Alan Deere had recommended me to take the unit
> and that's what made me accept; after that I couldn't go wrong.

One of 485's sergeant pilots during this time was Jack Rae, who served with
great distinction and became an ace while serving in 485. He remembers
this period:

> When we heard that our squadron was moving to Biggin Hill
> and that Alan Deere was to be our Wing Co, there was not a
> pilot who was not thrilled with the news. His skill as a fighter
> pilot was legendary and his ability to relate to us as a New
> Zealander was without question. When the action started, the
> squadron, now equipped with the fabulous Spitfire IXBs,
> proved to be more than a match for the Focke-Wulf 190s. It
> was exciting to attend our pre-operation briefing – to know
> who was leading us – yes, we enjoyed flying behind our
> charismatic Al Deere.

Another New Zealander, Sergeant Pilot Douglas Brown, also met Deere
when serving with 485. He recalls:

> No one meeting Al Deere for the first time could possibly
> guess he was one of the most brilliant of fighter pilots in the
> Battle of Britain; that was because his courage and ability were
> matched by his modesty. He never regarded himself as a hero.
> 'Bravery,' he once told me, 'is a greatly over-rated word. I
> wasn't brave. Most of the time I was up there I was bloody
> scared.' I knew exactly what Al meant. All of us Spitfire pilots,
> who at that time were operating out of Biggin Hill, felt the
> same way. Al was a quality wing commander and he often
> commented he was like an army general directing the wing on
> operations, but he usually missed out on the action as 485 were
> too efficient and beat him to the punch.

Over two days in July, Alan Deere's luck was definitely working overtime
when he suffered engine problems with his Spitfire. On 6th, he was leading

the Wing while flying with 485 Squadron. Setting course at 6.55 pm with 341 in company, the squadrons climbed to make altitude crossing the French coast, but just before reaching the coastline at 22,000 feet, Deere suddenly experienced problems with his engine, which began to run unevenly. He signalled to Johnny Checketts over the R/T and handed over command. Deere then set course for Manston and managed to land there safely. The following day, he was leading 11 Spitfires of 485 Squadron on Rodeo 242 on 7th July, when he again became the victim of engine failure. The squadron took off at 12.45 pm, but just before he was about to get airborne, three cylinders on the port side of his Rolls-Royce engine burst. Deere immediately pushed the aircraft down and switched off the engine in case of fire. Johnny Checketts again took over the lead role and the raid was carried out according to plan. Seven days later on 14th July, Deere claimed another Focke-Wulf 190 during a mission covering American B17 Fortress bombers on a raid near Paris. His combat report states:

> Green 1 and 2 (myself and Flight Sergeant Clarke) had become engaged just north of Bernay with about eight to 10 enemy aircraft, and were left behind. We were making our way out at about 1,000 feet, when about 10 miles west of Le Havre, two FW190s were noticed diving on the section from behind. I gave the order to break and each Spitfire singled out an FW190. A general dogfight followed in which both our Spitfires were fired at and we returned fire. I only managed one burst in a tight diving turn using approximately two rings deflection, when I had to break off as another two FW190s came on my tail. I was able to observe the enemy aircraft at which I fired gliding towards France with white and black smoke pouring from it, at about 500 feet.
>
> I do not consider that he had a chance of reaching the French coast as it was losing height rapidly. I noticed Green 2 firing at an aircraft, but his bullets appeared to be going into the water behind the Hun. I claimed 1 FW190 probably destroyed in this combat.

This claim was to be Deere's last enemy aircraft claim of the war.

The following day, the *London Gazette* carried the announcement of Deere's award of his DSO, which he had been granted in June. Dated 15th July 1943 it read:

> *Since being awarded the Bar to his DFC in September 1940, this officer has destroyed seven aircraft, probably destroyed two and damaged four others. He has taken part in approximately 120 sweeps and led the Kenley or Biggin Hill Wings approximately 50 times. His total operational hours stand at over 500 hours.*

On 9th August, Deere led 485 and 341 Squadrons on Ramrod 191. Taking off from Biggin at 8.30 am, the wing made rendezvous with the bombers at North Foreland as arranged before setting course to cross over the French coast at Gravelines at a height of 17,000 feet. It was while crossing the coast that the two bomber formations became widely separated and as they flew further inland, one formation turned completely away from the other. Deere reacted to the situation immediately and detailed 485 Squadron to escort one formation, while 341 escorted the other. Both the two squadrons had to reduce height to 14,000 feet. No enemy fighter aircraft were seen or engaged by 341, but 485 was soon confronted by Me109s. Jack Rae flying that day remembers what happened next:

> August 9th was a day that I vividly remember, when Alan's agreement [for the attack] was followed by his wise concern and caution, which made the operation an amazing success. Johnny Checketts was leading our squadron and Red Flight. The Marauder bombers that we were escorting broke into two sections and we stayed with the section that moved off our planned course. While escorting this group, a flight of eight Me109s appeared below. Johnny called up Alan over the R/T asking if it was OK to attack. Al agreed, and he took over the escort of the Marauders and we went down to attack the enemy fighters. The result was amazing – they were apparently practising formation — and we shot down six of the eight, plus one probable. Johnny Checketts got three and one each between the other three of us.
>
> That operation was a remarkable success; but is not the part of the story, which I wish to emphasise. Those few moments of staggering success were intoxicating – I know it was for me and I'm sure it was for the others. We thought that we were four invincibles flying in an area where the enemy just did not expect us. Afterwards I sighted another two enemy fighters not far way and a third stooging far below. We were about to launch into another attack when I heard Alan Deere's urgent voice saying, 'Get the hell out of there.' I have thought about Alan's urgent, deeply concerned call, often; he was probably right and a wise leader, who guessed we would at any moment run into deep trouble. It needed someone like our Wing Co, who could measure aggression with caution.

27th August 1943 was to be a fateful day for the Biggin Hill Wing and especially 341 Alsace Squadron. Michael Donnet was flying with the wing that day and he records:

> On 27th August 64 Squadron was detailed with 341 and 485 Squadron to escort four boxes of 60 B17 Fortresses, attacking V1 sites in the vicinity of St Omer.
>
> Alan Deere had briefed us on the importance of the

operation as he told the pilots. He was to lead the escort force – when we joined up with the Fortresses as close escort.

I was surprised to hear that it was René Mouchette and not Alan who was leading the wing. We witnessed the fierce dogfight, which took place above the bombers between 341 Spitfires and the FW190s. At one time I heard Mouchette calling and announcing he was by himself, wounded and pleading for help.

This was the end of him, a very sad blow as he was an outstanding fighter pilot and first class leader. The next day I learned that Alan Deere had a narrow escape when the engine of his Spitfire stopped on take-off and he had finished off at the bottom of the cliff at Biggin Hill airfield. Once again he escaped with only a great fright. But he was most upset and really very sad by the loss of René Mouchette, a friend and pilot whom he very much admired. He was really feeling guilty at not being there to give a hand and protect his wounded friend.

It was in September that Pierre Clostermann of 341 Squadron left to take up his new posting to Deere's old squadron 602. Clostermann recalls:

Al Deere always kept an eye on me and he called me up, because he knew I wouldn't get along with the new commanding officer of 341. He said to me, 'Look, Clostermann, you are quite a good fighter pilot, sometimes you are a little bit crazy, try not to play the game of going on your own after the Germans. Because one of these days you will be eaten alive.' He then asked me what squadron I would like to go to. I said, 'I would like to go to 602 with my friend Jacques Remlinger.' So he arranged my posting, which was very nice of him.

On 6th September one of Deere's closest friends and fighter leaders, Johnny Checketts, was shot down during a raid over Cambrai. Checketts was leading 485 Squadron that day as high cover escort to American Marauder bombers, which had been tasked with attacking the marshalling yards at Cambrai. Just as the squadron turned for home, they were set upon from above by 20 FW190s. As combat was met by the two opposing sides, Checketts managed to manoeuvre himself onto one of the enemy fighters and shoot it down. But suddenly the role of hunter was changed to being that of the hunted as Checketts later described:

I then saw five FW190s at three o'clock above me and coming down to attack us, so I called to my No.2 to break. We fought for altitude and finally got it, when to my surprise I saw two more FW190s above me. One of them came for me in a port turn, the same as mine and the other took the other turn and

attacked head on. The first attack was miles out and I thought
I would get a shot at him next time round, but we both missed.
His third attack was terrific and I saw all his cannon firing, also
his spinner and engine cowlings. There was a violent explosion
at my feet and my cockpit filled with flames. I frantically
clutched at my hood release and dragged the hood open. The
flames gushed round my face and I released my harness and
stepped out into the slipstream. The stench of burning flesh
was sickening and I seemed to be hours trying to escape the
inferno. At last my body was wholly out, but the toe of my
flying boot caught on my windscreen catch and I was dragged
swiftly down; a terrific kick and I was hurtling head over heels
down and down. I clutched at my ripcord and pulled hard and
my parachute opened with a hard jerk.

On landing, Checketts was helped away by a young boy who had seen his
descent by parachute and took him to his father's house, where he was
hidden. The local Resistance was contacted and soon Checketts was moved
to various safe houses along the Resistance routes. At one of the safe houses
he even met another 485 pilot, Sergeant 'Terry' Kearins, who had been shot
down on 15th July 1943. After recovering from his burns, Checketts and
nine others travelled to a French port and were secretly taken aboard a
lobster boat named the *Suzette* and sailed out to rendezvous with a Royal
Naval vessel at a pre-set point out at sea. Checketts arrived back in England
seven weeks after being shot down.

At the end of September 1943, the aerodrome at Biggin Hill was
suddenly struck down with a severe outbreak of dysentery, which affected a
lot of the pilots. One of these was Al Deere. Al had been suffering for a
couple of weeks from tiredness and severe stomach pains, but had not
sought any medical advice. Doug Brown had also developed the same
symptoms and remembers:

> A few of us in the wing at Biggin, including some of the 341
> French Squadron, contracted severe dysentery. I recall my last
> week at Biggin – Al and I were endeavouring to enjoy a beer at
> the bar (not very palatable, for the beer was always watered
> down), when suddenly the doctor (Station Medical Officer
> Flight Lieutenant Thomson) came up to us and told Al he had
> to go to hospital. Al objected strongly, but the Doc held his
> ground and said; 'If you do not receive treatment immediately
> you may not be in the land of the living for very long.' We were
> both admitted that night and thanks to drugs that had become
> available, we were cured within a month.

Douglas and Al were both admitted to the hospital at East Grinstead, Surrey,
where a specialist saw them straight away. Al was diagnosed as having
developed acute enteritis. During his recuperation, he was visited by Air

Vice-Marshal Saunders, who together with Group Captain 'Sailor' Malan had come to the conclusion that Al should be taken off operational flying for good. Malan himself had decided enough was enough a couple of years earlier, when the strain and tiredness was beginning to show. After a further three weeks in East Grinstead, Al was released and given two weeks' sick leave, which he spent with Joan Fenton, at her parents' home in Harrogate, Yorkshire.

Good news arrived on 13th October 1943, when Deere received a communiqué from the Headquarters of the US Eighth Air Force which relayed the following:

> Under the provisions of Army Regulations 600-45, 8th August 1932, as amended, and pursuant to authority contained in Section I, Circular 36.
>
> The Distinguished Flying Cross is awarded to the following officer.
>
> A.C. Deere Wing Commander, Royal Air Force.
> For extraordinary achievement, while leading his Wing as fighter escort for medium bombers of the Eighth Air Force on more than fifteen missions over enemy occupied Europe. Wing Commander Deere devoted untiring energy assisting in the development of new, untried tactics for medium bombardment aircraft. In order to observe the effectiveness of the new tactics, he personally led his Wing as cover for the bombers on the first mission. The successful bombing of a heavily defended target without loss of an aeroplane is in a large measure due to the planning, skill and leadership of Wing Commander Deere.
>
> His actions reflect highest credit upon himself and the Armed Forces of His Majesty's Government.
>
> By the command of Lieutenant General Eaker

A few days later Deere received a package from Colonel L.W. Sweetser, Deputy Chief of Staff, Ops at Headquarters 8th Air Support Command United States Air Force. In the package were two copies of *Stars and Stripes* magazine and an accompanying letter which read:

My Dear Al,

Enclosed for your inspection are two copies of the Stars and Stripes of Monday October 18th 1943, which contains a story of the joint British and American decoration ceremony and mentions the award of the American Distinguished Flying Cross to you.

It goes without saying that I am personally delighted that you have been given this American decoration and in addition, the entire command is also most pleased. As I have already mentioned to you and your superiors, I feel that the work that you have done for the

Americans both on the ground and in the air, has been outstanding.

As you already undoubtedly know, I will be stationed at Hawkinge until November 4th and if, by any chance, you are able to fly down, please do so. Group Captain Malan hopes to come down also within the next week or so, to have lunch with me.

I remain, respectfully yours

L.W. Sweetser, JR

Following this award from the Americans, Deere was asked if he would undertake a radio interview for the BBC Overseas Service. He agreed and gave a highly descriptive talk on his time at Biggin Hill and of the pilots and operations they had participated in. The following is a transcript of the broadcast:

> I came to Biggin Hill early this year as supernumerary squadron leader, attached to one of the Spitfire squadrons. A supernumerary squadron leader is one who, after six months off operations, is required to go back to a squadron and to act as a stooge until he gets his hand in again. Then you normally get command of a squadron; I got command of the Biggin Hill Wing.
>
> For six weeks after I arrived at the station, I flew as No.2 and No.4 positions. These are the stooge positions in a fighter squadron. On two or three occasions I was following sergeant pilots who were leading my section, and during the attacks I often had to follow my sergeant pilots in to attack the Hun. One day when the wing was flying at 32,000 feet near St Omer, I spotted and reported 15 enemy aircraft. They were about 10,000 feet below. I received permission from the wing commander to attack, and followed the section leader, who was a flight sergeant. When the leader of the enemy formation saw me, he dived to the ground. This is a typical Hun evasive tactic, but knowing their tactics I followed him eventually showing about 480 miles an hour on the clock. When my first burst hit him, great chunks flew off and after the second burst, it was all over. To make sure I gave him a further burst. He completely disintegrated.
>
> Our most recent activities have been concerned with escorting the American Flying Fortresses. It is a wonderful sight to see, this great gaggle of Fortresses flying in formation. I remember quite clearly going out to pick up these Fortresses returning from their first daylight raid on the Ruhr. We met some 200 of them coming back as if they had been on a pleasure cruise. It was a breathtaking sight. We could see them about 60 miles away. Somewhere south of Rotterdam we met them. They were in boxes of about 20 strong, and the whole

distance covered by this formation was something like 20 miles. It took this formation 15 minutes to pass a given point – 20 miles of four-engine bombers. When I saw them I felt sorry for the Huns' fighter pilots, who are ordered to attack these formations, as the Fortresses' fire power is deadly.

To get back to the wing again, I must say I enjoy being with the Biggin Wing very much, particularly as it has such a record. We have a French squadron who are looking forward to the day when we shall all be back in France, fighting from their own soil and fighting over Hun territory. We are a fairly mixed wing at Biggin. The group captain, as you probably know, is a South African; I'm a New Zealander, Jack Charles a Canadian. There are also Czechs, Poles, and Australians – in other words, pilots from all over the British Empire including our Allies. I was asked the other day at Biggin by an American pilot if I would like to fly a Flying Fortress. I think my reply was typical of every pilot on this station. Give me a single-engine aircraft any day – preferably a Spitfire.

All we New Zealanders over here hope that before long, and I'm sure it won't be long, we shall be out in the Pacific operating our Spitfires from Australia or New Zealand giving the Japs a beating, until the great day comes when the Armistice arrives.

At the end of the radio broadcast Deere sent a message to his parents and friends in Wanganui. Fortunately for Al and many other New Zealand fighter pilots operating in Europe their services were not required later to fight the Japanese.

Back in his native home of New Zealand, the newspaper press were keeping the citizens up to date with his activities and awards. His mother was interviewed and featured in the local Wanganui newspaper. In the article she proudly spoke of Al's achievements and of her other four sons:

'We are just as proud of each of our other sons as we are of Alan.' These were the introductory words spoken by Mrs T.J. Deere, mother of the most decorated New Zealand fighter pilot, Wing Commander Alan Deere, DSO, DFC and bar, DFC awarded by the United States Army Air Force and Croix de Guerre and Palme awarded by the Fighting Free French. Modest and retiring, Mrs Deere shares with her husband an intense dislike of publicity and a deep love of quiet home family life. In the happy atmosphere of the attractive living room, where Mr Deere and Mrs Deere and their family of six sons and their sons' friends had shared many jolly times together, Mrs Deere, who is slight in appearance, chatted about her sons. 'The newspapers have kept the public posted on Alan's decorations,' she said, 'and he certainly has had amazing experiences of all kinds since he left the solicitors' office where he was working in 1938, when he elected to don RAF uniform.' 'Yes,' she added in an almost unbelieving tone. 'I suppose he must be a great airman.'

Leaving the discussion of her illustrious son at that, Mrs Deere went on to say that for the past 12 months Sergeant L.W. Deere had been a prisoner of war in Italy and her other son Brian has also been a prisoner since the Greece-Crete campaign. He had been sent to Germany and with other New Zealanders and Australians had been working on a farm belonging to an elderly German woman, who, Private Deere wrote, was kind to them and had given them traditional food for their Christmas dinner. Another of her sons, Pat, had been in the Middle East for some months. After naval training in New Zealand followed by two years' further training in England, Able Seaman Deere was at home for his recent 21st birthday. Desmond, the Deere's youngest son, is still a student at the technical college, but he is fitting himself to follow in his five brothers' footsteps as soon as he is old enough by performing a sergeant's duties in the school platoon.

Following his recovery from his illness, Deere was posted as Chief Instructor of the Fighter Wing of the Central Gunnery School at Sutton Bridge on 21st October 1943; and while here he was further delighted, when his friend Johnny Checketts, now a squadron leader, was posted in to command one of the squadrons.

While at Sutton Bridge, Deere received a card of invitation to attend Buckingham Palace for the investiture of the Distinguished Service Order from His Majesty King George VI. On 9th November, he arrived at the Palace to accept the award, and with him he brought his fiancée and her mother. Also attending that day was his fellow countryman and friend Colin Gray, who also received an award. After the investiture, they all dined at the New Zealand Forces Club in Charing Cross Road as guests of the High Commissioner, Bill Jordan.

Deere received a letter from an officer of the Free French Air Force on 17th November 1943, with reference to the award Deere had received earlier that year in June. It read:

Dear Wing Commander Deere,

I received a few days ago your French wings and the certificate of an honorary French military pilot. All the boys and myself would have appreciated to be able to give you these wings at their dispersal, unfortunately some red tape delay has made it quite impossible for they are at the present moment much too far away from your station. Nevertheless, I wish you to receive this testimony of our admiration and respect for the leader who so brilliantly and so many times took the 'Alsace' Squadron into action.

CHAPTER 7

VICTORY IN SIGHT
1944

On 20th March 1944, Alan Deere was posted to 11 Group Headquarters as a member of the air staff. His commander was his good and old friend Cecil Bouchier, now the Senior Air Staff Officer of the Group. It was here that he was to receive another award, this time presented by the Free French Forces; it was the French Croix de Guerre with palm. The citation read:

> *Wing Commander Deere took part in protective operations covering the Dunkirk evacuation, securing four victories and, two days later, two victories. He participated in the Battle of Britain. On 53 occasions he led the French fighter groups 'Ile de France' and 'Alsace' in operations over occupied territory. His total victories are 21 with an addition of seven probables.*

Meanwhile back in New Zealand, Deere's younger brother Kevin was about to become controversial headline news. Kevin had served in the navy since 1941 and had returned to New Zealand in April 1943. For a further year he served in the Royal New Zealand Navy on shore duties and was discharged on compassionate grounds in May 1944, when their father became seriously ill. The condition of the discharge was that Kevin should return to employment in the New Zealand Railways, which he did as a porter. But soon after this the Wanganui Armed Services wanted him to return to active service. Cousin Erin Englert explains:

> When uncle Joe took very ill, Kevin was sent back, he had done 2 years and 11 months in the Navy. He was sent back on compassionate leave because his father was ill and he said he would not go back. Had he stayed in the navy a month longer it would have been all right, because after a three-year tour you were entitled to come home. But because of this it went to court, where the Judge suggested that if Kevin stayed at home, Desmond the youngest brother could be taken out of college and put into the air force. That caused uproar and the Wanganui people rose up and supported the family in this matter.

Fortunately the war ended and Desmond didn't have to go.

The local papers carried the story as it progressed and as appeals against the Court's decision were submitted, newspapers carried the following reports:

> The recent decision of the Wanganui Armed Forces Appeal Board must surely arouse the fighting spirit of every woman in New Zealand. That brave mother Mrs Deere whose four sons are still overseas must once again bid goodbye to her fifth son who has already given three and half years service as a volunteer. One is forced to wonder how many sons those members of the Appeal Board have given? To them it is not enough that the health of two courageous parents should break under the strain, but that five brave sons should serve and serve again until the end.
> While the name of Wing Commander A.C. Deere DSO, DFC and Bar, rings from one end of the world to the other, thousands of other New Zealanders can hide behind the cloak of essential industries and conscientious scruples. Surely the women of New Zealand will not let this pass without comment.

The case continued well into 1945 before Kevin Deere finally won his appeal and by then the war in Europe was coming to a close.

Back in Britain the build-up to the forthcoming Allied invasion of Europe was well underway, with the south of England becoming more and more like one giant army camp, as the flow of men, machines and supplies for the invasion began to envelope every small village and free field space.

To the average Briton, it seemed like the coming together of all the world's nations, as troops from all countries who had escaped during the German occupation of Europe in 1939/40 joined by those of the United States of America, had now united to hurl their might against the evil Nazi empire.

In April 1944, while working at 11 Group Headquarters, Alan Deere received the amazing news that he was again to become operational. Cecil Bouchier told him that the Air Officer Commanding 84 Group had contacted him with regard to Deere taking command of the French fighter squadrons' airfield in his group. Later, Deere found that the Chief of Staff of the Free French Air Forces, General Valin, had personally requested him.

After being released from his duties, Deere arrived on 1st May at Merston airfield near Chichester in Sussex to take command of 145 Wing, which was part of 2nd Tactical Air Force. He and his men settled in at their new, but basic camp and waited for Operation Overlord, the invasion of mainland Europe, to begin. They moved to an advanced airfield at Selsey at the beginning of June, and while there Deere and other senior RAF officers of his group were requested to travel up to RAF Uxbridge on 4th June, where two hundred congregated in the station cinema to await details of the operation.

After a few minutes, Air Marshal Arthur Coningham, the Commander-in-Chief of 2nd TAF (Tactical Air Force) walked in and made his way to the stage. After thanking his officers for attending, he quickly directed their attention to the large operational map of the Normandy area, where the invasion would take place, and outlined its precise details. Following the briefing, Deere and the other officers returned to their bases that day, sworn to secrecy not to give any information out to their men before they had received a signal telling them the invasion's go-ahead.

It was scheduled for 5th June, but bad weather in the Channel had caused a 24-hour postponement. General Eisenhower, after much deliberation with his other commanders finally gave the go-ahead, and during the early hours of 6th June 1944, the Allied invasion of Normandy began. D-Day had arrived.

Deere recalls this time when at last, the Allied invasion was at hand, and they knew they would set foot again on French soil:

> I was asked by the Free French Air Force to command their wing of Spitfires to take them into France, because when I was the wing leader at Biggin Hill in 1943, I had two French squadrons under me. They made a special request, so I was sent down to lead their wing up to and including D-Day. I can remember the expressions on the faces of those gallant Frenchmen when I briefed them about the invasion. Many had tears running down their faces, full of hope and joy. On D-Day the weather was particularly bad and we didn't see very much along the beachhead; we actually went over as cover over the British beaches just north of Caen. But the weather was too bad for the German Air Force and they hadn't reacted at that stage anyhow. It was a marvellous sight though to see all those ships below. The French pilots were very good, but sometimes a bit excitable in the air. If you got into combat and they sighted something, they used to get a bit carried away and I would have to say to them, 'You are not to use the R/T under any circumstances unless it's an emergency or you've got a real sighting.' But having said that, I got on really well with them although I could not speak a word of French. Straight afterwards I was taken off operations and put into the planning side of the Tactical Air Force, so I went over to France, but didn't actually fly any more.

In a letter home to his parents, Deere wrote about this momentous event:

> You all have your wish at last. The second front has opened. It is a thrilling sight to stand on this advance base and watch the continuous stream of all types of Allied aircraft flying towards the beachhead. One formation was forty miles long and consisted of the biggest and best tugs and gliders the Allies

possessed. The sea was just crammed with boats, from battleships with 15-inch guns down to high-speed launches. The beaches in Normandy were blackened with Allied soldiers moving up the beachhead, while the coast for miles was dotted with fires from the air assault and the effective naval shelling.

What a contrast to that day four years ago, when I patrolled the Dunkirk beaches and saw our beaten army in retreat with the German Air Force dominating the skies and the burning oil tanks of Dunkirk town. So far very few Luftwaffe have appeared, and those that have are accorded such a hot reception and are so ineffective, that they might as well have stayed on the ground. From the air, the land battle is hard to observe because of the advance and the art of camouflage. Occasionally one sees a tank formation locked in battle and the answering spurt of one or two anti-tank guns dotted around the countryside. I will have to close now, as I will be taking off again soon to go over the area.

During his time in France, Deere would meet with Johnny Checketts who recalls:

I was leading a wing at that time and the tempo was pretty intense. It wasn't so much the fighting; it was patrolling all the time and doing a lot of ground strafing. I was pretty busy until Boulogne was liberated [on 22nd September] and by this time Al's crowd was already in France. I wanted to go and see the people who had nursed me when I had got shot down, so I flew into his airfield and we both went together to a small village near Lille and they put on a party for us.

Deere remembered his visit with Johnny to the village:

I got a great welcome and we learned what had occurred after he had been shot down. A married couple had nursed him to recovery, but the husband's mother, treated to champagne by the Germans, had talked too much and the Gestapo found Johnny's uniform hidden in the garden. The couple were taken away and were not heard of again. The Gestapo told the villagers that if the Allied army broke through, that they would burn down the village as a reprisal for helping Checketts. The Germans actually started fires, but the manner of their leaving was so hurried that they could not make a good job of the destruction.

Soon after, Deere was taken off operations and on 21st July posted to the Headquarters of 84 Group, Control Centre in his new role as Wing Commander Plans. This job entailed moving forward with a mobile unit when the army advanced and co-ordinating air to ground strikes against the

Germans. The job also had dangers of its own, as Deere was to find out, when the Allies' advance came to a halt outside the town of Caen. He was given orders to go up to the most forward Allied positions and report his findings regarding the situation. He was driven up in an armoured car to where the Canadians were positioned, and only just escaped with his life, when a German 88 millimetre shell landed nearby, killing some of the troops, while a large splinter whizzed past his legs.

A second incident occurred when Deere was driving down a small country road, when suddenly he was confronted with a Frenchman standing in the middle of the road with his cycle. Deere drew to the side to avoid the Frenchman and as he did so the back wheel of his motor vehicle exploded with an almighty bang. This blew the Frenchman over into the back seat of the open vehicle. Which in turn startled Deere and the other passengers. He quickly slammed on the brakes and came to a sudden halt. Everybody was uninjured, but suffering from a bad fright, thinking that they had set off a landmine.

He continued in his role as Wing Commander Plans right through France and into Germany, until the Germans finally surrendered in May 1945. At that time, Deere was billeted at a town called Celle and was the head of the joint planning team. With the war in Europe now over, he remained with his unit in Germany. In June Deere received good news regarding two of his brothers who had been captured and made prisoners of war. His brother Brian, who had been captured in Greece and had been a prisoner for the last four and a half years, was safe and now in Rumania. His brother 'Jimmy' was also alive and well and in Germany. Deere made a flight to Hanover to be reunited with him and learned what had befallen him over the last three years.

The 21st Panzer Division had captured Jim, a sergeant in the 2nd New Zealand Division at El Alamein on 21st July 1942, along with many others. For six months they were in a camp at Benghazi, where conditions were very bad, and there were many cases of beri-beri and malnutrition. Eventually, Jim was sent to Titarano, in southern Italy, and stayed in Italy for 13 months; while there he learned Italian. After the Allies had invaded Italy, the camp was moved to Udine, which was notorious for jailing men for the slightest offence. He was then moved to Austria and then to Gorlitz in Czechoslovakia. When the Germans ordered the prisoners in the camp to be moved away from the Russians, Jim and seven South Africans hid in a ceiling above the barracks used by the Serb prisoners.

The Serbs were very kind and helpful, when the Russians did not arrive and the German guards returned. One Serb prisoner took the blame for the New Zealander and the South Africans being in the camp and was sent off to jail. Jim was himself sent off to a punishment camp at Hohe-Elbe, but after he had been there for only a few days, the Germans decided the camp should be moved in case Czech partisans attacked it. When the Germans finally vacated the camp, Jim volunteered to remain behind with the sick. He made very good friends with the partisans once they arrived at the camp and after sending the sick to Prague, he lived with the Czechs for nearly three weeks. He then went to Pilsen via Prague and there was liberated by the Americans. Jim Deere finally reached England via Rheims.

Alan Deere remained in Germany until 4th June, when he was flown back to Britain and was given a new posting – he returned to his old aerodrome, Biggin Hill in Kent and was made Station Commander on 5th June 1945. During this period he received the good news that he had awaited; he had been granted a permanent commission in the peacetime Royal Air Force and would also retain his wartime rank of wing commander. But this would also mean a new posting and his first new command was the Polish Mustang Wing based at Andrew's Field, in Essex, which he took up on 2nd July 1945.

CHAPTER 8

PEACE – A NEW BEGINNING

On 18th September 1945, Alan Deere and his fiancée Joan Fenton were married at the Register Office, St Pancras, London. The reception held afterwards was attended by many of Deere's RAF colleagues, including Group Captains Jamie Rankin, John Cunningham and Denys Gillam and Wing Commanders Archie Winskill, Denis Crowley-Milling and Bob Blake, with whom Deere had flown in 54 Squadron during early 1940. It was a joyous occasion.

On his return to Andrew's Field after a short leave, Deere was given notice that the Polish Wing was to be disbanded in October. In November that year, both Deere and his wife Joan were overjoyed to learn that she was to become a mother and could expect their first child sometime the following July. More good news followed when he was given command of RAF Duxford in Cambridgeshire on 1st December 1945. Here he was in charge of the first postwar active RAF squadrons, which arrived at the aerodrome on 18th January 1946. The first squadron was 165 Squadron, which was operating Spitfire LFIXs at the time. Another squadron that arrived to take up residence was 91, which flew in during April.

Many of Deere's wartime colleagues had remained in the service after the war and many would attain high rank during the following years; one of his closest friends and wartime leaders, 'Sailor' Malan, did not however. Malan decided that a peacetime air force would not suit him, so he returned to his native South Africa to take up farming. In February 1946, he boarded the steamship *Caernarvon Castle* at the port of Southampton to return home, but the ship suffered some engine problems and docked again at Plymouth. On 25th February, he wrote the following farewell letter to Deere:

Dear Al,

We have called in here after sailing from Southampton in order to undergo a few minor engine repairs. This gives me a chance to catch up with a million and one letters which I meant to write before leaving England, but which, for many reasons, I failed to accomplish.

I am very sorry I was unable to see you before we left, but honestly I was in a constant rush right up to the end and couldn't spare either the petrol or the time to see you on the last Saturday night, when you were in town. Besides, I seem to remember that I had a previous engagement as well as a hell of a lot of packing to do – I remember now, it was that two of Lynda's married brothers and families had to come over to Ruislip on that night.

Well Al, we have had a long and happy association together which I shall never forget, and I do hope we shall meet again some day. I hear you are to receive the OBE which of course you thoroughly deserve; many congratulations.

I am very pleased that you have taken a permanent commission; the service could do with as many of your type as they can lay their hands on. I don't think I could have faced a peacetime service, even had I not got myself fixed up as well as I have. I flatter myself that I could have improved my position and circumstances in several other walks of life, since I am still young enough to be adaptable and yet old enough to exploit my experiences. What an ego!

I hope Joan is bearing up well under the strain as D-Day approaches. I expect you are constantly telling her that giving birth is a perfectly natural phenomenon and a perfectly normal function of a woman. Nevertheless I expect you will be as nervous as a kitten when her time arrives. But I can picture you strutting about with pride when your infant arrives. I hope it is a boy because I expect you are both hoping for a son. Nevertheless you will be equally pleased if it turns out to be a girl. Our own girl is far more entertaining and attractive than the boy who inherits a lot of my bloody mindedness, obstinacy and general faults.

Should you ever feel disposed to drop me a line my address will be:

c/o The Anglo American Corporation
41 Main Street,
Johannesburg

Yours ever

'Sailor'

On 1st June 1946 Alan Deere was awarded the Order of the British Empire. It was indeed a great honour for him as well as for his family; he received the award for his outstanding service to his King and Country. Seven days later Deere's Duxford squadrons took part in the giant Victory flypast over London. The following month, on 8th July 1946, while living at the station commander's house at Duxford, Joan Deere gave birth to their first child, a girl, who they named Jacqueline Elizabeth. Douglas Bader was later chosen to be a godparent at the baby's christening.

On 24th August 1946, Deere was sent on a nine-month course to the US Air University in the town of Montgomery, Alabama. Here and at Maxwell airbase, he undertook a course, which dealt with air strategy based on operations during the war. While in America, he sent for his wife and new baby to join him, and Joan and Jacqueline boarded a liner for New York. Alan Deere's son John recalls:

> My mother and sister went out to Alabama on one of those returning ships which had a lot of those English ladies aboard who were going to get married to GIs they had met during the war. She said that there was not a drop of drink on board during the whole trip and it was pretty miserable. When she arrived at New York, her geography was not too good and she thought she could get a train out of New York, which ended up being a three or four day trip.

On his return from America in June 1947 Deere was given his next appointment, on 17th July, which would again take him overseas. This was as a member of the air staff of Air Headquarters Malta, with the reduced rank of squadron leader. During his time in Malta, Deere was given leave and this gave him the chance to make a visit to New Zealand, the first time back there in ten years. On 27th February 1948 at 6.55 pm, Alan Deere landed at Ohakea airport, where a grand welcoming party of family and friends were gathered to meet him. After having tea at the airport the family travelled by car to Deere's family home at Wanganui. Also at the airport that day on hand to report on one of New Zealand's greatest wartime aces were reporters from various newspapers. One newspaper, the *New Zealand Free Lance*, interviewed him and reported on the visit:

> Besides having a most distinguished war record, Squadron Leader Deere has also acquired a very charming wife and sweet little 19-month-old daughter Jacqueline, who has inherited the Deere curls and is distinctly like her father in appearance with his slanting deep-set eyes. Mrs Deere was formerly Joan Fenton of Harrowgate and she looks forward to the time she can accompany her husband to New Zealand to introduce her to the family and favourite haunts of his childhood. During the last seven months the Deeres have been stationed at Malta, where they reside at Sliema, the residential part of Valetta.

Deere stated:

> 'Life in Malta is not all it might be. The cost of living is exorbitant – imagine paying 9/- per dozen for eggs and not having any butter at all – but there is of course plenty of social life as Malta is the most important British naval base at present and extremely important from an air defence point of view.'

The newspaper report continued:

> He expects to remain in Malta for another 18 months before an

RAF posting elsewhere. Also awaiting the aircraft's arrival at Ohakea was his great pal, Wing Commander Johnny Checketts, who was in New Zealand on leave from Suva, and who spent the weekend as the guest of Mr and Mrs Deere. Although Alan Deere is considered by many as the world's number one air ace, he has not changed in simplicity of manner. He is tremendously interested to hear of old Wanganui friends. Unfortunately his stay in New Zealand is so short, barely eight days, and essentially to see his people after all these years. Great is his delight to see his mother, still so amazingly youthful. His breastful of medals incidentally also includes the French Croix de Guerre with palm.'

Erin Englert, Alan's cousin remembers his visit back to the 'Old Country':

After the war he came back a few times and he always visited my mother if he could. I was a young girl in my first job and he came to see me on one occasion. I think at that time he was stationed in Germany. I remember he commented on the fact that I had plaits in my hair, which was the fashion in New Zealand at the time, and he said that I looked like the German girls. I think that that was actually the last time I saw him. My mother was very fond of him, he was a great favourite with her, because he had stayed with us when he was young and he and my father had got on very well.

Following his return from New Zealand, Deere continued with his tour of duties in Malta and seven months later while still there, his wife Joan gave birth to their second child, John, on 13th September 1948. John Deere recalls his mother's memories of his entrance into the world:

I was born in Valetta, Malta, at the Officers' Hospital during the evening, because I can remember mother saying that father was down the pub and had missed the show, which was a good judge of form in my opinion. Father had been on a two-year posting and I was born towards the end of it.

His tour finally ended and on his return from Malta, Deere was again promoted in rank to wing commander on the staff of 61 Group at RAF Kenley on 12th September 1949. His duties here included the joint planning in co-operation with Headquarters, Southern Army Command, based at Hounslow. On 26th September, he was attached on temporary duty to the School of Land/Air Warfare until 8th October 1949.

On 12th December 1951, Deere was posted as Wing Commander Operations for Headquarters, Northern Sector, 11 Group Fighter Command based at Linton-on-Ouse, where he stayed until 7th May 1952, when he was given command of RAF Station, North Weald in Essex, taking over from Wing Commander Peter Wykeham-Barnes. There were two squadrons based at the aerodrome at this time, 72 and 601, equipped with De Havilland Vampire jet aircraft, although both were about to convert to Meteor 8s.

Soon after his arrival, he quickly had to get the station ready for the Air Officer Commanding 11 Group's Annual Inspection, for which a full ceremonial parade was to be required. With full co-operation from his staff, the inspection on 24th May was a success and Deere was asked to convey the AOC's message of congratulation to the men and women at the station for putting on a first class show.

During that month Deere's comments in the Station's Operations Record Book stated some of the tasks, which had to be undertaken:

> Works services on the airfield are proceeding satisfactorily and the first new type of dispersal should be ready for occupation at the end of July. The new Air Traffic Control building is still very much behind schedule. No.72 Squadron had a very successful month's flying, despite an all-time low in pilots and ground crews. The position re pilots is steadily improving, but the ground crews are deteriorating to a serious degree.

In June, 601 Squadron together with 604, which had arrived to operate from North Weald, flew off to Malta for summer camp and afterwards were stood down for two weeks. The aerodrome played host to a member of the Norwegian royal family on 19th June 1952. The occasion was the official unveiling of a memorial stone in memory of the Norwegian airmen who had died fighting whilst operating from Britain during the war.

The monument was designed by Norwegian sculptor Roar Carlsen and was cast in Norway, then flown in for the ceremony. Alan Deere and other high-ranking RAF officers, which included Air Marshal the Earl of Bandon and Air Marshal Sir Basil Embry, met Princess Astrid, the daughter of Crown Prince Olaf, as she arrived for the ceremony. The princess was 20 years old at the time and studying at Oxford. After inspecting a guard of honour, she was led to where the monument was sited and after speeches were made, she unveiled the monument on which the following inscription read: 'A gift from the Norwegians of 331 and 332 Squadrons, in gratitude for the hope and opportunities so kindly given at a difficult time.'

Pilot Officer D.J. Keats was with 72 Squadron and he remembers Alan Deere's time at North Weald:

> As commanding officer of North Weald, Al Deere was extremely popular with the officers of 72 Squadron. He was always very welcome during his frequent visits to the crew-room and it was a marvellous experience to fly with him on several occasions.
>
> I had contact with him whilst I was squadron adjutant, for some six months, when he was always very helpful and understanding. He was very keen on sport. I was officer-in-charge of station cricket and a member of the team and also a

member of the station rugby and squash teams. He gave tremendous support to all the teams, particularly the rugby in which he was on the touchline for all the home matches, shouting loudly in support.

One experience I had with him still sends shudders down my spine. On the day I arrived at North Weald as a pilot officer starting my first operational tour, I was instructed to report to the station commander. I had only just learned that Al Deere was the commanding officer of North Weald and as a young boy I had followed his exploits very enthusiastically – so this occasion for me was rather like being called before the Pope. He was immediately very friendly and put me at ease, such that when he asked me if 72 Squadron had been my first choice, I said 'No' and that my first choice had been 41 Squadron at Biggin Hill, because my girlfriend lived near there. I immediately realized I had made an almighty clanger, but he laughed it off. In summary, he was a perfect officer and gentleman.

Other aircrew of 72 Squadron such as A.E Sweetman also fondly recall their station commander:

When Al Deere became CO of North Weald 'Dining in Night' became a night to be viewed with trepidation. For as soon as the meal and port were over, the floor was cleared to enable the night's festivities to begin. Al would pick the roughest of games for us to lose ourselves in. One of which had to be abandoned as too many of the lads were having back problems. He was a marvellous guy in spite of that!

R. W. Needham:

I can sum up Al Deere in a nutshell. If you think of the actor, Kenneth More in the film Genevieve and the Douglas Bader film, he acted the part, Al Deere lived it!

Mr F. James:

Nice chap, down to earth. I used to play tennis with him and his wife. A great couple!

During July 1952, 72 Squadron was re-equipped with Meteor 8s, while the Vampire aircraft had to be modified and prepared for disposal, which caused normal flying to be curtailed. That month Deere had to write letters of commiseration to families of two pilots, Flight Lieutenant Wyborn and Sergeant Randell, of 72 Squadron when they were killed on 12th July while practising aerobatics for flying displays. A full military funeral was held at the village church on 18th July.

Deere continued to write his comments in the station logbook for that month:

The re-equipping with Meteors is going ahead rapidly, but as usual the planned Works Program entered into for the additional accommodation brought about by re-equipment to a larger type aircraft is well behind schedule. The new Air Traffic building is as far from completion as ever, and will definitely not be ready for the Autumn Air Defence Exercises. The 'Scramble' installation is fairly well advanced and should be ready on time. Flying tasks over the past month have been disregarded due to re-equipment.

Jim Barton was an engineer mechanic with 72 Squadron and remembers the station commander:

My recollection of Al Deere? My stomach full of butterflies from the minute the corporal, Tam Cousins, ran over from the flight office and said, 'You'd better spruce your kite up, Jim, the station commander is flying after lunch.' Bloody Hell, I was still nervous of all officers as I still had the 'Sprog Marks' on me and now I had the boss man of the station thrust on me!

Very anxiously waiting for him to arrive and get it over with, I suddenly heard, 'Good afternoon, is she ready?' The great man was holding his parachute for me to place it in the cockpit. 'Afternoon, sir, she's all ready,' I answered. My fears left me in a flash on seeing the grin on his face. He flew in my kite on several occasions after that. A smashing, reserved and very polite man, and I felt Cock o' the North!

During September, Deere and his team of staff directed their efforts towards arranging not only the ongoing work of running the airfield, but towards putting together a successful Battle of Britain Open Day, which was scheduled for 20th September.

This proved to pay dividends, when 40,000 people attended and commented on the high standard of flying by the squadrons participating. The last week in September was spent working up for Exercise Ardent which was to take place on 4th/5th October. This was a postwar Air Defence Exercise and according to the exercise, North Weald had received minor damage and for the duration the domestic lighting was switched off and emergency lighting was used. In fact during the exercise 400 lamps, 20 lbs of candles and 130 gallons of paraffin were used for the emergency lighting.

On 20th March 1953 601 Squadron held a dining-in night with the retiring Commander-in-Chief of Fighter Command, Sir Basil Embry, as guest of honour. Other guests included Air Vice-Marshal The Earl of Bandon, Air Commodore Morris (Met Sector Commander) and the station commander.

During September that year the aerodrome again played host to the annual Battle of Britain Open Day and again the squadrons put on a marvellous display. Deere himself was flying one of the Meteor jet aircraft and he led a formation over to Hornchurch, where the station was also celebrating the Battle of Britain anniversary. In Deere's autobiography he recalled as he neared the aerodrome some of Hornchurch's landmarks, which included the tall laundry chimney, which belonged to St George's Hospital, which was situated right next door to the aerodrome and the grass flightpaths, which now were non-operational as far as the RAF was concerned. It obviously brought many memories flooding back to him as he led the jets on the final run, and of his many comrades he had known in 54 Squadron who had taken off from there in 1940. It also triggered the idea in him of writing his own book and telling his and their story at Hornchurch.

Mike Druitt of 72 Squadron remembers that the squadron held a special party for two of their pilots on the station:

> When Jack Browne and Bob 'Chuck' Breeze of the United States Marine Corps decided to have a double celebration for the arrival of 'Chuck' to 72 Squadron and the departure of Jack, they decided to invite Al Deere and his wife to attend.
>
> Al immediately accepted and couldn't wait for the event. Jack and Chuck obtained the gallons of booze from a part exchange store on one of the American bases. I actually watched them mix a special brew; everything went into it including the Mess sofa, you've never seen such a brew. They called it 'Sneaky Pete' and sneaky it was!
>
> It tasted like fruit juice, but within minutes it was sneaking straight up to your brain and you were completely sure that you could walk on the ceiling; I'm sure a few of the lads tried.
>
> The party blasted off into the night and throughout the evening I caught sight of Al Deere looking thoroughly fed up as the party raved on, but he stayed until the bitter end. I was told later, that Al had been informed by his doctor to lay off the booze for a while. It must have been awful for him not to be able to try the brew.
>
> Jack Browne was found asleep in his Hillman car at six o'clock in the morning. He had missed the right turning from the Mess and the two front wheels were in the ditch with the back wheels up in the air still turning. What a night to remember!

Towards the end of 1953, Deere commented on the hard work that he and his men had undertaken in keeping the aerodrome fully operational including the new control tower:

> After two and half years of work and the last 12 months made up of frustrated attempts by me to get the job done, the new Air Traffic Control Tower has at last opened. Even now, however the job is only partly completed as the ORDF display in the

tower is not yet working. It only remains for the airfield lighting to be set in operation, particularly the high intensity lighting and the controller's and pilots' jobs will be made that much easier.

John W. Meddows was doing his National Service and the duties he had been assigned required that he confer with the station commander on certain points of detail. He recalls the following:

In those days, apart from the usual section inspections and parades, we ordinary airmen seldom had the opportunity to interact with the likes of station commanders. However, it came to pass that the Duke of Edinburgh was appointed Commander-in-Chief of 601 Auxiliary Squadron, and in his honour, it was decided to refurbish the Mess bar in preparation for an impending visit by him. As a result of this decision, various sections were trawled for airmen who had some knowledge and skills connected with cabinet making, joinery and French polishing. This produced a grand total of three National Service airmen with the abilities required, and we soon set about the task of obtaining most of the materials from Edmonds of Epping (no expense spared!) and we were granted permission to use the facilities of the station workshops, given the use of a 'Queen Mary' transporter to collect the large oak timbers and a cash float for anything else needed to help produce the right ambience during the visit of such an important VIP.

If my memory serves me correctly, I believe we had about five to six weeks before the visit, during which time Alan Deere paid us short informal visits, usually entering the bar by way of the French windows, dressed for tennis with his racquet tucked under one arm. He always seemed to have a quiet confident manner and listened with interest when we described slight changes to the original design – none of us had actually worked on bar construction before, but we were pooling our experience to obtain the desired result.

As the work progressed, we were particularly fortunate to have both technical and practical assistance from one of the auxiliary pilots from 601 Squadron, who apparently worked for a firm, which supplied soft secluded lighting units, and was willing to supply them! This variable colour secluded lighting worked magic, and certainly the visual effect on our behind the bar shelving units, created a new atmospheric dimension.

Thanks to the cheerful support and encouragement of Alan Deere and the senior technical officer, we completed the work on time. Both appeared happy and delighted with our efforts. Whether the new commander-in-chief of 601 enjoyed his visit,

I will never know, as I was due for two weeks' leave and gratefully took it.

On 2nd December 1953, Deere was on hand to see the arrival and re-formation of 111 Squadron under the command of Squadron Leader Pears DFC.

On 16th June 1954 Wing Commander Alan Deere's time as station commander came to a close as he handed over command of North Weald to Group Captain G.C. Eveleight OBE, ADC. Deere was given a new position as Wing Commander Administration at 2nd Tactical Air Force Headquarters based at Wildenrath in Germany on 23rd June. It was here that his son John recalls his first taste of education and his father spending time with him:

I can remember knocking his fence down while dressed as a Red Indian and getting a clip round the ear for my troubles, that was one of my earliest recollections of father. We used to kick the ball around the garden and he used to try to teach me how to play sports of various sorts. I went to a local school while I was there. But I was taken away for filling all the toilets up with coal, which took me all morning. But then after that I was sent off to boarding school and he flew with me actually from Bruggen to Northolt. Germany was the place I remember him best on a day-to-day basis. He'd get up and get dressed in his uniform and off he'd go to fly his desk or whatever else he did. He wasn't an ostentatious man, he never spoke about war exploits unless you specifically questioned him or showed some interest. He was not secretive, but not disclosive about it.

During our upbringing he was strict, he had pretty clear rules on what was right and what was wrong, which was a good thing. I remember I must have pinched something from the NAAFI once and he made me go and confess, then go and work there for a week stacking all the shelves. I wouldn't say he was a disciplinarian, but he made sure I didn't get out of line. My mother on the other hand was as soft as butter.

One incident I recall was when we went on holiday from Germany to Italy. We got to the border and the border post wouldn't let him through because he needed a visa as a New Zealander. So he had to travel back to Germany and I know he was very pissed off about it. He had only wanted to spend a couple of days there.

In March 1957, Deere finished his tour of Germany and was recalled to Britain. One person who remembers meeting him at this time was Gerry Mobb:

I worked as an Operations Clerk (Air Traffic Control) during my National Service from 1957 to 1958 and after initial training I was posted to RAF Wattisham in Suffolk. At that time Wattisham was on a 24-hour fighter readiness, with day and night fighter squadrons being deployed for a week at a time from all Fighter Command stations. One late afternoon in March 1957, we had an emergency call from an Avro Anson on route from Germany to, I believe, Northolt. The aircraft was experiencing some engine trouble and made an unscheduled landing, which it did without any problem.

The crew of two came to the control tower while the station mechanics had a look at the problem. When the two aircrew arrived at the tower, I recognised from photos and books that I had read as a youngster that one of them was in fact Alan Deere, who was by now a wing commander. It was explained to them that according to 'the rules' we were obliged to inform Customs and Excise*, who were based at Ipswich, that an aircraft had landed from abroad and needed clearance to continue. Wing Commander Deere asked me to get him some people at the Air Ministry before ringing Customs, which I did. After making his calls, we were informed that the Anson aircraft was now ready. Alan Deere then gave me a packet of cigarettes, which I noted were duty free service issue, for my troubles! I suspect there were a lot more on board the Anson!!

This incident stays in my mind because not only had I come face to face with a real fighter ace, but, even though I was only a LAC at the time, he was so polite and friendly to all he came in contact with during that short period.

On 26th March 1957, Deere was selected as an instructor to teach at the RAF Staff College at Bracknell, Berkshire. On 1st October, he was promoted to group captain and appointed the Group Director at the college. It was while at Bracknell, that Deere began to put pen to paper and began writing a manuscript of his wartime memoirs, *Nine Lives*. John Deere remembers seeing his father spend time working on the project:

He would sit at the back of his study with this little typewriter going 'click, click, click' and he'd spend hours in that room, because he did the whole thing himself manually. I think mother helped him go through it and she read it for him. When it was eventually published it sold quite well. One thing that arose from the book's publication was that in it he talks about going to a HMV factory during the war and making a morale-boosting speech and the management saying that they would give him a radio for coming along, but they never did. [See Chapter 4]. But the then managing director of the company had read the book and thought that this was something that they

---

*Although we phoned Customs, I don't recall them ever turning up!

ought to right. So they came round with this amazing state of the art stereogram, which had just come in. It had a big cabinet with independent mahogany speakers; I mean huge things, not like the things you get today. I remember seeing these two guys in brown overalls walking in with this and in order to demonstrate the stereo sound, they had a record which played a table tennis recording in which you could hear the ball go from one speaker to the other. It was quite amusing.

With the book finally finished, he presented the manuscript to a list of possible interested publishers and finally secured a contract with Hodder and Stoughton Limited of London, who published the book in 1959. The response to the work by the press was varied, but on the whole the reviews were very positive. The *Daily Telegraph* columnist John Chappell wrote:

> Group Captain Alan Deere is a 'Kiwi' to use his contemporaries' expression, who joined the RAF in time to fly in the Battle of Britain. His account is the first to be written by one of the 'Few.' Its title *Nine Lives* is a misnomer. The author appears to have used up this quota in the first few chapters, but has nevertheless survived to tell us the tale.
>
> The book recaptures the experience for those who shared it and for those who know the feel of fighter controls, perhaps more successfully than it conveys the atmosphere to those otherwise engaged in those times. A slight reticence in language may have something to do with this. As the nine lives go down like ninepins, one has the feeling that the conversation was rather more vivid than as reported.
>
> The RAF College at Cranwell may not regard Group Captain Deere's story as a textbook, but it contains history, and lessons can be drawn. As early as page 55, fighting area attacks – the standardised methods of fighter squadrons before the war – are shown to be inappropriate.

The *Evening Star* reviewed the book in the newspaper's Saturday Magazine section and concluded:

> In this book one can trace the transformation from a 'sprog' pilot, reckless and eager for the kill, to a responsible wing leader, still eager for the kill, but with almost paternal feeling of responsibility for his 'youngsters' being blooded for the first time.
>
> Unfortunately only a few had the opportunity of maturing like him. In these pages of *Nine Lives* the reader will meet likeable young men only to read a little further on of their death or disappearance. In fact there is almost off-hand callousness about the manner and frequency with which the names are introduced then killed throughout the book. But this in itself

gives the real clue to the life of the fighter pilot of those days, a mere 19 years ago. Life was valuable, but short. Friendships were valuable, but short. An air of callousness was almost essential to live through those times.

Whatever the attitude of mind, however, here is a first rate story, seen through the eyes of a now famous New Zealander, of a period which will long be remembered in history. It is a book devoted to courage and a shining example of endurance and determination. No reader should be disappointed in *Nine Lives*.

That same year, he again managed to visit his native New Zealand and was again treated like a VIP on news of his arrival in his hometown of Wanganui. When questioned about future writing activities by the local *Wanganui Herald*, he smiled and said that writing was hard work and despite the success of his autobiography, it had not left him with any ambition for a repeat performance. During his stay, he attended a reception at the Army Headquarters, Maria Place, as the guest of the Wanganui Hospital Board's Miss Personality candidate, Miss Rachel Lavulo. He also attended the official opening of the Wellington Airport on the South Island.

On 17th October 1959, he left the Staff College and was posted on attachment to Headquarters, Transport Command, on liaison and lecture duties. His stay was short and he had left by 8th November. That same month a new role was found for him at Air Ministry, when he was made Director of Postings. It was here that he met Air Commodore David M. Strong CB, AFC:

> I first met Al Deere when I had become an Air Commodore and he was a Group Captain, and he came to work for me at the Air Ministry. His job was as postings officer for group captains in Britain and overseas. I at that time was Director of Personnel. However, the first time I had actually heard of him was just after the war, when I was posted to Rhodesia. I travelled by ship to Capetown and on my arrival, Sailor Malan the famous wartime fighter pilot met me. Malan and I had learnt to fly together at 3 Flying Training School at Grantham, Lincolnshire, before the war, so I knew him well. By this time, he had left the air force and was working in business in South Africa. He said to me, 'If you come across a chap named Al Deere, he is a very good chap.' Al Deere had such a very good reputation and his reports were so good that he was just the sort of chap you needed to post group captains; they needed someone they could trust, and who was honest and they got it with Al Deere.

John Deere recalls this period in his father's career:

> We had moved the family home to Northwood by this time and

he would commute into London by train wearing his bowler hat, looking like the gentleman from the Spillers flour advert. It was the done thing at that time, that if you weren't wearing a uniform you would be wearing a suit with a hat and an umbrella, very stereotypical today, but that's how it was.

I remember one amusing incident, which happened to him on the way into London.

My mother always said to him that he was too reserved and shy and that he must make an effort to speak to people, and engage them in conversation and so on. He was sitting in his carriage travelling down to Liverpool Street Station, and there was a lady sitting opposite him who was reading a book. He suddenly said to her, 'What a nice day it is and it is nice to have the sun out.' The lady didn't reply. Five or ten minutes later, he plucked up courage again and said, 'That's a very nice tweed skirt you're wearing.' With which she replied, 'If there's any more nonsense like that, young man, I'm going to pull the communication cord.' So that put him off for life.

On 4th March 1961, Deere opened his daily post to find a letter from the Air Ministry, which read:

Dear Sir,

I am commanded by the Air Council to inform you that The Queen has been graciously pleased to appoint you as one of Her Majesty's Aides-de-Camp with effect from 22nd March 1961. Notification of the appointment will appear in the Royal Air Force Supplement to the *London Gazette* on 21st March.

How did Deere and his family react to such an honour being bestowed upon him?

His son John recalls:

I remember mother talking about it rather than him, and saying what a good honour this was and as a result of that they would go to a few tea parties at Buckingham Palace, all dressed up in their finery. Part of his function was to represent the service he was in, when the Queen visited around the country on special occasions.

Deere continued in his post at the Air Ministry until 1962, when he undertook another 12-month course starting on 8th January 1962 at the Imperial Defence College. Air Commodore David Strong remembers:

I recommended Al to go to the Imperial Defence College at Belgrave Square, which is now called the Royal College of Defence Studies. This was a course of about one year with other top Navy, Army and Civil Service people, where they studied all the things that top people should know about. This included trips to various parts of the world to follow up their studies.

After finishing the course successfully, Deere was appointed Assistant Commandant at RAF Cranwell on 3rd February 1963 and further promotion followed ten months later, when he was made Air Commodore. He was posted to command the East Anglia Fighter Sector on 23rd March 1964 and continued there until the sectors were disbanded in August 1965.

Because of Deere's passion for golf, his son John used to help out on occasions at the local golf club, and it was here that he got to meet some of the RAF's famous wartime heroes:

> I met Bader a lot. I used to caddy for him when they played together at Wentworth. To me as a young lad his fame preceded him even though he was a close friend of father's. I was always obviously respectful of him and he was good with me. I had heard he could be a bit cussed, but I never had any experience of that.
>
> When my father got his final appointment at Halton, he thought it was marvellous, because sports was his favourite pastime, particularly rugby and golf which were his two great loves and in golf he could participate. He played at Ashridge, which was his second home, his heaven where he would play with his mates and RAF people. He had been to this course in 1937 when he had first arrived in this country during the time that the famous golfer Henry Cotton had won the British Open. He was also very good friends with Geoffrey Page, Jeffrey Quill and Paddy Barthropp.

The nation went into mourning when it was announced that Britain's great wartime leader and statesman Sir Winston Spencer Churchill had died on 24th January 1965.

The country honoured Churchill with a state funeral and arrangements were put into motion for the funeral to take place at St Paul's Cathedral on Saturday 30th January. It was decided that RAF officers who had fought during the Battle of Britain would lead the main funeral cortège procession with Churchill's coffin carried on a gun carriage, and Alan Deere was chosen to pick and lead the officers on that day. One of the officers selected to march at the head of the funeral procession was Air Commodore John Ellacombe CB, DFC, who recalls:

> The Royal Air Force kept a logbook of people who were available for such occasions and this was updated every six months, we were told. They had about 20 chaps on the list, and at this time they grabbed whoever was available, because some of the officers had been posted overseas. During this time, I was a Group Captain Ops of the Central Fighter Establishment

at RAF Binbrook.

The gathering point for the rehearsals for the funeral was at RAF Uxbridge. Alan Deere had been chosen to lead as they wanted a senior chap and he was an Air Commodore at that time. Al was a fine chap, very nice and very much admired by everybody, but also a quiet bloke who never wanted to talk much about his wartime career.

When we got to Uxbridge, there was a briefing; in fact warrant officers carried this out, who were the chaps who organised the drill. We were driven up to London on the day of the funeral to our start point at Horse Guards parade. The weather on that day was bloody cold, something like minus four degrees. The mood was a very sombre one and the one thing that struck me was, that as the band started the funeral march and we moved off, it was very emotional and pretty well all of us had tears in our eyes. It was a tremendous historical moment.

Winston Churchill, the man we had all known about and had heard throughout the war, was being taken on his final journey. I remember being at Rochford airfield during the Battle of Britain with 151 and sitting at dispersal at readiness, when he made his speech of 'Never in the field of human conflict was so much owed by so many to so Few.' After we had walked in the procession to St Paul's Cathedral, we all climbed aboard a coach and were taken back to Uxbridge and were given a late lunch and had a group photograph taken.

Alan Deere and John Ellacombe were joined that day by other notable Battle of Britain pilots including Leonard Bartlett, Ronald Berry, Ernest Wootten, Richard Haine, Desmond Sheen, George Westlake, Geoffrey Brunner, Peter Brothers, Roy Dutton, Robert Wright, Alec Ingle and Bobby Oxspring.

Alan Deere's final appointment came in November 1965, when he was made commandant of RAF Halton, the Aircraft and Boy Entrant training establishment in Buckinghamshire. Here he was also a very popular and well-respected commander. The family home was situated off the camp in the nearby town of Wendover.

During his time at Halton, the camp was visited by many VIPs including the Chief of the Malaysian Armed Forces who had an incredibly long and difficult name to remember, Lieutenant General Tan Sri Tunku Osman bin Tunka Mohamed Jewa. He inspected a guard of honour mounted by apprentices of the 202nd Entry and afterwards made a tour of the camp. Accompanied by Alan Deere and Air Vice-Marshal B. Robinson, Air Officer Commanding 24 Group, the General was shown around the airfield workshops, apprentice schools, domestic areas and playing fields before lunching in the officers' mess. After this he met some of the Malaysian apprentices at the camp.

After a year and half at Halton and after being in the service of King and Queen for 30 years, Alan Deere decided that Halton would be his last appointment and he would retire and seek a post within the service, but as a civilian. His last ceremonial function as Commandant was to give out the prizes to the apprentices of the 207th entry. It was during this ceremony that he publicly announced his retirement. Deere's replacement would be Air Commodore H.F. Connelly, who was an ex-Halton apprentice.

Tribute was paid to him on the day of the apprentices' prizegiving by Air Marshal Sir William Coles, Air Officer Commanding-in-Chief of Headquarters Technical Training Command, who stated:

> Air Commodore Deere is retiring from the service after a most distinguished, courageous and splendid career. He was one of the great band of fighter pilots who took part in the Battle of Britain and shot down no fewer than 22 aircraft. He displayed throughout the whole of his service the tremendous qualities of leadership, which we all admire. I am delighted to say that Air Commodore Deere's services are not being lost to the RAF. He is taking up an appointment in the Ministry of Defence, where he will be responsible for sport in the Service and where he will continue to have a very close relationship and association with youth. I can think of no man who is more suited to such an appointment.

His official date for retirement from the RAF was 12th December 1968. That same month, he was officially offered the job as Civilian Director of Sports Royal Air Force, which he accepted without hesitation. Air Commodore David Strong remembers Deere's enthusiasm for his new role:

> I was the chairman of the Royal Air Force Rugby Committee and I knew Al was quite keen on that sort of thing and eventually he too became chairman. This included picking all the teams, which meant we had a lot to do. Another sport that Al was keen on was golf. We played together at the same course at Ashridge and they eventually chose Al in 1976 to be the captain of the club, which was a high honour and he did it very well, as you would expect. His handicap was something around eleven. Sometimes Al and I would recall our wartime experiences; Al would say to me: 'Look, Strong, while I was fighting the war, you were having a holiday in Hitler's holiday camp.' With that we would burst out laughing.

On 2nd December 1967, Alan Deere returned to Hornchurch as a special guest for the inauguration of a new school built on the grounds of what was once RAF Hornchurch.

The aerodrome had been closed down in 1962 and sold at auction. What the Luftwaffe had failed to achieve during the Second World War, the housing developers and gravel extraction companies now achieved by razing the aerodrome's buildings to the ground. The new school was built on the site of the aerodrome's main entrance and parade ground. The school would be named after the designer of the Spitfire, Mitchell. With Deere at the ceremony was Air Vice-Marshal Richard Jones CB, AFC, who commanded 11 Group, Fighter Command, who presented the school with a two-foot replica of the station badge. Deere's visit to the school was a great success, especially the response that he evoked from the young children, when they were told who he was and what he had done at Hornchurch. Over the following years to come, he would support the school with many such happy visits.

CHAPTER 9

THE BIG WING CONTROVERSY

Alan Deere's previously unpublished views

In 1969, with the release of the much-publicised United Artists' film The Battle of Britain, the public interest in the men and machines that fought in one of the greatest air battles in history, and the controversy regarding the use of the Big Wings during the latter part of the battle was again brought to the fore.

Alan Deere decided he would write a paper on the subject and titled it 'Tactics in Dispute'. Below in full for the first time is the paper he presented with his own personal views:

Public interest in the Battle of Britain has been aroused by United Artists' recent film on this famous air battle, and the tactics employed in the Battle by the air defence forces of Fighter Command are again in dispute.

Pilots of the time who were followers of Keith Park as AOC 11 Group and those of 12 Group who supported their Group Commander, Leigh-Mallory, are arraigned in re-awakened argument on the merits of small and large formations for defence, the root cause of the tactical disagreement between the two group commanders.

As a flight commander, who led both flight and squadron in the Battle, I have decided views on the subject of the tactics used. Naturally, therefore, I was interested to see if the tactical controversy was introduced into the film, and how it was slanted.

In the event, it was touched on only briefly in a fictitious scene – one of the few in the film – played in the commander-in-chief's office. Personally, I was glad that this was so, because to have laid so much stress on what was in fact a personality clash between two commanders would have detracted from what was otherwise a magnificent team effort, and one which achieved an historic victory in the first and perhaps the last classic air battle.

135

However, to coincide with the film's release Robert Wright's book *Dowding and the Battle of Britain* appeared in the bookshops. In essence a potted biography of Lord Dowding, it is concerned chiefly with the strategic and tactical issues in Fighter Command before and during the Battle. From his researches and personal contact as aide to Dowding at the time, Wright reveals much that was not previously known about the controversy. And he confirms the belief long held by Park's supporters that his tactical handling of the Battle was in accordance with the aims of the Commander-in-Chief; aims of which Park had first hand knowledge by virtue of his previous appointment as Senior Air Staff Officer to Dowding in the formative years of Fighter Command's existence.

In the light of this re-awakened controversy and these new disclosures, I have been moved to restate my views, which hold firm on the side of the small formation as the basic element in fighter defence operations, at least in the conditions, that pertained in the Battle of Britain. In fairness, however, to those who supported Leigh-Mallory at the time I confess I write with the advantage of hindsight; nevertheless, hindsight has served to strengthen a viewpoint already held and not to change it.

When in May 1940, Dowding wrote his now historically famous letter to the Under Secretary of State at the Air Ministry to express his resistance to the plan to send home-based fighter squadrons to France, he was motivated by the necessity to have in being in the United Kingdom the minimum number of squadrons he considered necessary for the defence of this country. He believed that 'if an adequate' fighter force was kept in this country to resist invasion we should be able to carry on for some time.

Dowding appreciated that, with the fall of France imminent, the full might of the Luftwaffe would be turned against England and in the time available, he could not hope to match the Germans in strength. The strategic disposition of his forces was therefore of paramount importance and it must be dictated by the ability to carry on for some time. In effect, 'some time' was that period from the opening of an air onslaught to, in German eyes, its successful culmination as a prelude to invasion.

If Dowding's fighter defence forces could hold out through the summer, the Germans would be forced to defer their plans for an invasion into the less favourable autumnal weather period or risk a seaborne assault without establishing the necessary air superiority. Thus time was the essence of Dowding's strategy, which resolved itself into a twofold aim:

1. To prevent the destruction of his forces
2. In the process, to inflict the maximum of destruction on the enemy air force.

To achieve this the husbanding of his force was the paramount consideration, but in order to ensure the second part of the aim, it was necessary to meet the immediate threat by committing at any one time only that portion of his force required to protect the vital targets. Only by so doing could Fighter Command still be an effective force at the climax of invasion.

It was this concept of operations which dictated Park's tactics wherein he endeavoured to combine the factors of maximum flexibility with minimum force, the latter scaled to meet the threat to his major airfields, which in the context of air superiority were of vital importance and, of course, whose serviceability would play an important part in mounting around-the-clock air operations over the invasion area expected to be in the south-east; as we now know was to be the case.

His plan was simple. To use an analogy, it was based on the premise that as the lightweight in the contest he could not expect to knock out his heavier opponent.

He could but hope to win either by a technical knockout or on a point's decision.

To knock out the Luftwaffe was indeed never possible, it had too much in its armoury. A technical knockout was possible but not probable in the expected time available. A point's decision seemed, therefore, the most likely solution and this meant staying the distance. In effect, this is what Fighter Command achieved.

Tactically, the Battle of Britain was a three-phase operation; the attacks on the peripheral targets including radar, on the Sector airfields, and those on London. As regards the first-named, it has never, I think, been disputed that the only way to combat these was by the use of small formations operating from forward airfields.

The short sea crossing to the target areas meant a minimum of radar warning and it was rarely possible to get more than a flight into the air to achieve effective interception. On hard-hit forward airfields, as for example Manston, a scramble was always a hazardous event, which usually resolved itself into an every man for himself take-off, as the only sure way of getting airborne before the bombs fell.

It was the two second phases that brought to light the tactical differences of opinion between Park and Leigh-Mallory. Only at this point in the Battle was there sufficient airborne time in hand to effect interception in reasonable strength before the target was reached. Moreover, up till this time, mid-August, the 12 Group squadrons had not been called upon to take part in the fighting which continued to be concentrated in the 11 Group areas.

In the meantime, back on the 12 Group airfields, the pilots were persistently harrying the Controllers at Sectors to get them into battle somehow. The Controllers in turn were complaining to Leigh-Mallory who was constantly ringing the 11 Group Controllers for permission to send his fighters into their area. But true to his policy of containment, Park was happy that for the time being he could handle the attack with his own resources. As, however, the raids moved inland and increased in frequency and strength, there was posed an altogether more serious problem, that of the defence of the base – the Sector Operations Room; the control link in the Air Defence System, and the Sector airfields, whose continued use was vital to successful air defence.

As this time too, another factor entered into the equation, that of raid filtering. Raids of shallow penetration were easily identifiable and tracked to interception, but as they moved further inland and so out of seaward radar coverage of our Chain Home stations, the plots became confused with those of our own fighters; both now the responsibility of the Observer Corps. With hopelessly inadequate detection devices the Corps relied mainly on visual sightings, and cloud cover quite often enabled an enemy raid to pass unidentified. Thus, raid filtering was early revealed as the 'Achilles' Heel' of our air defence system, and more and more as the tracks of the enemy and those of our own fighters coalesced over southeast England.

The raid picture in the Group and Sector operations rooms became one of confusion; and, moreover, one of the principal Chain Home stations in the south had been knocked out thus allowing undetected penetration of the perimeter defences, which served to aggravate the problem confronting the by now harassed Group Controllers.

Clearly, Keith Park's chief concern, the defence of his Sector airfields apart, was now one of over-commitment. He dare not take unrestrained action on the picture presented to him on the operations table because of the danger of 'spoofing' either intentionally by the Germans, who were now splitting their raids and also making diversion attacks to draw off the defences for a big raid sneaking in through the radar gap in the south; or unintentionally by wrong identification both in numbers and as friend or foe. The only safe tactic was, therefore, to operate his force in small formations, which because of their flexibility could both delay their take-off time until raid information became more positive, and yet be mutually self-supporting in the target area. Whatever tactic he adopted the problem of defence of the airfields was paramount, and it was this undertaking, which was assigned to the 12 Group squadrons at Park's request.

By now it was well into August, and the 12 Group squadrons, though becoming increasingly more involved in the Battle, were being used principally to defend the 11 Group airfields and to meet 12 Group's allotted responsibility 'of defence of its own area, including some highly industrial districts.' Fighter Command therefore strictly controlled incursions into the 11 Group areas in accordance with Dowding's directive that Park was in sole control of the tactical battle, for so long as the main weight of attack was concentrated in the 11 Group areas of operations.

Circumscribed, at least as he saw it by these instructions, it is easy to understand Leigh-Mallory's feelings of frustration, and no less those of his pilots who were at constant readiness, and contended that they were being deliberately kept out of the battle. It was in this atmosphere that the tactic of using Wings was first put forward by Douglas Bader, in the hope, I suspect, that by adopting the large formation, that more 12 Group fighters would get into the battle. It was a natural reaction from an aggressive leader of Bader's calibre who, says his biographer, 'found it intolerable that others should be plunging into fire of battle while he was held impotently on the ground.' Bader's persuasive personality soon won over Leigh-Mallory to the concept; although initially he reputedly countered the suggestion by replying, 'We can't put all our eggs in one basket, Bader. You've got to hang on and wait. No doubt the enemy would be delighted to draw our fighter cover away from the Midlands.'

Sound advice, and based on Leigh-Mallory's knowledge of his Commander-in-Chief's aims; knowledge not of course disseminated down to the squadrons and even if it had been, it was indigestible stuff to Bader and his restless followers.

By the last week in August, when the fighting was at an intense stage, tempers at all levels had become somewhat frayed, and not least those of Park and Leigh-Mallory. The latter was now solidly lined up behind Bader who, again to quote his biographer, 'skulked and stormed in the dispersal hut at Coltishall.' But Park was not to be intimidated because he was both confident that the tactics he was adopting were paying off, and ever mindful of his directive, to call for outside help only when absolutely essential.

More and more Park was finding that flexibility was his

chief weapon in countering new German tactics of spilt-raids, spoof attacks and diversions, all of which tended to swamp the raid-reporting system. Operating at squadron strength, he now introduced the tactic of using specified Spitfire squadrons to get airborne early to engage and draw-off the escort fighters and at the same time to report back on the direction of the raids. This allowed Park to hold other squadrons on the ground at a high state of readiness until the enemy plan of attack was established; and then to engage the bomber force under more advantageous terms. Using these tactics, he quite often had all his squadrons in the air at once thus leaving his Sector airfields unprotected. Now was the time to request assistance from 12 Group.

At first all this meant to the 12 Group squadrons was a higher state and longer hours of readiness, but as the weight and fury of the raids intensified they more and more got into the fighting; and with some success. Bader had by this time, won his point for on 7th September, when in accordance with Leigh-Mallory's phoned instructions, 'Next time 11 Group calls on you, take your whole team,' the Duxford Wing of three squadrons took the air. In the ensuing climb to height the two supporting squadrons got so far behind that they virtually missed the fight. One wonders therefore, if operating independently with less time to form up, a greater number of fighter aircraft could have been brought to bear. Bader's answer to this was to complain on landing 'If only we could get off earlier we could get on top of them.' A valid comment, but Bader, ignorant of Park's tactics, could not know that as a reserve-cover force it would have been folly to commit the 12 Group squadrons too early in the raid build-up. Time to height when ordered off was therefore overriding, and any formation scramble greater than squadron strength would clearly operate against this consideration.

Curiously, it was on this day, 7th September, that the Germans switched their attacks to London and 12 Group was now virtually freed of its cover commitment. This fact plus a certain amount of success – and one must be fair the Duxford Wing did have its successes – led Bader to press for more squadrons en masse, until finally the operating strength of the Wing was raised to five squadrons.

Although a larger force would inevitably slow down the interception time, this factor was no longer of quite such importance because it was to some extent offset by the deeper penetration of the raiders. If there ever was a time for using big formations it was now, and the Duxford Wing certainly delivered some telling blows, albeit that a number of interceptions were made after the enemy bombers had reached their target.

As is now known, however, the Germans had already decided that invasion was no longer a possibility. August had come and gone, and with it the good weather; the Royal Air Force was still a force to be reckoned with. The attacks on London were in effect the last throw of a beaten opponent, carried out as much in anger at the Royal Air Force's bombing of Berlin as a desperate last attempt to deliver a knockout blow. But the knockout blow never came and a tired and disillusioned Luftwaffe retreated to its corner, leaving the ring to Fighter Command, victors on a point's decision. Thus whatever impact the Duxford Wing had on the subsequent fighting, it had none on the outcome of the Battle proper, which in the words of Lord Dowding, 'ended when Hitler cancelled the orders for invasion.'

It will be argued by the protagonists of the Duxford Wing enthusiasts that because 12 Group squadrons were held back so long before getting into the fighting, the effectiveness of the Wing concept as a tactic in fighter defence could not be proven. There is of course some merit in the argument. However, it ignores the main problem facing Keith Park, that of fighting and surviving throughout the period leading up to and including an expected invasion, while at the same time keeping intact the Sector airfields. This latter task, assigned to 12 Group when the airfields came under heavy attack, was a vital one and its fulfilment could not have been guaranteed had the bulk of the 12 Group forces been committed to the Battle from the outset. Furthermore, and as already stated, Dowding's directive to the air officer commanding 12 Group, charged him with the defence of the Midlands as his prime task; and unrestricted entry into the fighting while it was confined to the 11 Group area and within the capacity of Park to handle, would have been in contravention of this stated task. In fact, Leigh-Mallory did partially ignore orders when without the knowledge of Fighter Command, he sent his five-squadron Wing into battle thus, to use his own phrase when earlier he resisted the temptation to do so 'putting all his eggs in one basket'. In doing so, he was wrong in principle, and in the matter of tactics unsound.

Air Vice-Marshal Johnnie Johnson had this to say on both points: 'The Duxford Wing had taken 17 minutes to leave the ground and a further 20 minutes before it set course from base. Also, because it absorbed five squadrons from a relatively weak Group, it left some highly important targets in the Midlands short of fighter cover.' A damning indictment by one who was not only a pilot in the Duxford Wing, but also at a later date an outstanding wing leader under Leigh-Mallory.

The Battle of Britain has gone down in history as a great victory, and it was due not so much to successful tactics as possession of an advanced air defence system backed by fine teamwork and inspired leadership at all levels. Tactics were of course important to the outcome, and in the finely balanced period of fighting towards the end of August, they were perhaps all important, and at that time the overriding factor that ensured final victory.

Victory proved Park's tactics to be right in the particular circumstances and however much one might lean towards the Wing concept, it is difficult to envisage success other than in the way it was achieved; a combination of flexibility and economy of force. Neither is an ingredient of the large formation; and I believe if used in 11 Group, the Wing concept would have foundered on its failure to observe these two basic principles. Admittedly, the concept never had a chance to wholly prove itself – nor I suppose to be wholly condemned – and we shall perhaps never know its true merit, because it is unlikely that two opposing air forces will ever again become engaged in a comparable classic.

It is, I think, fitting to leave the last word on the subject with an historian, Sir Basil Liddell Hart, who wrote, 'The Germans' bid to gain command of the air, as a preliminary to invasion was frustrated by the superb efforts of fifty-odd squadrons of Fighter Command under the masterly direction of Air Chief Marshal Sir Hugh Dowding and Air Vice-Marshal Keith Park.'

CHAPTER 10

THE TWILIGHT YEARS

On 21st March 1972, Deere received a letter addressed from Hornchurch. It was from the headmaster of the Mitchell Junior School:

Dear Group Captain Deere,

As this school is named after R. J. Mitchell, designer of the Spitfire, and stands on the site of the now demolished RAF Station, Hornchurch, I feel it would be most fitting, as we are beginning a House system at the school, to name the Houses after four famous Spitfire pilots who served in squadrons which were based at this station during the war.

I am sure this would be more significant to children of Junior School age, if the names chosen were those of persons still living, and the children and I would regard it a great honour if you would consent to the use of your name as a title for one of the Houses along with those of Wing Commander H.M. Stephen, DSO, DFC and Bar, Wing Commander R.R.S Tuck, DSO, DFC and 2 Bars, DFC (USA), and Air Chief Marshal Sir Harry Broadhurst, KCB, KBE, DSO, DFC, AFC.

The choice of names follows a little research I have pursued, aided by Squadron Leader Martin at the Ministry of Defence. They commemorate, in addition to their deeds and squadrons, various other attributes not only of themselves, but also of others who served at Hornchurch.

Thus yourself, as a New Zealander, represents the aid given by Commonwealth countries in the war effort. Sir Harry Broadhurst was Station Commander, Wing Commander Stephen, a Scot, reminds us that the United Kingdom comprises other races besides the English. Sir Harry Broadhurst and yourself remained in the Air Force after the war and rose to even greater eminence in the Service, whilst Wing Commanders Stephen and Tuck returned to the civilian life for which they had fought so valiantly.

You will know that we already have links between the school and the RAF, as I understand you visited the school on the occasion of the

143

presentation of the badge of RAF Hornchurch. The badges of the four squadrons based at Hornchurch are used as trophies for House competitions and a scale model is used as an overall trophy for the Champion House. I think from the foregoing you will realise that our links with the history of this area would be near completion, if you would agree to the use of your name.

If in addition, you were able to visit the school and talk to the children in 'your' House, either with the three other gentlemen or on a separate occasion, this would indeed be an honour and help to make that history a reality.

Should you accept this invitation, I have one further request, that you might either present the school with an unframed copy of your favourite uniformed portrait photograph of yourself at about the time of the Battle of Britain, or lend a picture or negative from which a copy may be taken, so that the House Badge mounted in the school hall may bear your portrait.

Yours Sincerely

R.A. French

Alan Deere put pen to paper the following day and wrote to the headmaster telling him of his delight in being chosen and that he would accept his invitation to attend the school again. The picture that he sent to the school was the pencil sketch drawing, which had been done by the famous wartime artist Cuthbert Orde. The Spitfire scale model that the school displayed carried Deere's code letters when with 54 Squadron: KL-B.

That June, Al Deere together with Wing Commanders Robert Stanford Tuck and H.M. Stephen arrived at Mitchell's School to see the inauguration of the new house system, where they were treated to a rendering of the Royal Air Force March by the school's recorder band. The new House Trophy, a silver cup engraved with 'Spitfire Pilots' was presented to the school by the veteran pilots. Also presented were the four copy framed sketches of each of the pilots and these still hang proudly today in the school hall either side of the RAF Hornchurch badge.

In fact Deere and his wife visited the school on several occasions over the following years, attending the children's annual 'Sports Day', which he always enjoyed. Following one such visit in 1972, he wrote:

My Dear Headmaster,

I am writing to say how much my wife and I enjoyed our day with you on Thursday.

We were truly impressed with all the arrangements, which ensured that we as your guests received maximum benefit from the visit with the minimum of protocol and fuss. It was just what we wanted and it made every minute an enjoyable one.

Please convey my thanks to your staff who were very considerate of our every wish, and to the Headmistress of the Infant's School for her conducted tour, which we found particularly interesting.

Finally, I send my very sincere good wishes to all the school children, particularly those who so able performed in the School Hall. And, of course, a special mention for the members of Deere House, who seemed to be headed for victory in the Inter-House sports, which I hope they won.

I look forward to a visit at some future date.

Yours Sincerely

Alan Deere

On 2nd March 1972, Alan Deere, with other distinguished Royal Air Force wartime pilots and celebrities from the world of entertainment and sport, had arrived at television studios in London to pay tribute to Sir Douglas Bader in a 'This is your Life' programme which was hosted by presenter Eamonn Andrews. Deere was one of the guests selected to talk about certain aspects of Bader's life, which he did, selecting the occasion when the RAF flew a new artificial leg over to France when Bader had lost one when he had been shot down and made a prisoner of war. Eamonn Andrews set the scene and introduced Deere as wartime friend and golfing partner. Deere related the following for the television audience:

> Well, it was decided in the circumstances of the recipient here, that we couldn't accept the German offer to have a free flight in and therefore a bombing raid on St Omer was laid on by Blenheims, one of which carried the new leg. I was the one unfortunate to be detailed to provide close escort with Spitfires and we had a hell of a job getting in and out, but Douglas got his new leg.

Alan Deere finally retired from his job as Director of Sports and Inspector of Recreational Grounds, Royal Air Force on 12th December 1972.

During the following years, he kept up his great interest and love for sport, playing golf matches for charities and always attending RAF anniversaries whenever possible. But Deere was always the modest gentleman and would not seek to talk about his wartime experiences unless he found the person was genuinely interested.

He always supported his beloved New Zealand and whenever the All Blacks were playing or the New Zealand team were participating in the yachting race of the America's Cup he would watch the television avidly.

In 1987, when American aviation artist Jerry Crandall began research for his series of paintings depicting events of the Battle of Britain, he contacted Deere and arranged to interview him regarding his collision with an Me109 on 9th July 1940. Jerry Crandall recalls:

> We travelled to England in November 1987, to interview Al

Deere for this project. It was delightful visiting him and his wonderful wife Joan. They really made us feel most welcome.

We went over every detail of this incident step by step and recorded an interview with him on a video camera, while he demonstrated with 1.72 scale models to show me the battle leading up to and including the collision. While working on the sketches, I played the video over and over to get the exact angles, attitudes etc in the final painting. After many letters and phone calls, I sent him a copy of the final sketch for his approval. The painting was finally finished and from it a special edition of 950 signed prints was released to coincide with the 50th Anniversary of the Battle of Britain in 1990.

It was in 1988 that Alan Deere's health had become a cause of concern, when after undergoing medical tests he was diagnosed as having cancer of the colon. After having chemotherapy, which appeared to keep the disease in check, he was told that it could recur. He felt that if it did so he would let events take their course, especially as he was having increasing problems with injuries he had sustained during wartime. Meanwhile with the treatment seeming a success, he continued to live a fairly normal lifestyle.

During 1989, he played an active part in helping to raise funds for the RAF Benevolent Fund, when he was asked to contribute to what became one of the world's most expensive books. The Limited Edition book entitled *So Few* was the brainchild of the late John Golley, historian Bill Gunston and photographer and artist Michael Pierce, and would tell the story of the Battle of Britain through the memories of 25 pilots who flew during that period. Each book would be made out of the finest paper and leather bound, with an original signature and a silhouette portrait of each veteran. The purchase price was £1,500 with only 401 copies being produced. This magnificent tome would be ready in 1990, in time to commemorate the 50th anniversary of the Battle of Britain. The book was an enormous success and raised over £300,000 for the Fund. Deere supplied the producers with photographs from his private collection and wrote two pages about his lucky escape at Hornchurch whilst taking off.

In April 1990 he visited his beloved New Zealand for the last time. The occasion was to participate in the New Zealand version of 'This is your Life' programme to honour his great friend and fellow wartime ace Johnny Checketts. The visit with his wife Joan, gave Deere the chance to see family, friends and many of his old comrades.

In 1991, Deere's autobiography was made available again, reprinted by Wingham Press, with a marvellous cover painting by renowned aviation artist Robert Taylor. The book sold well. Deere was to be found at many of the air shows that summer signing copies for the public with friend and RAF colleague 'Laddie' Lucas, who had just released another book of his own.

On 8th July 1993, I was privileged to meet Alan Deere for the first time. The occasion was the official opening and unveiling of the monument to the men of the Battle of Britain by Her Majesty Queen Elizabeth, Queen Mother, at Capel le Ferne, Folkestone. The previous day had been a typical summer's day with beautiful blue skies; but the day of the ceremony however could not have been more different.

As the veterans arrived, the weather worsened until it was almost a full-blown gale.

Walking amongst so many distinguished airmen, I noticed to one side of one of the marquees, a gentleman appropriately dressed in a hat and raincoat; it was Alan Deere with his wife Joan. I had written to Alan previously regarding my interest in his time at Hornchurch, and so introduced myself. His reaction was instant and enthusiastic. 'Hello, how are you? At last we meet.' He asked how I was getting on with my research and was very interested in the local preservation of RAF Hornchurch's history. My time with him was only brief, but during our time together my friend John Cox, another ex-Hornchurch veteran, posed proudly with Al in order for me to take a photograph. The meeting still stands out brightly in my memory.

Sadly, I did not meet Alan again, but we corresponded occasionally. It was at this time that his cancer reoccurred, and the illness was now becoming stressful to him, so the last thing he needed was visits from historians and researchers.

Alan's son John remembers this final period of his father's life:

> My father felt it was something he just had to deal with. He was forever saying that 'I've done well to last this long,' and he was perfectly philosophical about it, but his main concern was for my mother and that she would be able to look after herself financially and otherwise when he was gone. My mother of course was extremely worried for him, as she lived for him. My only great regret as is common with most children is not doing more with him when I was younger, and when he was younger.

Deere continued to battle against his illness and kept himself busy still undertaking smaller requests from historians and publishers. His two final pieces of work were for a new book to commemorate the 60th anniversary of the Spitfire and a five-part television documentary series entitled New Zealand at War for which he agreed to be interviewed. This was the first and only time that he been filmed to tell his own story.

His contribution for *Spitfire – The Legend* was to write the foreword, which he did eloquently. The book was not released until 1996.

On 21st September 1995, after a long and hard-fought battle against his illness, Alan Christopher Deere died. John Deere recalls:

> Mother and I were there when he passed away. A couple of months earlier, he had bought a golden wedding ring to give to her on their anniversary. He had been to Aylesbury to buy the ring and had said to me, 'You must remind me to give it to her

and here it is.' So I took charge of it and when the day arrived, which was the 18th September, I gave it to him as he was lying in bed and he gave it to her that day.

He expressly willed that there be no funeral service and in fact I was the only one present at the cremation. His wishes were that his ashes be scattered over the Thames estuary from a Spitfire, and this was done with the co-operation of the Battle of Britain Memorial Flight. There was no memorial service held, but what I did do was get a lot of his close friends and immediate relatives to come to a reception at Halton House, which is the officers' mess at RAF Halton.

During the days following Alan Deere's death many tributes were paid by fellow colleagues and newspapers around the world, which carried obituaries telling of the outstanding life of this fine gentleman.

What memorials stand in memory of this most notable of airmen? In Hornchurch, there is a road named Deere Avenue and the school House at Mitchell's School. The RAF Museum Hendon now hold his medals and a large archive of documents and photographs, which were purchased at an auction organised by Dix Noonan Webb on April 2nd 2003 for the sum of £138,000, amongst the items being his original notes and manuscript for *Nine Lives*. At the Hornchurch Wing Collection housed within the Purfleet Heritage and Military Centre, Purfleet in Essex, one can view Deere's wartime flying boots, pre-war RAF Boxing Cup, Caterpillar Club Tie and other memorabilia, which were kindly donated to the collection by Joan Deere prior to her death in 1998. The Kent Battle of Britain Museum at Hawkinge, Kent, has on display the Rolls-Royce Merlin engine and other assorted remains from Spitfire R6832 which was shot down on 28th August 1940, together with a full size replica Spitfire representing KL-B. In New Zealand, the Royal New Zealand Air Force Museum at Ohakea also hold a boxing cup award, which was given to the museum by his late wife. A flying tribute to the great man will take shape in the next five to seven years, when a Spitfire aircraft, which is being restored in New Zealand, is finally completed. The Spitfire Mk IXc, PV270, is owned by Al Deere's nephew Brendon Deere and once completed will carry the code letters used by Deere when he led the Biggin Hill Wing.

In final assessment, one could say that Alan Deere led a charmed life. He had fulfilled his boyhood dreams of flying and had an RAF career that was exceptional, albeit with a number of major life-threatening escapades along the way. He respected and was respected in turn by his fellow men. He was an unassuming and modest man, and although the majority of people saw him as an outstanding WW2 fighter pilot, he felt he was nothing out of the ordinary and had only done as many others had, a job for which he had been trained. His courage and strength however, showed that the human spirit could survive against overwhelming odds, which lifted his standing well above the average although he never sought this.

Lord Dowding summed up the character of Alan Deere perfectly when he wrote the foreword for Deere's autobiography:

> He will always stand to me as an example of the best type of fighter pilot, whose endurance and determination brought this country of ours through the greatest immediate danger, which had threatened it since Napoleon's armies stood along the Channel shore.

It was fitting tribute from his commander-in-chief during the Battle and is still valid today. The name of Alan Deere will always be held in esteem within the annals of air combat and the proud history of the Royal Air Force.

PART TWO

Escape

by

Air Commodore Alan Deere

A previously unpublished wartime adventure story

INTRODUCTION

After the publication and good reaction from reviewers and the public in general to his autobiography, *Nine Lives*, it is possible that Al Deere decided to follow up his first book with an attempt to try his hand at writing for a more wider audience.

The following fictional short story titled *Escape* was to be an adventure wartime story for boys, and was aimed at a younger market. During the 1960s, accounts of wartime heroics and deeds were available, some true, some fictional.

The Victor, *Commando* and *Air Ace* were just a few of the magazines that many young boys bought with their precious pocket money.

In *Escape*, Deere has provided the reader with the main ingredients for such an adventure book, the main heroic character, his trusty friend, and the elements of imminent danger. Deere himself could easily relate and write about danger and its many guises, which in an instant could materialise from a seemingly normal situation.

What was the inspiration for the story? For those who have read widely the exploits of fighter pilots of World War II, many will perhaps recognize the main character on whom Deere has based the story. The gentleman in question was Johnny Checketts, who was a very good friend of Deere's, and the initial opening to this story is based on fact. The remainder of the book and dialogue between the story's main characters is the author's own work.

Today's youth is now far removed from the youngsters of the 1960s for which this short story was intended, and in retrospect although now dated, I hope the reader will find it has the charm and content of a bygone age, now unrecognisable in today's literary world. The passages describing flying and air fighting are excellent and have certainly more than stood the test of time.

Richard C. Smith
May 2003

CHAPTER 1

On the outskirts of the village of Tours-en-Vimeu, some twenty kilometres east of Le Tréport in the province of Picardy, a small boy on his bicycle bumped his way along the high crowned cobbled road, which passed through the village and continued on its tree-lined way towards the Channel coast. The boy's progress was slow. For on the front wheel of his bicycle was a half deflated threadbare tyre which spread itself uncertainly over the cobbles, while the rear wheel was devoid of any tyre or tube, but generously bound with sacking tied on with string. This gave out a clonking sound as it turned on every uneven surface.

Pierre was fourteen years of age, and in the two years that the bicycle had been in his possession (he had found it abandoned in a weed-covered ditch which skirted the village) he had looked after it and replaced worn out tyres from the village dump. He now reached a particularly bad stretch of the road, ravaged by the severe frosts of the previous winter. This caused more than the usual discomfort to him, although adept as he had become in negotiating the potholes in the road, Pierre could not wholly avoid the occasional spine-jarring bump; and when this occurred he jerked violently at the handle-bars and muttered angrily to himself.

Suddenly a noise broke his concentration and they were overhead. 'Spitfires,' the word jumped from his lips in an expression of both chagrin and pleasure; chagrin because he had confused their sound with that of the Focke-Wulf 190s he was so accustomed to seeing and the pleasure at the hard, clean lines the two Spitfires presented in plain view as they passed overhead, their duck-egg blue bellies contrasting with the darkening sky, as they hurtled westwards towards the setting sun. Hardly had the reassuring purr of their Merlin engines died away, when a harsher and more menacing note followed it. There was no doubt this time. Overhead sped a formation of enemy 190s – nine in all, and although the watching boy could not know it, almost in range to open fire on the Spitfires.

The Spitfire pilots knew they were in danger, for at that moment they wheeled up in a long sweeping curve to give battle. A dogfight had begun.

Violently, the sleepy evening sky woke to the bark of cannon and the hot lick of tracer bullets; all speeding towards their target, as determined German fought desperate Briton. The bark of the German oerlikons contrasting with the thud of the slower firing British cannons.

In the cockpit of the leading Spitfire, a grim-faced pilot cursed into his oxygen mask. 'Fool, fool I knew I shouldn't have chased that blighter down so far inland.

Now look what's happened – outnumbered, damn-all fuel and for all I know, no ammo.'

Not that George was frightened, but he knew that he and his number two were in serious trouble, simply because he had disobeyed the golden rule of aerial combat; 'Never follow the enemy down when deep in his territory.'

Too late now for self-recrimination he thought, action was imperative. The 190s were in range to fire. Thought was now thus transferred into a long sweeping curve that Pierre was witnessing from the ground. The hunted was turning on the hunter.

George shouted out over the R/T: 'We'll have to get out pretty quickly, Blue 2, I'm short of gravy. Have a quick squirt and go like hell for home. You must be damn low on fuel too. Don't worry about me, I'll keep them at bay for a bit.'

'OK, Blue 1. Yes, I'm pretty low; I'll break away at the first opportunity. See you at base.'

A violent manoeuvre, a quick flick to the left and George was behind two fast-climbing 190s. Out of the corner of his eye he could see two other Germans about to repeat the manoeuvre on him; careful aim was not possible, a quick glance at his reflector sight, a jerky adjustment of rudder and stick, with firm pressure on the firing button and the two cannons and four machine guns thudded and spattered into life in a mixture of smoke and searing tracer shells. As suddenly as they had started the guns stopped; there was no longer any purpose in continuing to press the button, all ammunition had been expended.

Savagely George pulled into the two attacking Focke-Wulfs, the blood rushing from his head as the mounting 'G' forces pushed him down into his seat. Just 'greying' but taking care not to 'black out' he kept up the tight turn, knowing that there was no German fighter built that could stay inside him at this rate of turn. As the attacking Focke-Wulfs juddered off his tail, the forces of gravity overcoming the skill of their pilots, George eased forward on his stick and with slowly clearing vision, observed four other Germans positioning for an attack.

Once again he turned towards his attackers, but as he did so there was a loud explosion in his earphones, and he knew he had been hit.

The fighter pilot's nightmare, the one-he-hadn't-seen, had struck. The control column jumped violently from his hands, the rudder pedals, normally solid when at speed, flopped uselessly under his feet and the airframe trembled protestingly as cannon shells tore through its proud body. The wounds were mortal.

'I must bale out.' He frantically tore at his cockpit harness, dragged at the hood release and choked by smoke and stroked by flames that now started to engulf the cockpit, he struggled free. As his hurtling body tumbled clear of the inferno that was once his Spitfire, the hungry flames, not to be cheated of their prey, reached out long tongues to lick his arms and legs.

No sooner had his parachute thankfully opened than he realised that he was on fire. With flaying arms he beat frantically at his body; anyhow, anywhere so long as he could prevent the flames from spreading upwards to the slender silken cords of his parachute, the life-lines of his descent. His efforts were rewarded; a smouldering trouser leg, burnt hands and searing pain in his face remained evidence that there had been flames. Numbed, burned and shocked, he sagged in the supporting harness and slowly drifted down to earth.

As soon as the dogfight had begun, Pierre had urged his bicycle forward in a straight line towards the nearest tree; bumps and discomforts were forgotten in his eagerness to find safe shelter from which he could watch the ensuing battle unseen. Silently he prayed for the Britishers, knowing that his prayers would be needed against such odds as they faced. He watched fascinated as Spitfires and 190s twisted and turned, darted and dived and spat at each other in the fury of aerial combat.

He saw the pair of Spitfires break formation; one to continue battle, the other to dive away westwards apparently unseen by the enemy. The silent watcher beneath the tree stood by helplessly as he observed the sneaking Focke-Wulfs creep up underneath the unsuspecting Spitfire.

'Watch out!'

Involuntarily Pierre cried out a warning, not knowing that he had uttered a sound. Even before the first burst of enemy fire found its target, he knew there was no hope and as the Spitfire buckled under the impact he felt the hot tears seeping from the corner of his eyes, tears of mortification and frustration. Then as the now burning fighter aircraft slowly doubled up in agony under the repeated impact of cannon strikes, he saw the pilot hurtle free of the aeroplane and almost simultaneously his parachute streamed and billowed above him.

'Thank God.'

Pierre brushed angrily at the tears now in full flow from his eyes, resolving to do something to help the British airman to escape from the German soldiers who would be sure to arrive on the scene before very long. Hastily, he cast his bike into a nearby ditch to hide it from prying German eyes and then ran towards the rapidly descending airman, observing as he did so that the pilot's clothes were smouldering. Away to his left the broken Spitfire had plummeted into a ploughed field, sending a ball of flames shooting skywards as it exploded on impact into a shower of metal and earth.

The explosion of the doomed British fighter signified the end; the aerial drama was now played out and that of an escape had begun. Only one thought remained in the young French boy's mind: I must help the RAF man to escape. 'How?' Pierre's mind echoed the question as he ran towards the plantation behind which the descending airman had drifted.

It was almost dark when Pierre reached the wood. To his right, and down the road he had just left, darting fingers of light denoted the approach of a German search party. Resolutely Pierre pushed his way into the wood with total disregard of the cruel clawing undergrowth. Inside it was silent and eerie; for the first time Pierre was afraid at what he had set out to do. The impulse that had prompted him to action was beginning to wane as the crowding silent trees pressed in around him, and fear speeded his hammering heart. Was he doing the right thing? Should he go on? Silently he asked himself these questions and sought his answer in a whispered prayer.

'Achtung Englander.'

A guttural shout from a searching German provided the answer; he knew he must help. Without further thought of the consequences, Pierre plunged purposely but nevertheless stealthily towards his objective.

'Anglais, Anglais!'

Every now and again he stopped to repeat this urgent whisper, hissing out the words as loud as he dare so as not to attract the Germans who, judging from sounds, seemed to be concentrating their search in the area of the crashed aircraft.

It was the faintly visible splurge of white made by the crumpled parachute that first attracted Pierre's attention when he emerged from the wood. At first he was a little suspicious, the shouts and answering shouts of the Germans now seemed to be all around him; but as his eyes became more attuned to the light he could see the blurred outline of a crumpled figure nearby. He knew he had found the pilot.

George lay in an agony of pain; his hands were burnt and peeling and his face – or that portion of it not protected by his helmet, which he still wore, was smarting unbearably. He could not open his eyes; the lids felt as if they were baked to his eyeballs. Unseeing, he had been unaware of his height while descending and was quite unprepared for the shock of landing; the impact left him too sore to attempt to release his chute which, robbed of its sustaining air pressure, rapidly deflated and sank to the ground alongside its wounded charge.

'Anglais, Anglais!'

The voice seemed to cry out to him through a mist of pain. But it had a ring of urgency and a promise of help. He must make an effort to identify himself. Agonisingly, he fumbled with burned hands to operate the quick release of his parachute harness, calling out as he did so.

'Here, here.'

He felt, for he could not see, the boy at his side and in response to gentle levering he managed to get into a sitting position. At the same time the parachute harness was eased free of his shoulders.

'Can you stand?'

The question was in French, but George understood the sense, if not the actual meaning, and responded by scrambling to his feet. Slowly, Pierre steered his charge towards the wood. And deeper and deeper into its darkening centre, the fugitives stumbled; one blind and wounded, the other afraid but providing the eyes. Once again Pierre spoke in French, but this time he spoke more slowly, and George, who had specialised in modern languages at school, was able to understand fully. He was to stay hidden here while the boy went back to the village to fetch help. Gratefully George sank down in the protective undergrowth and almost at once lapsed into unconsciousness.

At about the time Pierre had left George hidden in the wood and had set off to fetch assistance, a formation of Spitfires arrived over one of London's famous fighter airfields, and breaking into ones and twos, the aircraft came into land.

The ground crews eagerly awaited news of the combat, which they knew had taken place, noticing the tattered fabric gun covers, which if the guns had been fired, were now just shreds. Wearily the pilots unstrapped and eased themselves out of their cramped cockpits, thankful once again to be safely back at base.

The ground crews always seemed to be able to sense if something had gone wrong; this occasion was no exception. The eagerness on their faces changed to concern as they sensed the loss of a popular pilot. Usually the pilots laughed and joked about their successes – losses being pushed into the background with resigned shrugs. But not this time. A grim-faced squadron commander pushed through their ranks and they trailed expectantly behind him as he approached the intelligence officer.

'Ring up operations, Tommy, and see if there's any news of George.'

'He was Blue 1.'

'Right away, sir.'

'I heard him tell Blue 2 to go it alone, so ask the Controller if there's any news of Blue 2.'

So it was George. Respectfully and affectionately the listening airmen murmured his name. Flying Officer George Allen had been with them for about a year and in that time had, by his daring, good humour and puckish pranks, endeared himself to officer and airman alike. Above all, and from the squadron commander's viewpoint, he was a brilliant fighter pilot and a born leader, if a bit too headstrong. It was this latter trait that had led to his eventual downfall, as his many admirers suspected it would do.

'No news of Allen, sir, but Blue 2 is in contact and should be overhead any moment.' 'Thanks Tommy. It sounds ominous. But we must wait and see what Preston has to say.'

A lone Spitfire appeared in the circuit and made a long run into land; it was obvious to the tensed spectators that the aircraft had been badly hit. Though there were no visible signs of damage, the pilot had not selected 'flaps down' and his long motoring approach was a sure indication that he was uncertain of his controls. Lower and lower he came until crossing the hedge at fifty feet, he throttled sharply back, to be answered with defiant spits from the revving Merlin engine. When the aircraft touched down there was an audible sigh of relief from the watchers (and from the pilot, had the watchers but known it) to be followed a few seconds later by 'Damn, he's punctured a tyre,' from the NCO in charge of the flight. As the aircraft now neared the end of its run, it suddenly slewed violently to starboard and in contrast to the first manoeuvre, stood gently on its nose.

The fire engine was there first – as it should have been – followed closely by the ambulance, but there was no real need for either. There was no resulting fire, and the uninjured pilot was already climbing out of his cockpit on to the wing.

Back in the dispersal hut, a cup of sticky NAAFI tea was clasped in one hand, in the other a cigarette. Pilot Officer Teddy Preston had safely but somewhat luckily returned from his first combat in six trips, and started to answer the Squadron Leader's probing questions.

'Where did you last see Blue 1?'

'I don't know, sir, about thirty miles inland, I think. I flew on 300 degrees, coming out and I think I crossed the French coast somewhere south of Cap Gris Nez.'

'Why the hell did you lose your leader, anyway,' the Squadron Leader continued.

'I didn't. He told me to get out when we were attacked. He said something to the effect that he was short of fuel and that I must be nearly out, and the best thing was for us to split and get out independently.'

'Well, what happened before that? How did your section become separated from the formation?'

Preston replied, 'We were just near the target when a couple of 190s came sailing below and across us. George immediately swung out and down and away from the rest of the section. At that moment someone switched on a radio transmitter and there was a babble of voices. I don't know, but I think George was warning you that he was going down to attack; but somebody transmitting at the same time blocked his message. Anyhow, I just clung on behind him and jolly difficult it was too.'

'Did he get the Hun?'

'Yes, I've never seen anything like it. One burst and the 190 just disintegrated. It certainly gave the German formation leader a fright. I don't think he had seen us up to that point, because his aircraft practically turned itself inside out as he jerked into action. We followed; or should I say that I just pushed everything forward and clung to George as he gave chase.'

'What height did this all take place?'

'I think we started at about 27,000 feet, but the next thing we knew we were hedge-hopping, going north I think. George was pumping odd bursts at the Focke-Wulf 190, but didn't appear to be hitting it. Then I heard him say, "Hell, we'd better get out of here." He then asked if I was still there, and when I answered "Sure" he swung to the left and headed out.'

'At what stage was this?'

'Shortly after we turned for home. George reported some Huns tailing us from behind, he said that we'd probably have to turn into them. I hadn't seen them, but when I looked behind I damn nearly jumped out of my seat. There seemed to be a dozen of them, about to mow me down. Just then George said, "Break left," and around we went.'

'I suppose the usual dogfight developed, or did George try to get back on course when he completed his turn?'

'No, he just shouted to me to get out alone and after a couple of tight turns to make certain I wasn't being followed I banged everything forward, hit the deck and beat it for the coast.'

'Were there any further transmissions from George?'

'No, I didn't hear or see him again. I got hit just as I levelled out near the deck. Where the blighter came from I don't know. One moment the sky around me was clear and the next, bang! And I was full of holes. I thought I'd had it but luckily the Hun must have sheered off after one attack because I didn't see him again.'

'Alright, Preston, I think you've had enough excitement for one day. Give a full report to Tommy, count yourself on stand-down tomorrow. Not your fault, you did your best.' Thus the cross-examination was concluded.

'Just have another check with Operations, Tommy, will you,' directed the Squadron Commander.

But there was no news; and tired aircrew and despondent ground crews made their way across to the messes and billets. Another day's work was done, and another gallant airman was posted as 'missing'.

CHAPTER 2

When George regained consciousness, which was some ten minutes after Pierre departed for help, he was at first unable to recall his whereabouts. As, however, his numbed senses returned he became aware of the smarting pain that attacked his burnt face and hands, and a realisation of the events that had led up to his present position flooded his tired mind.

Slowly, but progressively more clearly as his full senses returned, his mind built up a complete picture of the day's events. In his mind's eye he could see quite clearly the squadron crew-room crowded with pilots sorting themselves out in a confusion of Mae Wests and flying impedimenta in readiness for the next operation. On the squadron state board were listed the names of the lucky twelve pilots arranged under the colours of Red, Blue and Yellow, the sections in which they were to fly. He could see his own name standing forth in bold relief as leader of Blue section.

In ones and twos he pictured the pilots as they left the crew-room and walked towards the aircraft dispersals. Some carried parachutes slung over their shoulders, others had flying helmets draped by the R/T cords around their necks, while a third category carried nothing; they were the fortunate ones who had been on the earlier 'show' and their equipment was already fitted and installed in the waiting Spitfires they were to fly.

Snugly tucked in their concrete dispersal pens, the armed and aggressive-looking Spitfires waited to be claimed by their pilots. With the pilots securely installed in the cockpits, the ground crews attending to the starter batteries waited with an air of quiet expectancy for the airscrew on the squadron leader's Spitfire to start turning; this was the sign to 'start up'. One minute all was quiet; the next was seeming pandemonium as the peace, which always seemed to settle over the airfield immediately prior to a wing take-off, was shattered and swamped in an increasing roar as in quick succession twenty-four Merlins fired into life.

Now the airfield was alive with movement and sound, quickly and purposely the two squadrons forming the wing, taxied into position on the runway, lining up in sections of two ready for the take-off. When all were ready and zero hour was at hand, the Wing Leader gave the signal to roll. As pair followed pair down the runway the throaty roar from the eager Merlins built up to a crescendo of sound, which reverberated from the two hangars and dispersal buildings. Section after section streamed out in a wide, climbing turn around the airfield, each section leader easing into his place in the formation as the Wing Leader rounded into an eastwards course towards France and the enemy. On the airfield, contrasting with the noise of the Wing's departure, quietness had descended and those left behind went silently about their various tasks.

Thus in reverie George recalled each significant detail; and as event crowded event in his mind he was soon led to a realisation of his present predicament.

His senses now fully on the alert, George could hear his would-be capturers searching the wood in which he lay concealed. Nearer and nearer moved the eager searchers; louder and louder grew the challenging sound of voices; and in tune with

159

both, the ever-brightening beams of powerful torches danced from branch to branch of the surrounding trees reflecting their rays in suffused pools of light onto the leafy foliage which concealed the prey. Stealthily, and painfully aware of his burns, George burrowed further into the undergrowth; now perfectly still and hardly daring to breathe he waited for the worst.

A crashing and banging near at hand signalled the uncomfortable closeness of a searcher. Tensely George waited for what seemed inevitable discovery, while all around him the bushes broke and parted under the enemy's approach. All seemed lost, but as quickly as he had come the German moved on, almost tramping his unseen quarry underfoot as he beat a way through the tangled undergrowth. Gradually, reassuringly, the menacing sounds moved away until, finally, the guttural voices could be heard no longer.

'What now?' queried George to himself. 'I wonder where the French boy has disappeared to?'

Pierre had not been idle. On leaving George he had stealthily reclaimed his bicycle and, well clear of the searchers, he was at that moment pedalling for all his worth back to the village. The potholes which had earlier so incommoded him were now ignored in his all-out effort to return with the least possible delay. Back in the village he quickly made his way along the darkening streets and between the shuttered houses to his home where, out of breath from his exertions, he burst into the well-lit kitchen to be greeted by his parents who were having supper.

Pierre's father was the village barber. He had returned to his home and trade soon after the occupation of France by the Germans, having served as a private in the French army since the outbreak of war. He had seen little fighting and, indeed, little of the conquering German armies, which had submerged all resistance as they swept ruthlessly and efficiently over French territory. Defeated and demoralised, he was an embittered man, and there was nothing he wouldn't do to clear the Germans from his beloved homeland. It was in this frame of mind that he joined the French resistance fighters who were doing so much to make the occupation as unpleasant as possible for the German troops. Helping Allied pilots to escape capture and so return to fight again was part and parcel of his underground activities. Pierre knew all this; his father had used him on numerous occasions as a trusted messenger, in his dealings with neighbouring partisans' leaders.

'Dad, I've found a British airman!'

Pierre's breathless outburst when safely behind a closed kitchen door brought a quick smile of amusement to his father's face, not at what the boy had done but at the way he put it.

'Well done, where is he?'

'About two kilometres along the Abbeville road, and hidden in that big wood just off to the right. You know the one?'

'Yes, I know where you mean. Is he injured?'

'He's burnt about the face and hands, but I don't think there are any other injuries. He seemed to walk alright when I led him towards the wood.'

'What about the Germans; are they out searching?'

'Yes, they are all over the place and seemed to be making towards the wood as I came away. It's pretty thick in there though, and I reckon that he'll be safe now that it's dark. I've hidden his parachute in the undergrowth so that it won't give him away.'

'Good' acknowledged the now serious father. 'I'll give them a good hour to clear the area and then we'll go and bring him in. You'd better come, in case there's difficulty in locating him. He might well have moved to a safer hiding place; unless of course the Germans have found him. Alright, get on with your supper while I go and find the priest and ask him to stand-by to look at the boy's burns.'

The reference to the priest was not without some meaning. He had in his younger days been a doctor before turning to the Church, and had on many occasions in the past been called for in a medical emergency. The doctor who tended the village lived some miles away and was not always available. In any event, the priest was in the confidence of the 'underground' and the doctor was not. About an hour after Pierre's return he set forth to accompany his father to the wood where, he prayed, the injured airman remained undiscovered by the Germans. The priest had been located and was now with Pierre's mother making preparations to receive the Britisher.

In the wood George was breathing more easily. The searchers appeared to have moved away across the fields and he was about to make a move when he heard someone approaching stealthily. The barely audible crack of a downtrodden twig warned him of danger in the immediate vicinity. He lay perfectly still and awaited developments.

'Anglais, anglais.'

Sibilantly and near at hand, the voice came like music to George's straining ears.

'Here, here', George hissed in return, hardly daring to raise his voice for fear of attracting the Germans.

George had by now shaken off the effects of the immediate relapse, which overcame him as soon as Pierre had safely hidden him before departing for help. Although in pain his burns didn't feel quite so bad and he could now see quite well, certainly well enough to discern the outlines of the two figures which moved in on his hiding place.

Identities established, the three set off through the woods. Skirting the edge of the wood farthest away from the German search party they quickly made their way across the fields and through the darkened and seemingly deserted village to the warmth and safety of Pierre's house.

Once inside the cosy kitchen George's normal ebullience overcame his weariness, at least for the time being, and he was able to relate his experience to his rescuers, avoiding of course any mention of his squadron and station; even to friendly Frenchmen this information was not divulged. The natural and obvious friendliness of the family was a great help to George in overcoming his shyness in speaking French, but he found that he could make himself understood with the aid of gestures and some help from the priest who spoke quite good English. Indeed, he had interrupted George's discourse in French to say in English.

'You'd better get undressed and into the bed prepared for you, young man, so that I can have a good look at those burns.'

'Oh, I feel alright and they don't seem too bad,' countered George.

'That may be, but there's generally a reaction and a high temperature resulting from the shock of burns and we can't have you bedridden too long here; it will be dangerous. When the Germans find that you have escaped their clutches they will, as they always do, search the village and surrounds, and it's not easy to hide a sick man. They'll probably find your parachute and know that you've landed safely and are being helped by loyal Frenchmen.'

'OK, I'll do as you suggest. Where do I go?'

'Maria will show you,' answered the priest and turning to Pierre's mother said in French, 'I think he should get some rest now. Could you show him to his room and find him something to sleep in? When he's tucked in I'll have a look at him and take his temperature and pulse.'

George's examination confirmed what the priest had suspected. Although his burns were most fortunately only superficial, his temperature was up and his pulse rate was a bit high. His scorched eyelids and hands were causing him the most trouble and the priest applied a little anti-burn ointment to the lids to prevent them from cracking. Otherwise, he judged it best to let nature take her course in the healing process which he told George would take two to three weeks, that is, before he would be fully fit to move. The actual healing process would, he explained, take much longer, but it should be without complication. Reassured and dog-tired, George lapsed into heavy sleep.

For five days, George was delirious, drifting from heavy sleep into semi-consciousness, from semi-consciousness into light sleep, and from light sleep into a full awareness, but for brief periods only, before again becoming unconscious. Throughout, he was tenderly cared for by Maria; in the rare moments when he was conscious and felt her bathing his smarting face, he smiled his weak thanks, at other times he was but vaguely aware of her presence in the room.

On the sixth day he woke from a deep and prolonged sleep, the prelude to final recovery and to a full awareness of his position. The priest was standing by the sunlit window and turning saw that his patient was conscious and seemingly free from fever.

'How long have I been here?'

'This is the sixth day, and right glad I am to hear you speak,' answered the priest.

'Have I been in danger then? countered George.

'No, but you have been delirious for most of the time, and we were worried about the delayed action of shock. It can be fatal.'

'Well, I feel OK now.'

'Good. All you need now is rest and care and you've already had plenty of both.'

'Yes, I know. I was aware from time to time of madame's nursing and I am most grateful to her and to everybody who has helped.'

'Well,' rejoined the priest. 'We are only doing what any humane person would do in the same circumstances. Anyhow, those of us interested in your welfare are also interested in victory for Free France.'

From now onwards George made rapid progress; the scabs, which had formed on his burns, gradually dried and fell away, although his eyes remained sore and troublesome. At the end of two weeks he was up and about; being confined of course in his movements for fear of detection. Within three weeks he was fit to travel and the important question now was, how to get back to England?

During his illness Pierre's father had been in touch with French underground agencies, who organised the escape of shot-down Allied fliers and he proceeded to bring George up to date on plans for an escape.

'There has been,' he said, 'a slight delay enforced on our escape plans because one of our agents in Paris has unfortunately been arrested by the Gestapo. Until we can check the security of his particular part of the escape route, we cannot feed any more airmen into the system. I'm afraid, young man, you must be prepared to spend a week or two more in our company.'

'Of course I'll do whatever you say, only I'm dying to get cracking again,' said a disappointed George. 'Is there anything useful I can do while I'm waiting for the word to go?'

The Frenchman thought for a moment and then said, 'There may be at that. We are organised into sabotage squads in this district and a willing pair of hands is more than welcome. Mind you, it's dangerous work and I must consult my colleagues who may not think it wise to expose you to the risk of capture, or even death.'

'Oh, do let me have a go,' an eager George countered. 'After all, this is a war and any risk is acceptable. I wish you'd speak to your friends. Tell them that I'm keen and with my moderate French I should be able to follow orders without jeopardy to fellow conspirators.'

'Alright I will, but,' said the Frenchman, 'you should be prepared for a refusal. We can't be too careful, and you are somewhat of a risk.'

Throughout the next three days, George occupied himself during the day by practising his French, talking to Pierre, who by now was a great admirer, and from him he learned that they were fairly close to Abbeville airfield. He knew that this was a German fighter base and he was anxious to know more about its operation. Pierre would know and he set about cross-examining the boy.

'What's at Abbeville airfield at the moment, do you know?' he asked the boy.

The answer came without hesitation. 'Focke Wulf 190s, I see them often coming from that direction. Anyhow Jacques – he's my uncle you know – is employed by the Germans as a labourer on the airfield and I heard him telling Papa that a new lot had recently moved in.'

'Is it well guarded, Pierre?'

'Oh yes. There are dogs, and German guards with guns are always on patrol.'

George's thoughts from now on were concerned almost solely with the problems of an escape in a Focke-Wulf 190.

'Wouldn't it be wonderful,' he thought, 'if I could manage to get away in one and fly it back to England. That would give the boys something to talk about.'

Normally the problem of starting a strange aircraft for a quick get-away would have made the attempt possible, but only a few weeks before George was shot down, a test pilot from Farnborough had toured the fighter airfields in a captured FW190 and all pilots had had a lesson on how to start this formidable German fighter. George, in fact had been allowed to fly it on a subsequent visit to Farnborough. The flying would therefore be easy enough, although a night attempt only would be possible and this could make it tricky.

'Good weather, a moon, a lot of luck and I reckon I could pull it off,' mused George.

Once the idea had caught on, George was impatient to explore the possibilities further. At the first opportunity he consulted Pierre's father. 'Pierre tells me that there are FW190s at Abbeville airfield.'

'Yes, I believe there are,' was the guarded answer.

'Well, I reckon I could get away in one if I could manage to get into the cockpit undetected. What do you think?'

'Very little chance, I feel,' answered the Frenchman. 'It's highly dangerous anywhere within a radius of a mile of a German airfield. However, it's a good idea and I'll consult my colleagues. By the way, I have spoken to them about you and they are quite prepared for you to come on one of our little jaunts.'

'Good, when do we go?' asked George eagerly

'There is something afoot in a day or two. I can't tell you more at the moment; anyhow, the less you know at this stage the better. The Germans are always on the alert for you chaps, especially when in your case, they must know that you are hiding somewhere in this area.'

Days went by, irksome ones for George who could only take outside exercise under cover of darkness, and then in the confined space of a small backyard; and still there was no mention of an attempted escape or sabotage raid. Unknown to George however, a scheme was in place for him to pay a visit to the German fighter airfield on the following evening.

The next night, a gathering of grim-faced French resistance fighters assembled to discuss a plan designed to give George all possible help in his attempt to steal a FW190. The plan was a simple one and it was to be put into operation on the following night, when there would be a full moon, and, according to the local weather prophets, a clear sky.

CHAPTER 3

All next day, George mooned about in the confines of his refuge in a state of animated suspension, one moment wildly optimistic and the next depressingly glum at the seeming impossibility of his daring venture. To make matters worse, it was a lovely day. One of those days that escorting fighter pilots dream about: unlimited visibility and high cirrus cloud against which aircraft are strikingly silhouetted, thus making surprise attack an almost impossibility.

Deep in his turbulent thoughts, George did not at first hear the summoning cry from Pierre, who was pottering about in the backyard to no particular purpose. He too was pent-up in anticipation of the forthcoming adventure, in which, said his father, he was to take part.

'George, George,' the urgency of the appeal broke through George's reverie.

'Yes, Pierre, what is it?' he answered peering from the door and not daring to venture outside in broad daylight for fear of detection. He had been repeatedly warned not to do so.

'Come and look. There's a huge formation of American bombers approaching. I'm sure there'll be a fight.'

An excited Pierre danced joyfully around the yard in expectation of this event. Taking care to observe that there were no Germans near the house, George, unable to resist the appeal and the chance of seeing the exhilarating spectacle of a day-bomber raid, joined Pierre and with his eyes followed the direction of the boy's pointing finger.

Yes, there they were. Very high (about 25,000 feet he estimated, and away to the west), he could see a formidable array of Fortress bombers and all around them the barely distinguishable black dots of the close-escort fighters.

Relentlessly, inevitably, the huge mass of bombers flying in their symmetrically spaced boxes of about 20 aircraft, ploughed their course eastwards. Nearer and nearer they came, larger and more distinct became their individual outlines, accompanied now by the purposeful drone of hundreds of motors. Ahead, to the sides, above and below innumerable fighter formations darted and dived, turned and weaved in their constant task of surveying the hostile skies. As the mighty armada winged its way overhead there welled up in George a feeling of frustration that he was but an on-looker, yet at the same time, a strong feeling of pride swelled up in his breast, its very intensity bringing moisture to his eyes.

'They're ours,' he muttered half aloud, 'now see what you can do Jerry.'

But this for the time being was Jerry territory and the challenge was about to be met. Towards the east they rose. At first the distant horizon stretching deep into France was unbroken by movement, but even as he muttered his words of exaltation, movement in the form of distant specs became visible to the naked eye. George was the first to notice the enemy fighter reaction.

'FW190s,' he exclaimed. 'Look.' George's trained eyes were on them in a second, his normally good long-range vision being assisted by the high cirrus cloud which provided a contrasting back cloth to the assembling German fighter formations.

'Not to worry, Pierre, we'll take care of these blighters,' said George as he patted the excited young Frenchman on the shoulder. 'In any case, I expect some of our diversion fighter wings are already positioned ahead to draw them away from the bombers.'

'The reception party has gone into action, Pierre. Look at the flak. As usual it's behind and below the target much to the relief of the bomber crews, I bet. That must be the guns around Le Tréport, I expect the bombers are crossing the coast.'

But the AA guns were not quite as ineffective or as inaccurate as George implied or hoped. Such a large and comparatively slow-moving formation could not change course easily and the gunners were thus able to find the range and height by a process of trial and error. Before the formation could move out of range the menacing black and white puffs of bursting AA shells liberally sprinkled the sky around it. Soon the bombers would be out of range but not, thought George, soon enough.

And then it happened. To the watchers on the ground there appeared at first but a tiny ball of fire sitting, as it were, on the starboard wing of one of the leading bombers. Gradually it enveloped one engine and then another until the stricken bomber lurched away and down from its protecting comrades. From its underbelly a series of black objects hurtled earthwards; clearly the captain was shedding his unfused bombs in the hope that with a decreased load he could maintain height on his two good engines. With the other two engines shut down and the fire under control, the pilot might make the comparative safety of the Channel should it become necessary to ditch or abandon the aircraft.

Before, however, he had completed his turn for home the enemy fighters were upon him. George had not noticed them sneak up from behind, nor so far as he could see had the escort; as seemed always to be the case the enemy had appeared as if from nowhere. Like angry wasps they stung the helpless bomber with long bursts of hot, punishing cannon fire; darting in, around and back again in a series of co-ordinated attacks, they delivered the coup-de-grace. But now the Spitfires were on to them. But in high-powered dives, for which the FW190s were ideally suited, the enemy planes escaped out of range and to the safety of reduced height. 'Live to fight another day,' was their motto: a sound one with bombers as their primary target.

For the stricken bomber there was now no hope. It hurtled earthwards in an inferno of flames, shedding pieces of fuselage through a combination of fire and excessive speed, until eventually it disappeared from the view of the watching friends; its grave signified by a slow-rising plume of black smoke on the far horizon.

'Poor devils,' muttered George aloud, 'they didn't have a chance. Did you see anyone get out of the bomber, Pierre?'

'No, I think they must've all been killed.'

'Anyhow, our boys have taken care of those blighters who got up ahead. Look at them, Pierre, giving the Jerries hell.'

In the far distance in the path of the raid, which had now passed overhead, the two watchers could see a changing pattern of antlike objects as attackers and attacked fought their desperate battle for local air supremacy while, seemingly unmindful of the outcome, the bomber formation ploughed on, for a short time at least untroubled by enemy defences.

CHAPTER 4

The pent-up emotion, engendered by the long wait for action and the events of the day's bomber raid made George more restless than ever. However, later that evening he met his helpers to lay final plans for the attempt to steal a Focke-Wulf 190 and it was not to be long now before waiting would give way to action.

As before they met in the parlour of Pierre's house. The same persons were present but in addition the priest was there, perhaps to ensure that George understood fully all that was being said. They could not afford any misunderstanding; this was often the cause of failure and death for those taking part. Pierre, too, was there because as George was soon to learn, it was he who was to guide George to Abbeville airfield. He knew the byways to the airfield and these were likely to prove the safest on a journey by foot from the village.

Pierre's father opened the meeting by again reiterating that they were gathered to discuss ways and means of assisting the *aviateur Anglais* (as he put it) to enter Abbeville airfield to steal a FW190 and fly back to England.

'As you know,' he said, addressing the gathering, 'we think the Englishman has a sporting chance of bringing this off, but only if we can create a suitable diversion to enable him to get into the airfield undetected. From then on there's little we can do to help.'

After lengthy discussion it was finally decided that the best way to create a diversion to attract attention away from the airfield was to stage a raid on a small factory, situated adjacent to the perimeter, which was producing component parts for railway engines. George was to enter the airfield perimeter fencing from the opposite side to the factory in the hope that, if not actually drawn towards the area of the disturbance, the airfield guards would at least be sufficiently diverted to allow him to penetrate the outer barrier unchallenged. If they could prolong the disturbance he would have a fair chance of reaching the aircraft lines undetected, even escaping the watchful eyes of the sentries in the guard towers.

'I think,' said the spokesman, continuing, 'that midnight would be a suitable zero hour. This will leave plenty of time after darkness falls for the English aviator and Pierre to cover the eight kilometres to the airfield. Also, it will allow time for the rest of us to assemble on different approach routes in the vicinity of the factory. Timing is, of course, vitally important, and we must all synchronise watches before we break up this meeting. I have here a map of the airfield and its approaches. Would you all gather around and I will outline my plan.'

All was soon settled and George and Pierre were confident that they understood fully their part in the plan.

'May I ask a question?' George addressed the assembled company. Silent assent encouraged him to go on. 'I appreciate fully that timing is important and that Pierre and I must not make a move from our final position outside the airfield until we observe the first explosion on the far side, which signifies that the attack on the factory is under way. But supposing something goes wrong with your plans and there is no explosion within a reasonable period of time after zero hour. What then?'

'Well,' answered Pierre's father, 'you must use your own discretion, but do nothing until zero hour plus 15 minutes; this is about the maximum time beyond which we are unlikely to act.'

'Fine, but I hope nothing goes wrong. I feel that I'll need the maximum assistance if I'm to get near a Jerry fighter undetected. Then, of course, I still have to start it. I hope they aren't picketed down, that'll really put the cat among the pigeons – or should I say George among the Germans?' said George laughingly. 'Does anyone know if the Jerries picket their aircraft overnight?'

'No, they don't,' responded a middle-aged Frenchman in the corner. 'I work on a farm near the airfield and I've noticed that their aircraft are never tied down and that even cockpit covers are not used in the summer.'

'Good-oh, that should make my job easier.'

'Everybody happy?' asked Pierre's father. 'Good, you all know the assembly point and the time to be there. See you all at 11.45 pm. Now to synchronise watches.' And turning to George, 'It should take you about an hour to get to Abbeville. Perhaps you could discuss your route with Pierre, who has been fully briefed by me, and decide when best to set out. Don't forget you must look as much like a French peasant as possible; the clothes are in your room. I suggest you go and have a rest when you have tied up details with Pierre. He'll call you at an arranged time. I have to go over details of our attack with my comrades. Good luck.'

'Thank you, and thank you all,' said George addressing the assembled company. '*Vive la France*' they replied in unison.

It was by now nine o'clock and there was not much time to rest if they were to set out in time to be at their destination by 11.45 pm. This would allow 15 minutes for emergencies and meant that with an hour's walk ahead of them, George and Pierre must leave around 10.45 at the latest. George, like all fighter pilots, knew the importance of a rendezvous on time and decided therefore that at 10.30 pm they should leave the house. He conveyed his thoughts to Pierre and together they studied the route laid by Pierre's father.

Satisfied that Pierre was fully briefed and confident of the part that he had to play and that an hour was sufficient time in which to make the journey, George retired to his room to change into the peasant clothes and to rest, having adjured Pierre to call him at 10.15 pm sharp. It was not yet 9.30 pm, and so he retired, to rest but not to sleep; there was too much at stake to sleep.

When George and Pierre set out that evening, both were filled with a sense of adventure: George by the thought of stealing a German fighter plane, Pierre by a feeling of at least playing an active part in the French resistance against the Germans.

The night was fine. A full moon sat serene and majestic, together with its escort of faintly visible stars embracing the expectant yet peaceful French countryside in a soft diffused light. A few scudding high-cirrus clouds moved majestically across the night sky, intermittently obscuring the moon and as they did so diminishing its light so that a corresponding darkness caused the immediate landscape to fuse into a darkened nonentity. The conditions, if they persisted through zero hour, were ideal for at least George's part of the plan.

In the shadowy sanctuary of the village streets, two ghostly figures slid silently through the back lanes, carefully skirting those buildings, which Pierre knew housed German soldiers. Pierre led. This had been decided because with his local knowledge of not only the village surrounds, but also the intervening countryside as far as Abbeville there was less chance of detection or of becoming lost than if George, with his greater knowledge of map-reading, were to lead.

Soon they were clear of the built-up areas and, less concerned about detection, making rapid progress; yet always keeping to the hedgerows and the more wooded areas. No words were spoken; none were necessary. So long as Pierre appeared confident of his route then George was happy to follow. And Pierre was much too excited and overcome by his responsibility to want to be diverted by small talk.

There were one or two villages to be skirted en route but these presented no problems. Under a German-enforced nine-o'clock curfew the inhabitants had long since retired within shuttered houses; even the Germans, if there were in fact any in the villages, sought sleep in preference to the solitude of each other's company.

As they approached their objective the two intruders became more conscious of a feeling of suspense. There was nothing tangible to account for this imperceptible but nevertheless noticeable change; it was just that somehow the atmosphere seemed different, as of course it always does when an impending event is charged with danger.

Now they were in sight of the airfield, its whereabouts pinpointed by the ghostly outlines of two blister-type hangars, which the Germans had erected for servicing their fighters.

Pierre stopped and signalled George to take the lead, as had been agreed when the airfield was sighted. Stealth was now absolutely essential and no words were spoken as, George leading, they made their way around the airfield keeping a respectable distance from the tangled-wire fence, which marked its boundary.

It was George's intention to hide outside the wire fence, but fairly close to it and conveniently near and in view of the nearest parked aircraft, until the synchronised attack on the factory was signalled. He soon found the ideal spot. A leafy tree abutted the airfield perimeter at a point not twenty yards from a parked German fighter, which, so far as he could ascertain, was neither picketed down nor closely guarded. Neither could he see, nor hear patrolling guards in the area. It all seemed too good to be true. As indeed it turned out to be.

Having selected his point of entry through the perimeter wire, George sought and found a nearby bush, which gave him adequate shelter.

'Go home now,' he whispered to Pierre, having settled himself to wait.

Pierre of course was reluctant to leave but there could be no question of him remaining in the area once trouble started. Should he be caught, he would bring suffering to the whole village from German reprisals. Reluctantly the young French boy retraced his steps, bitterly disappointed that he could not be in, as it were, 'at the kill'.

He had not gone far, however, when the peace of the night was shattered by a loud explosion followed immediately by a leaping orange flame, which lit the surrounding countryside with an eerie kind of glow.

'Good,' muttered Pierre as momentarily he halted to observe the effect of what was obviously the attack on the factory under way, 'Now George will be making his way into the airfield.'

George was indeed making his way through the sharp and tangled wire fence; no easy task at the best of times let alone when keyed up with excitement, and in a hurry. Through at last he poised to re-locate his objective and having sighted the Focke-Wulf he stood up and ran towards it. Speed at this juncture was more important than concealment. Alas, neither was to be of any use. At the precise moment he started forward the whole airfield was illuminated in the harsh and revealing glare of powerful searchlights, which beamed out from the many Guard towers around its perimeter.

Momentarily, George stopped, nonplussed by this unexpected happening. Unexpected because this was one contingency which had been overlooked at the briefing. The presence of searchlights in the guard towers had not been mentioned, if indeed their presence was known to the French labourer, who worked on the airfield, and had furnished all the information about its defences.

Such an oversight, if oversight it was, can ruin the best-laid plans. And thus it was. Before George could gain his objective he was spotted from a nearby tower and a loud bellow from a German guard signalled this unwelcome news to him. There was nothing for it but to turn and run, on the principle of 'living to fight another day'.

With his heart thumping madly George dived for the wire but as he did so a hail of bullets ploughed up the earth around. Miraculously he was not hit. Frantically he scrambled and tore his way through the grasping wire, leaving in his wake a trail of torn clothing, but barely feeling the stinging cuts and scratches of the needle-sharp barbs which tore at his exposed hands and face.

At last he stood up and ran for cover, the fear and the urge to survive lending added strength to his limbs. Again a whining hail of bullets spattered around him, but this time to more effect. A numbing searing pain in his leg told him that he had been hit but he determined to keep going. As he stumbled on with the pain in his leg becoming more and more acute he could hear behind him the clamour of excited voices, the piercing shrill of sirens and the crack of rifle fire; all combining to convey to him a desperate sense of the urgency of his predicament. Quite obviously the Germans thought the airfield was under some type of full-scale attack, and they were taking no chances; everybody and everything was thrown into the alert.

Fortunately for the fleeing George, their efforts were concentrated on the far side of the airfield nearest the area of the explosion and this served to divert any co-ordinated attack and follow-up search on him. Thus a much-weakened George eventually reached the nearby woods, and for the time being at least he was free from pursuit. But he knew he must keep going because once the Germans realised that there was no attack developing they would send out a search party to comb the woods in which he was now hiding. Keep going he must.

However, it was imperative that he stop the bleeding because further loss of blood would so weaken him that he would be unlikely to sustain the long trek back to the village and safety. Now deep in the wood he sat down to examine his wound which turned out to be a bullet through his calf, or so it felt to his groping fingers as he sought the source of the bleeding, unable in the darkness of the woods to see well enough to examine it. Hastily he divested himself of his shirt from which he tore a strip to act as a tourniquet.

With the bleeding temporarily stemmed by the hastily provisioned tourniquet bound tightly around the leg just above the wound, he limped off towards the village using the woods and hedges to avoid detection. His leg gradually stiffened up and his progress became slower and more painful with each succeeding yard. He willed himself not to stop and rest for he knew that if he did so he would be in grave danger of being overtaken before he could get clear of the danger area.

He was forced to stop repeatedly to adjust the tourniquet which kept working loose causing a consequent loss of blood as it did so. After a time his journey became a nightmare of dizziness, but gamely he struggled on, determined whatever happened to keep going. And keep going he did, sheer willpower overcoming sickness and fatigue.

Determination and courage were, as always, justly rewarded. Unknown to George, Pierre had decided to wait outside the village just in case the attempt was unsuccessful and George was forced to return. And it was at this point, a few hundred yards outside the village, that Pierre sighted a by now desperate George staggering towards him. Once again he was to be the saviour lending his support, without which George would have undoubtedly collapsed, as he guided the weary airman to a safe refuge.

With admirable foresight for one so young, Pierre realised that it would probably be too dangerous to take George into the village, which was bound to be thoroughly searched by the Germans as soon as daylight came, so he sought refuge in a partially derelict barn nearby. He had often used the barn as a place to hide when playing with his friends in the happy days of peace and he knew it had a hayloft with a good supply of hay, old and musty perhaps but offering warmth and security nevertheless.

With George bedded down in the warm hay, Pierre set off for the priest's house. He thought that medical attention might be urgent, as even to Pierre's inexperienced eyes George seemed to be dangerously weak from loss of blood. And the priest was, he knew, the best person to give first-aid.

When the priest did arrive some hours later, George was sound asleep and it took Pierre some time to wake him. With him the priest had brought a thermos of hot water, antiseptic and dressings. In next to no time he had washed and cleaned the wound and George, who throughout had barely awakened, was soon again bedded down for the night. It was thought wise to leave him where he was and to move him at first light to a safer hideout.

So it was that once again George found himself in the role of an injured fugitive entirely dependent on the loyal and patriotic French villagers for succour and safety. For the remainder of that night he slept undisturbed in his warm bed of hay but as dawn stole across the countryside, he was awakened by Pierre's father who had come to take him to another and safer hideout. The Germans were bound to search the village and its immediate surrounds and a hayloft was too obvious a place in which to remain undetected for long.

In old French cottages it was not unusual to have a small cellar beneath the kitchen in which French peasants of earlier days used to store their wine, gathered from their own small holdings, for maturing and safe-keeping. Access to these cellars was a carefully guarded family secret but it was usually by means of a trapdoor concealed beneath one of the large stone flags, which made up the floor. As an extra safety precaution, this particular flagstone was invariably covered by the careful positioning of a heavy and not-easily-moved French dresser, which was a standard item of equipment in most French village homes.

It was in just one such cellar, long since disused, that George was to be hidden; not this time in Pierre's house but in that of a neighbour. It was not the most cheerful of places in which to be hidden, being only twelve feet square, and with hardly room to stand upright it was both damp and dark. However, the occupants of the house had been pre-warned of George's coming and an improvised bunk with some heavy blankets had been made ready in the cellar.

The ever-faithful priest was in the house to greet George on his arrival and to again wash and dress his wound and the abrasions received when he fought his way through the barbed wire surrounding the airfield. It was a relief to learn from the priest that the bullet wound was but a flesh one, and provided it could be cleansed and dressed regularly it should heal in a matter of weeks.

All that day as George fitfully dozed in his safe retreat, the German search squads roamed the village and surrounds. During one of his periods of wakefulness, George became aware of a commotion in the room above his head and could faintly hear guttural and angry German voices. For what seemed to him an eternity, but which in reality was only about ten minutes, the sounds of search penetrated to his confined space. However, the Germans obviously suspected nothing and they soon departed for other fields of search.

And search they did with typical teutonic thoroughness as they moved from house to house sparing none and accepting no protestations of innocence from the householders.

They could not know exactly for whom they were searching, but it soon became evident to the villagers that they were determined to find someone or something, which would implicate the village in the previous night's factory explosion. And by an odd coincidence they did find something but not directly connected with the most recent event.

When George was first hidden in Pierre's house his uniform had been taken from him and buried safely, as was thought, in the corner of the garden. Unhappily, the sharp eyes of a German soldier searching the house and garden noticed the newly dug earth and ordered two of his henchmen to investigate. It took but little digging to reveal this most damning evidence; Pierre's father was arrested forthwith and taken off under escort to the local German headquarters for interrogation. It was later learned that he had been deported to a German concentration camp where he was to spend the rest of the war, but happily to survive the horrors of his internment.

Undaunted by this setback and suffering even more stringent restrictions imposed on them by the German commander of the area, the villagers continued to plot and plan to the embarrassment of the occupying forces. True Frenchmen would not easily be daunted by German threats.

For three long weeks George was confined, for the most part to his miniature dungeon, the monotony relieved only by periods after dark when he shared the comfort and warmth of the kitchen, under which he was incarcerated, with its inhabitants.

German security forces continued from time to time to pay unexpected visits to the village and it was not considered safe to allow George any freedom of movement by day. During the hours of darkness there was more chance of hiding him elsewhere should the villagers be caught by surprise when he was up from his cellar-hiding place. On most evenings the kindly priest was there to continue the dressings to the wound, which was healing fast. Otherwise, George had little to occupy him and the long hours in the darkness of his cell were beginning to tell on his normally exuberant spirit. He was assailed by long periods of depression and on each and every occasion when released to the homely comfort of the kitchen he pleaded to be allowed to make an attempt to work his way southwards into the unoccupied zone of France, travelling on foot and under cover of darkness.

However, through the common sense arguments of the priest that not only was he not fit to travel but he was in no fit condition to do it alone, he was persuaded to bide his time. A big incentive to be patient was the firm promise that the French underground helpers were determined that he should get at least one more chance to attempt to steal a German fighter from Abbeville. If for no other reason George was prepared to stick it out to achieve this most desirable objective; his keenness to do so was in no way dampened by his recent abortive and near fatal attempt to get off with a Focke-Wulf 190.

When at last it was considered safe to release him permanently, after the German search parties had, it seemed, finally given up, he was moved to yet another house, this time on the outskirts of the village and nearer to the airfield. As before a conference was arranged to decide on how best to steal a German fighter. On this occasion there were fewer Frenchmen present, only three in all, for it had already been decided that the next attempt should be made without a co-ordinated sabotage attack in the airfield vicinity. The Frenchman chairing the meeting explained this to George when they were assembled.

'I'm afraid,' he said, 'that we made a mistake last time. The factory explosion only served to alert the whole base and cause the perimeter searchlights to be switched on which, of course, we had overlooked. Our next attempt should be carried out completely unaided and under cover of a dark sky to give maximum surprise. Do you agree?'

'Yes,' answered George, 'I do. I would rather have a moonlit night so that I would have some light, both to see to start the aircraft and to avoid any aircraft obstructions during take-off. However, I think I can manage the starting and I'll take a chance on taking off in indifferent light.'

'Well, you know best,' said the Frenchman. 'We can of course do a preliminary reconnaissance of the airfield to ascertain the best direction. You won't have to taxi, I take it?

'No, that's the last thing I want to do. The aircraft will of course be parked into wind. Anyhow, provided the wind is not too strong, I can go off downwind should the necessity arise; at worst, I can always swing the aircraft across wind after starting at the same time as I open up for take-off.'

'Good. And now let's get down to a few specific details of date and timings,' said the French spokesman.

After a good hour's discussion it was finally agreed that George would make the attempt on the first suitable night in the forthcoming week, when there would be no moon, but on, it was hoped, a night clear of cloud. This condition was essential, because he could not risk entering cloud after a take-off. Due to his unfamiliarity with the Focke-Wulf's instrumentation this would be suicidal and moreover, he needed some light to aid his take-off run. A sky full of stars provided the ideal conditions.

As there was to be no co-ordinated diversion attack, George could afford to await these conditions, postponing the attempt from night to night until he was satisfied that the weather was favourable for the attempt.

Although he didn't voice his fears, George was also concerned about the weather en route and over England, particularly the latter. He knew that he must have good weather over England, not only to enable him to navigate visually by reference to the coastline, but also to make possible a safe landing. He had already decided on Manston airfield in Kent as his destination. With no parachute being available, he had no alternative but to stay in the aircraft and to attempt a landing wherever he finished up over England.

The plan was a simple one, a day and night reconnaissance of the airfield to ascertain a suitable aircraft, parking arrangements and areas of obstruction in the possible take-off area would be undertaken on the day prior to the attempt by one of the Frenchmen. This information would be relayed to George in the form of a sketched drawing of the airfield, and from this, he would decide where to make his entry and what aircraft parking area to make for. On the night of the attempt, a final early reconnaissance would be made to confirm that aircraft were dispersed on the airfield as expected and a last-minute report was to be made to George at an agreed rendezvous not far from the airfield, fifteen minutes before he was due to make his entry attempt. The hour chosen was midnight.

Before the conference broke up, he was told about the Germans arresting Pierre's father. It was the first he knew that during their search they had arrested someone and he was most upset to learn that it was Pierre's father, and that his discarded uniform was the cause.

'I must go and see Maria,' he thought. And aloud, 'Do you think it would be alright if I visit their house tonight?' he asked of the French spokesman.

'Yes, but do take care. We'll arrange for Pierre to come and meet you and lead the way. He knows how to keep away from danger spots.'

'Oh thanks,' he responded. 'One further request: if you think it not too risky and his mother agrees, could Pierre accompany me as far as the rendezvous point on Monday? He's been so much part of my survival and planned escape that I would like him to be in on what I hope is the final act.'

'I'm sure that can be arranged.'

'Good, so long as he is in no danger by accompanying me, I'd really like to have him along and I'm sure he would like to come.'

And thus it was arranged, much to the delight of Pierre. All was now set as George put it, for the final act.

CHAPTER 5

Throughout the next two days of waiting George was in a fever of anxiety. He somehow felt that if on this attempt he was not successful there would be no further opportunity; he could not reason why this should be so, it was just a feeling he had.

'It must work this time,' he kept muttering fiercely to himself.

He repeatedly went over in his mind what he would do when once he got airborne. He knew that it was important to remain at low altitude throughout the flight to escape detection not only from German radar but also from our own British coastal radar. In the former case once the alarm had been sounded German controllers would almost certainly attempt to intercept him on the way to the French coast, probably by diverting night-fighters already airborne on other tasks. If he could stay below radar control height – and he reasoned up to 500 feet would be safe – there was little chance of a casual interception by a German night-fighter using only its own airborne radar.

In the latter case, that of arriving over the United Kingdom undetected, it was equally important that he approached over the sea below radar detection height. And this would need to be really at sea level because George knew that our coastal radars had the ability to detect aircraft approaching over the sea well below five hundred feet. Should he be picked up by British radar, he would of course be plotted as an enemy aircraft and he had no wish to be at the receiving end of one of the RAF's heavily armed night-fighters which were constantly on patrol to deal with sneak raiders.

Then, of course, there was the problem of finding and landing safely at one of the coastal airfields. Having crossed the coast the sooner he got down the better, as the anti-aircraft defences further inland were formidable. The airfield defences, wherever he landed, were a problem too because like the radar operators, the airfield defence gunners could not know that there was a British airman flying the German fighter and however much his initial approach surprised them, they would see him on the final approach to land. George could only hope that when they realised he was actually approaching land – having, he hoped, seen that his wheels were down – the gunners would hold their fire on the assumption that the pilot had either lost his way and was under the impression that he was landing on a German-held airfield in France or that he was a deserter. Both were possibilities: the airfield defence commander would know that in fact there had been two such instances in the past year and this could be another one. And it was important to capture the enemy aircraft intact, if at all possible. This latter possibility gave George some measure of hope.

All this and more George reasoned out as he waited for the great day. There was a lot to think about, not least of which was the best course to steer to the French coast and from there to England. And where to aim for to make landfall in England. All British fighter pilots operating over northern France at that time knew that if lost or separated from the formation, a course of 300 degrees would normally ensure a fairly short exit route from France and a landfall somewhere in south-east England. In George's case however, he had the advantage of knowing his exact position at take-off and there was no need to resort to a random course of 300 degrees.

Moreover, there were important considerations, which he had to bear in mind. In the first place he must fly the shortest route to the French coast thus reducing his time over enemy territory and minimising the chances of interception by enemy night fighters and, of course, the length of time he would be exposed to ground defence fire. This latter was always a big factor with low-flying aircraft and once George managed to get airborne the whole ground-defence complex would be alerted along possible routes to the coast. Even within the period of about four minutes, which he estimated it would take him to reach and clear the coast, there would be time for the defences to pick up his course.

The second consideration was to choose a crossing-out point on the coast where there was not likely to be a heavy concentration of anti-aircraft guns. Two such places, both roughly on his route out, he knew, from past experience he must avoid. These were St Valéry and Le Tréport, both heavily defended by the Germans.

After turning over in his mind the various possibilities, he decided that if he steered about 280° after take-off he should pass over the French coast near the small town of Cayeux and within sight of a distinctly broken stretch of coastline, a sea basin between St Valéry and le Crotoy. This natural feature would be a good checkpoint and provided there was no cloud it should show up quite clearly, even on a moonless night.

From this point he would continue on a course of 280° until he estimated he was sufficiently well clear of the French coast to avoid light anti-aircraft fire. To be on the safe side he reckoned about five miles out would be sufficient. Finally, he planned to turn on to a northerly course which would bring him to the south coast in sight of the Dover cliffs which, even on a darkish night, should be visible a good way off. Anyhow, he was confident that in fair conditions, he would spot the famous white cliffs of Dover, ever a beacon of hope to British fighter pilots returning from operations over France.

Having worked this route plan out in his mind he decided that Manston airfield, on the tip of the North Foreland, was the obvious place to land. He knew the airfield well, all its approaches were familiar to him and above all it had an extra large runway (built especially for Bomber Command aircraft on emergency diversion) and a generous grass area on which one could land safely from almost any direction. Moreover, and this was the important point, George knew that if he could make landfall over Pegwell Bay, which was only just south of the airfield, a straight-in approach free from obstructions was ensured. He would then need only to turn a few degrees to starboard from a northerly heading, which he would be flying at the time, to line up with the main runway. With over 3000 yards of runway and good grass verges there was plenty of room for error.

Again and again George went over in his head the plans and the more he thought about them the more he became convinced that he could, with a little luck, pull off what must be the almost impossible feat of stealing a fighter from under the enemy's very nose. The big 'If' was getting into the aircraft and being able to start it undetected.

'I must pull it off, I must.' Time and time again George muttered these words to himself as he reviewed his plan of escape.

The time of waiting was nearly at an end. Sunday had come and gone now there was only Monday to see out. During this day George received confirmation from his Resistance friends – by word of mouth via the ever-faithful Pierre – that all was as expected at the airfield and that there were FW190s aplenty to be stolen. Having studied the sketch map of the airfield and its dispersed aircraft, George decided which dispersal area to go for. This information was conveyed by Pierre back to the Frenchman who was to undertake the final reconnaissance that night. It was now a matter of fixing the rendezvous point where George and Pierre would meet up with this man for final briefing.

The stage was set: and George was now the principal actor.

Monday night was good. A completely cloudless sky was canopied under a myriad of stars whose combined brilliance gave off just enough light to make the venture possible and yet not enough to provide long-range vision for the guards at the airfield. Certainly from a flying point of view it was ideal, and George had every hope that weather conditions over England would be similar.

He had been concerned about wind conditions because too strong a surface wind would make the take-off a most hazardous undertaking if he should be forced to take off other than into wind. As it was there was but a light breeze and the direction of take-off would not matter; he would simply take off in the direction the parked aircraft faced, provided of course there was sufficient distance for a take-off run.

Pierre arrived at the house early, tense and excited, yet outwardly he appeared to George to be somewhat subdued and a little sad.

'What's the matter, Pierre?' asked George. 'Are you afraid we won't make it?'

'No, it's not that,' said the boy, 'I just wish that I could come with you to England.'

'Sorry about that, I wish you could too. What could you do in England though?'

'Join up with the Free French Air Force and in some way avenge my father. I'd just love to shoot down a German fighter.'

'Too bad you are so young, Pierre, because even if you did get to England you wouldn't be allowed to join up in the forces. Anyhow, you're doing a wonderful job here helping chaps like me to escape, and a most dangerous one too. Always remember that, Pierre, when you feel that you are not doing sufficient to help the cause of freedom. Everyone has his particular job and for the time being at least yours is here doing exactly what you are doing.'

A somewhat mollified Pierre countered with, 'Well, when you get back promise me that you will avenge my father.'

'You bet I will, young fellow. The very first chance I get on returning to the squadron I'll make it my lot to bag a German aircraft specially for you on that score.'

At last the time of waiting was over. The hour on the kitchen clock was 10.30 pm and after farewells all round – there was quite a gathering at the house to see him off – George and Pierre set off for the rendezvous where they were to meet the Frenchman at 11.30 pm. This would allow them plenty of time to get there should they be forced to make a detour to avoid unexpected patrols of German troops.

As with the first attempt, Pierre proudly led the way, picking his way through the silent night, sheltered by hedge and bush whenever and wherever possible. Much was at stake and Pierre set great store by his part in the enterprise, which was to get to the rendezvous safely and on time.

The journey was not without excitement. Scarcely a mile from the starting point they were forced to seek cover through the unexpected appearance on the road ahead of them of a German staff car proceeding at high speed in their direction. At the time, they were walking along a tree-lined country lane safe in the belief that there was not likely to be any vehicular traffic in that part of the country at that hour of the night.

Strangely, they had not heard the car approaching perhaps because the road twisted away from them at that point to disappear into a wood from which the car suddenly appeared, its screened headlights producing a diffused but revealing light along the roadway ahead of it.

There was barely time to throw themselves headlong into the roadside ditch before it was upon them. Crouched in the ditch, which fortunately was dry, the two escapers offered up a silent prayer as the large black Mercedes roared past their hiding place and on into the night, presumably unaware of their presence.

'We'll lie low for about five minutes,' whispered George. 'You never know, they might just have seen us and could well turn round further down the road where there is room and come back to investigate.'

But no. All remained silent long after the last purring note of the Mercedes had faded away and, with a sigh of relief, they once again set off, both tensely alert now and determined not to be surprised a second time. It was just as well because very shortly after, Pierre's straining ears picked up the sound of voices somewhere ahead and he at once halted George with a sibilant 'Ssh'.

Quietly and quickly the two moved into the shelter of the nearby trees, and standing perfectly still they listened to what were clearly German voices.

'It sounds like a search party,' whispered Pierre. 'Yes, it does,' replied George, 'and in this wood too. We'd better make ourselves scarce. I wonder who they are looking for now?'

Pierre at once set off at right angles to the wood, the same one from which the staff car had suddenly appeared, in a large detour designed to bring them back on their route some few hundred yards further down the road.

The detour safely completed and the dangerous wood now someway behind them, Pierre increased the pace to make up for lost time.

Without further incident to interrupt their progress they finally made the rendezvous with ten minutes to spare, but as yet there was no Frenchman there to meet them.

'Let's sit behind this bush and wait, Pierre, I'm sure he will be here soon,' suggested a confident and expectant George.

'Oh, there you are.' George and Pierre almost jumped out of their skins as the cheerful but guarded voice addressed them from the other side of the bush. Skilled in silent movement the French patriot had stolen up on them unheard; amused by their obvious fright, he was yet quick to reassure them of his good intentions.

'Good heavens, you gave me a scare,' whispered George. 'I thought the game was up.'

'Sorry,' answered the Frenchman, 'I couldn't resist my fun. Anyhow, I've good news. All is well and with a little luck you should at least get as far as the aircraft undetected.'

'Why so confident?' asked the now excited airman.

'Well, I've not only marked out a place for you to get through the wire, I've also spent the last hour – undetected I'm pleased to say – cutting a path through the wire for you.'

George could faintly detect the Frenchman's smiling pride as he made this announcement, producing as he did so the wire clippers with which he had done the job.

'Gosh, that's marvellous. Is there a FW190 fairly near there?' queried George.

'Yes indeed, and unguarded, though there is a patrol in the area. However, he shouldn't cause you much bother and the nearest guard-tower is some distance away.'

'How do you suggest I go about it then?' asked George. 'Well, I'll lead you to the spot I've cut in the wire and you just lie low there and bide your time. Time your final dash to the aircraft when you have assessed the guard's movements.'

For Pierre the adventure was at an end; it was but five minutes for H-hour (midnight, the time agreed for the attempt) and, as in the previous attempt, Pierre's instructions were to be well away from the vicinity of the airfield before things started and the alarm was sounded.

'Well, goodbye Pierre, and thank you very much for all you've done to help,' whispered George as he clasped the boy around the shoulders in a farewell embrace.

Poor Pierre was too overcome to say much. He simply said 'Good luck.' And not trusting himself to say more he at once moved off towards home.

A few minutes later the big adventure was really on.

'Keep close behind me,' whispered the Frenchman to George as he set off towards the airfield in a crouching but deliberate attitude and at a fairly fast pace. Obviously, the quicker they could reach their entry point the less chance of detection, provided of course they were careful to make no noise and use the maximum cover available. On a still, clear night the smallest sound travels great distances and any unusual noise might alert the watchful guards and make entry into the airfield that much more difficult.

Almost on the dot of midnight, they reached their objective – the carefully cut tangled wire on the airfield perimeter through which George was to make his entry. No words were spoken, a quick pat on the back from the French patriot and George was alone, the faint silhouette of a German Focke-Wulf fighter seemingly beckoning him forward.

Up till this point he had felt no emotion, no fear. Now, however, in his solitude he could feel and hear his heart pounding and, as with most persons before an exciting event, he seemed to be short of breath and there was a sickly feeling in his tummy.

Silently and apprehensively he waited, his eyes fixed firmly on the fighter whose shape became more pronounced as with each succeeding minute his eyes grew more accustomed to the starry darkness. He could see that the aircraft was neither picketed (an unlikely precaution in such fair-weather conditions) nor covered, but the hood, as expected, was closed. This, however presented no problems as he knew it was a simple operation to release the catch and slide it back. But, best of all, the fighter faced into the slight breeze which was blowing in from the open airfield and he knew from the Frenchman's briefing that there were no obstructions in the path of a take-off run in the direction of the parked aircraft's heading.

To his right some two hundred yards away, George could see the faint outline of the nearest guard tower but he was not too worried about detection from there, at least up till the time of his attempting to start the FW190. The patrolling guard was his chief concern. He waited what seemed to him an age, but which was in reality about two minutes, before he heard the guard tramping towards him from the opposite direction of the guard tower.

'Good,' George muttered to himself. 'I reckon he'll go at least as far as the tower and beyond I hope, and when he reaches it, I'll make my dash.'

Purposely, menacingly the guard came on, a dim figure at first but very much alive as shouldering his rifle he bore down and finally passed the unsuspected British airman lying prone on the far side of the perimeter fence.

As the guard approached George's heart began to thump so loudly it seemed to him that the guard could not possibly fail to hear it as he tramped by. But as he came abreast of George there was no tell-tale sideways movement of the head or any slowing down in his walk, both sure signs that his suspicions were in no way aroused. As his figure receded in size and shape against the airfield darkness so George's heart beats returned to normal, but he was naturally tense and breathless.

As if it was a prearranged signal for the attempt to be made, the silence of the night was unexpectedly broken by the crowing of a cock from a nearby farmhouse. 'Gosh, he's early,' muttered George, 'but I'll take that as a good omen, I'm off.'

And putting action into words he moved in and under the wire, wriggling his way through the gaps cleared for him, halted only momentarily by the barbs which despite his care caught at various parts of his clothing.

When through he gave a quick look to left and right, saw that all was clear, and ran doubled-over towards the Focke-Wulf. This time there was no warning shout, no hurrying feet and no searchlight. So far so good.

In a matter of seconds he was there, crouched beneath and sheltered by the wing of the German fighter in a position from which a quick step up onto the wing, where it joined the fuselage, would enable him to slide back the canopy and scramble into the cockpit. He noted with satisfaction that the fighter was parked without steel chocks and he therefore made a mental note to release the parking brake which would have been left on for safety.

He was now breathing much more heavily than the short dash to the aircraft warranted, but once again the breathless excitement of fear was the cause, for it made normal breathing impossible.

'This is it,' muttered George desperately, as he stepped onto the wing and felt for the canopy release button.

With a sigh of relief he felt the canopy begin to slide back as pressing the button with his left hand he eased the hood back with his right. Hastily he scrambled into the cockpit, disappointed but not dismayed to find that the pilot's parachute had been removed for the night. This meant of course that he would not be able to bale out if for any reason he needed to abandon the aircraft. Also he would have to half stand in the cockpit, by bracing himself against the back of the seat, in order to get a good enough forward view to fly the aircraft visually.

Silently he slid the hood forward knowing that an open cockpit might be seen by the guard, should he return before George could get airborne. He needed a little time in the cockpit to get his eyes accustomed to the greater darkness and also of course to refresh his mind on the cockpit lay-out. And with the hood closed, and crouched well forward in the cockpit, there was less likelihood of being spotted at what had now become the critical stage of the attempt.

With relief he noted that the cockpit was as he had remembered it from his briefing at Biggin Hill in the captured Focke-Wulf, and best of all the starter button was in the same position. Carefully, he unscrewed the engine priming pump and as carefully as he could he pumped it back and forth until it came under pressure denoting that the line was filled with petrol ready for priming.

'About three I reckon,' muttered George as he continued priming. 'Now she's ready, here's hoping that she'll start first go. A flat battery and I'm done for.'

But luck was still on his side. At the first press on the starter button the propeller turned, the engine fired and in response to a quick throttle movement from George the radial engine roared into life, shattering the peace of the night.

'England here we come!' shouted an exultant George, no longer caring about detection. He was homeward bound, God willing.

CHAPTER 6

One of the dangers of a take-off immediately after starting-up was of course the likelihood of an unwarmed engine cutting out under power. Well aware of this risk, George gave the engine a quick half-throttle burst of about three seconds to clear the plugs before releasing the brake. When he did so the aircraft moved forward on its take-off run.

As the fighter shot forward, under its increasing power the German defences, only now realising that something was amiss, sprung into life. The searchlight on the nearest tower stabbed the darkness of the airfield as its operator tried to focus its beam on the fast disappearing aircraft. In the cockpit George was not finding things easy. The uneven grass surface was causing the Focke-Wulf to buck badly and, hampered by no settled seated position, he found it difficult to co-ordinate the rudder movements to counteract this effect and that of swing, the latter a most pronounced characteristic of the German fighter on take-off. To add to his worries he had no clearly defined take-off run to assist directional stability. However, by concentrating on one particularly bright star in the night sky ahead, he was able to maintain a reasonable heading.

He did not want to lift the aircraft off the ground too soon thereby putting the cold engine under more strain and so enhancing the chances of an engine cut, so he merely held the control column in the centre position which would allow the fighter to fly off at its safest speed. This manoeuvre meant a longer take-off run but it also allowed just that much more time for the engine to get warm.

He was at the critical part of the take-off run (just before the aircraft becomes airborne) when the probing searchlight beam caught the aircraft, its tangential rays flooding through the canopy and temporarily blinding the unhappy airman in the cockpit. The abrupt contrast between the now lighted cockpit and the darkness ahead was such that George could no longer see his guiding star, lost to sight now in the sharply contrasting blackness ahead. By feel alone he kept his heading until in a few more seconds, with fully flying speed attained, the Focke-Wulf leapt into the air assisted at the vital moment by an unintended bounce on a particularly rough spot on the airfield. Immediately it bounced, George eased the stick back slightly thus causing the aircraft to rise sharply and the offending beam to fall away as sharply, the sudden change in height being beyond the compensatory powers of the searchlight operator. With the speed now building up rapidly George flung the fighter into a turn, and as he did so he glanced at the phosphorous-tipped compass needle as it moved towards his intended course of 280 degrees.

But he was not to be allowed to clear the airfield without some attempt to bring him down and as he commenced his turn he was met with an alarming barrage of light machine-gun fire, the flaming red tracers stabbing towards his accelerating aircraft as it levelled from the turn onto its final height and heading. George was no stranger to light flak but this was the first time he had seen it by night and the effect was much more alarming. But the fire was ill-directed and for the most part, behind him, the gunners were firing blind on sound alone because the frantically sweeping searchlight was unable to relocate its target. It was never again to do so as the

Focke-Wulf under full-power sped away westwards into the safety of the enveloping darkness.

With course and height now set and safe, at least for the time being, George throttled back to a fast cruising speed of 240 mph, noting as he did so that the oil and coolant temperature gauges were at the 'normal' mark; the phosphorous-tipped needles and figures on the dials of the instruments showed up quite clearly in the dark cockpit.

'That's that,' muttered the relieved airman as he cleared the danger area of the airfield defences. 'But I bet I'll get a hot reception at the coast.'

As the stolen Focke-Wulf with the determined George at the controls thundered through the night, the sound of its racing engine carried to a group of silent watchers on the ground. Grouped around the house where George had sought his last safe refuge in France, a knot of figures gazed into the night sky trying to locate the unlighted fighter, as it sped over past and away towards the coast. Each offered up a silent prayer for the safety of the gallant British airman, whom they correctly supposed from the direction and timing of the aircraft flight was at the controls.

Much nearer to the scene of action, Pierre too had been halted by the tell-tale noise of an aircraft taking off from what he guessed and hoped was Abbeville airfield. Now the aircraft was airborne and settled on course, a course which took it just to the north of where Pierre now stood, he recognised the throbbing note of the Focke-Wulf and knew that George had pulled off the impossible.

'Good luck, George, and happy landings,' Pierre muttered aloud, a catch in his voice betraying his emotions.

The good and loyal Frenchman who had planned the escape could do no more. Alone in the vastness of the night, the ultimate success of the daring escapade rested entirely with George. He was happy that it was so; enough patriots had placed themselves in grave danger of arrest by assisting him thus far and he was in a sense relieved that he alone would be answerable for anything that might go wrong henceforth. He hoped nothing would.

But the Germans were not yet finished with him. Warnings had already been flashed to their network of defence posts and though he was flying too low to be seen on the air defence radar in the area, sound detectors from observer posts were plotting his course sufficiently accurately to be able to estimate his crossing-out point on the coast where the light anti-aircraft defences were alerted. At such a low altitude and with the little warning they would get, the gun predictors would not be much use to the Germans, and their barrage technique of all guns firing simultaneously ahead of the line of flight of the aircraft was therefore the Germans' only hope of scoring a hit. This ploy did, however, produce a most lethal area through which an aircraft was usually lucky to escape undamaged.

In the short time taken to reach the coast, George had little hope on a moonless night of pinpointing his position, and it was not necessary to do so. In the circumstances the shortest route was the best route and in the few minutes flight involved he was unlikely to be much off course. He did however hope to pick up the tell-tale light in the coastline near Le Tréport, and he was peering ahead of him looking for this landmark when suddenly and alarmingly, the star-studded horizon leaped into life as hundreds of tracer shells from the light-gun defences seared their way upwards in a seemingly impenetrable wall of hot lead. And the next moment he was in it, and the next moment he was through, left with no scars but a lingering impression of myriads of hot fingers reaching up out of the dark to touch his aircraft, stationary momentarily when first seen as they emanated from the gun barrels, but quickly forming themselves into long tracers of light as simultaneously, it seemed, they rushed at him and past into the receding darkness.

He did not pick up his coastal landmark; he could not do so, being blinded as he was by the flashing of guns, but at least he knew for certain that he had crossed the French coast. From behind him a few hopeful gunners sprayed lead after his rapidly disappearing aircraft, but to no avail.

Over the protective neutrality of the sea George concentrated on his instruments, a very necessary precaution when flying over the sea at night at low level when sea and sky merge into an indefinable horizon making it almost impossible for the pilot to maintain a steady height and aircraft attitude.

Clear now of all enemy defences, apart perhaps from an unlucky encounter over the sea with a German night-fighter – a remote possibility – he breathed freely and with relief when turning onto his predetermined northerly heading, and set his final course for England and home.

George estimated that his flight time to making landfall at Pegwell Bay on the English coast would be about 25 minutes. Not long; but in the pent-up circumstances of such a flight every second seemed like a minute and every minute an hour. But twenty minutes soon passes – time is no respecter of circumstances – and very soon the illuminated hands on his watch showed that he had been airborne for this length of time. Sure enough ahead of him now he could see a faint blurred outline of the white welcoming cliffs of Dover, which from time immemorial had gladdened the hearts of Englishmen returning to their native land from ventures and adventures, some perhaps as spectacular as now being undertaken by this young Royal Air Force fighter pilot.

As George's pulse quickened in the excitement of his first sight of home, a tiny warning signal flashed to his alert brain. And in response to it he veered his aircraft sharply to the right so as to keep well away from the coast, and possible danger, until the right moment came to turn inland according to his preconceived plan of landing at Manston. In the starboard turn he gradually reduced his speed so that he was better able to fly the aircraft safely at such a low altitude and at the same to keep the smudgy outline of the Kent coast always in sight. Also he wanted to select undercarriage and flaps down at a moment's notice and to do this it was essential to keep his speed below the safe maximum allowed for this operation.

With eyes straining to follow the coast as it first curved out, around and then back from Dover to Deal, he knew that the sound of the Focke-Wulf's engine must be carrying to the coastal defences which, always on the alert, would be seeking information and guidance from the operations room at Hillingdon where all aircraft movements were plotted and filtered. There would, George hoped, be no continuous radar plot; flying now almost at sea level he knew that though the coastal radar would detect his presence the plots would not be sufficiently positive to more than give an indication of the course he was steering and certainly the height could at best be assessed as 'below 500 feet'.

He felt quite safe from interception by night-fighters but he expected a hot reception from the airfield defences at Manston as he came in to land. It would only be light machine-gun fire (heavier guns could not be brought to bear at such a low altitude) and the gunners would be firing blind. Nevertheless, at the low speed he would be committed to for a landing and the fact that there could be no alteration of his heading immediately prior to touch-down, his aircraft would be an extremely vulnerable target. Of course George had foreseen all this but he could not stop such frightening thoughts racing through his mind as he neared the grand finale of his escape; a safe landing on British soil now, as it were, just around the corner.

At long, long last he sighted the eagerly awaited break in the steadily curving coastline, indicating that he was now abreast of his point of landfall – Pegwell Bay. A sharp but slight turn to port, a positive reduction in power and he was making good a heading of 020 degrees which he reckoned would bring his aircraft roughly into line with the runway. There was hardly enough wind to affect his landing direction and he could thankfully ignore this normally important factor.

Back came the cockpit canopy, down went the undercarriage, out came the flaps; a steady increase in power to counteract the resultant drag and he was set steady at 200 feet and about to cross the coast. This was the difficult part of the flying. It will be remembered that there was no parachute in the aircraft by which the pilot was raised to an extra height to see about him. Without it George was forced to half-stand in the cockpit by pressing his feet firmly on the rudder pedals and bracing himself against the back of the seat. To make matters worse the motoring approach to which he was committed produced the usual nose-up attitude in the Focke-Wulf, and this fact combined with its radial nose meant that he could see very little ahead and not a great deal to the side. Moreover, the extent to which he could move the rudder pedals was severely curtailed by the necessity to keep both his legs straightened, to afford the leverage necessary to maintain a half-standing position in the cockpit. But by a combination of constant throttle movement, coarse use of aileron, and a somewhat restricted rudder control he managed to keep the aircraft on a straight enough heading.

As he crossed the coast George could see the smudgy outline of a darkened town on his right, which he knew was Ramsgate, which meant that in about one minute he should see the airfield. But at that precise moment things began to happen; the darkness ahead previously unbroken except for the twinkling stars was in an instant dissected by pin-pricks of light as the light anti-aircraft guns around the airfield perimeter opened fire. Streams of light-gun fire raced towards the approaching aircraft as the gun crews, firing on sound alone, directed their guns into a concentrated wall of fire in the path of the Focke-Wulf, blinding the pilot to all ahead of him. To make matters worse, an airfield searchlight had by now added its penetrating beam to the conflagration, its searching rays playing all-round the approach lane seeking to illuminate the target.

In the midst of such turmoil George was thrown into momentary panic and very nearly lost control of his aircraft. He quickly recovered however and, a visual approach no longer possible, he eased back on the throttle and settled the aircraft into an engine-assisted glide using the instruments to maintain directional and lateral stability. He must now hope to touch down somewhere on the airfield which he knew must be fairly close and when he felt the wheels touch to cut the engine switches, try and control the inevitable bounce from such a landing attitude, and in the slang used by fighter pilots to 'hope for the best'. The best would be to settle down again after the first bounce on all three points and so run to a controlled stop: the worst would be to continue to bounce with an ultimate loss of control from which almost anything could result.

It was too much to hope that he could fly through a second barrage of fire unscathed. The luck was against him this time. A blinding flash on his starboard wing, which caused the Focke-Wulf to dip alarmingly and George to let go of the control column momentarily, was almost his undoing. Somehow, he regained a measure of control and continued his blind approach. At this juncture the hitherto troublesome searchlight came to his aid. The wandering beam found its target which now clearly illuminated was seen by the airfield gunners, who, though recognising it as an enemy, ceased firing. They had strict orders to do this if it was obvious that an enemy aircraft was attempting to land.

In the cockpit George was completely blinded by the powerful beam, he could neither see ahead nor to the side. There was only one course now open to him; throttle back fully and carry on in a glide in the hope that he would touch inside the airfield boundary. He did, but it was no touch. The wheels hit the ground so heavily that the aircraft bounced about twenty feet into the air, remained airborne for a good fifty yards, and then landed again wheels first. George was quick to react. He realised that he was likely to lose control on the subsequent touch down and landing run, so at the first bounce he reached forward and switched off the engine, thus reducing the risk of fire should the fighter eventually turn over out of control.

At the second bounce he fought to regain some measure of control but in his unnatural self-standing position he could not use full rudder, let alone operate the unfamiliar toe-brakes on the German fighter, and the aircraft merely slewed further and further to the right finally adopting a crabwise movement across the grass. The undercarriage could not take the strain and the starboard leg collapsed causing the wing-tip to bite into the ground; this in turn swivelled the fighter onto its nose, its wind-milling airscrew carving great furrows in the earth before, robbed of its motive power, it ceased to turn. This final breaking force was sufficient to halt the forward impetus of the now crippled fighter.

The sudden reversal of movement was too much for both the aircraft and George. The fighter reared up onto its rounded nose and George shot forward in the cockpit striking his forehead a severe blow on the armoured-glass windscreen. Fortunately for the now unconscious airman slumped in the cockpit the aircraft did not turn over but stood firmly on its nose, now brightly illuminated by the ever-watchful searchlight. Across the airfield darting fingers of light signified the approach of the fire engine, the ambulance and an excited airfield guard. The deed was accomplished: George had made it, for although unconscious he was soon to be rescued and identified to the amazement of his would-be captors.

'Welcome back to England, Allen.'

Thus some twenty minutes later, when consciousness had returned, was George greeted on his safe return.

At first his shocked mind could not assimilate these words but as the fog of confusion began slowly to lift he became aware of his surroundings and the fact that he was safely tucked up in bed. At its foot stood a group of men, none of whom he recognised. Gradually they and the room came into focus. Among the group, one person was clearly recognisable by his gold braided hat and the four stripes on his arm as the Station Commander. The others not known to George were in fact, the Medical Officer, the Intelligence Officer and the Station Duty Officer.

'How did you know my name, sir?' asked a now fully conscious George addressing his remarks to the Group Captain.

In explanation and before the Group Captain could reply, the Medical Officer reached forward and touched the identity disc, which George carried suspended on a thin silver chain around his neck.

'Oh yes, I forgot. It's a good thing I held on to that.'

'Yes, I suppose it is,' responded the Station Commander, 'but I doubt that we would have shot you on sight without first making sure of your identity.'

Responding to the quick humour of this remark George countered, 'No, not you perhaps but some trigger-happy airfield gunner might have done so.'

'Well, you needn't worry about that now. Indeed don't worry about a thing, but just rest until that bump on your forehead subsides.'

'Gosh,' exclaimed George as his groping fingers found and tenderly caressed his forehead. 'Is it bad?'

'No, just a bad bruise,' answered the MO. 'It will be gone in a day or two, and you needn't worry about it keeping you off flying. A week or two to rest and you'll be fully fit to go.'

'Good-oh'.

'I'd first like a short statement for the Intelligence Officer here,' said the CO, indicating the officer next to him, 'and then you can get some sleep. We'll need to send a preliminary signal to Air Ministry with brief details. The full report can follow when you're well enough to make it.'

Alone with the Intelligence Officer, George told him briefly of his experiences from the fateful day when he was shot down to the exciting moment of his arrival over England.

'Quite a story. I look forward to hearing the full details, but that will be enough for now; you get some sleep and we'll see how you feel tomorrow. In the meantime, I'll get a signal off to Command and Air Ministry. I'll bet it causes a stir up there and I shouldn't be surprised if the old man himself [meaning Churchill] is roused from his bed to be told of it.' So saying, the Intelligence Officer folded his notebook and prepared to depart.

'I couldn't care about that, but do you think you could ring Biggin and ask them to let my squadron commander know that I'm back, and you might add a-raring to go.' 'I'll do that. Now you get some rest. Goodnight.'

'Goodnight.'

Mentally and physically fatigued, George soon drifted into a profound sleep from which he was awakened some ten hours later by the noise of many aircraft taking off.

'Just like old times,' he muttered sleepily as responding to the day's awakening he reached up for the bell, which dangled above his head to summon the orderly.

He was famished and a good old English breakfast of bacon and eggs was going to be a pleasant change from French rolls and ersatz coffee.

George remained at Manston for three days during which time he made a full report and was visited by no less a personage than the Air Officer Commanding his Group and his delighted squadron commander. The former promised an early return to flying and the latter a welcome back to the squadron.

With these assurances given George happily departed on three weeks' leave, already excited at the prospect of a return to the fray. 'I must avenge Pierre's father,' were his parting words to his squadron commander. 'He'll expect it.'

'And so you shall, but all in good time,' was the comforting rejoinder.

It was in the small fishing village of Port Melon in Cornwall that George spent his leave. His parents owned a small cottage there, one of a row clustered along the sea front and but a road's width from the sea.

He was always at ease in the peace of these restful surroundings where he had sailed and fished as a schoolboy, both sports conducive to peace of mind. For one whole week he did nothing else, lost to all other cares but that of his sailing dinghy and his fishing line. Cold and often wet, he paid little regard to the elements, intent only on enjoying himself to the exclusion of all else – yes, even to thoughts of war and air fighting. Now and again as he fought and wrestled with his dinghy in the rough sea under full sail he was struck by the similarity of his reactions to that experienced in a Spitfire when in a dogfight. These were but fleeting thoughts and not seriously diverting.

A young, healthy body and mind cannot for long be content with the more mundane pursuits of sport when elsewhere friend and enemy are locked in mortal combat. Thus it was that after the first week a restlessness gradually asserted itself and George spent less and less time sailing and more and more time listening to the news and devouring the papers for tit-bits of the war, particularly the Royal Air Force daylight operations over the Channel. He knew it was time to get back to the job and he knew that he was now fit to do so.

It was in the middle of the second week of leave that he received a telegram from his CO which read: 'Congratulations on the immediate award of the Distinguished Flying Cross.'

George could hardly believe the good news as he read and re-read the telegram. Excitedly he showed it to his mother who, though justly proud of his achievements, merely smiled and said, 'Well, you earned it.'

Earned it he certainly had. Proudly he wore it – that small strip of white and purple striped ribbon, which was the secret desire of all wartime pilots. A true symbol of flying achievement in the face of the enemy.

It was early November before a rested and refreshed George reported back to Biggin Hill to the delight of air and ground crews alike. His cheerful presence in their ranks had been greatly missed and all looked forward to having him around again; his fellow pilots for the welcome sense of humour he brought into the crew-room, and the ground crews for the constant, good-humoured raillery to which he subjected them. George himself couldn't have been happier; he would soon again be behind the controls of his beloved Spitfire and, he hoped, very soon in combat with an opportunity to avenge Pierre's father as he had promised the boy he would do.

'Well, George, it's good to see you back.'

'It's good to be back, sir.'

George sat at ease in the squadron commander's office on the first morning of his return, being briefed on events since he was shot down. He learned that four pilots had been lost in the period and that the squadron and wing had been having a fairly heavy time of it.

'We can do with your experience,' said the CO. 'Although our losses have been negligible some of the section leaders could do with a break, and this is where you come in.'

'I'm ready to go anytime, sir. I've had enough time off to last me for the rest of the year. A few local trips to get my hand in again and I'll be ready to go.'

'Good, we'll go and see your flight commander and expect your name on the list for the first operation the day after tomorrow.'

'You bet, I can't wait,' responded George.

In the event, the weather was unsuitable for operations on the day named and he had to wait five days before finally together with other pilots, he assembled in the briefing room to hear the Wing Commander Flying run through the operation to be undertaken that morning.

Sixty Flying Fortresses of the American Eighth Air Force with an RAF Spitfire escort were to bomb Amiens airfield. The Biggin Hill Wing was to be in its favourite position of high-cover, which in brief meant it would be the highest flying wing actually accompanying the bombers throughout the mission.

Although not free to divert much from the bomber route, it did however have much more freedom of action than the closer and lower escort wings and squadrons. Within the wing, George's squadron was to fly top cover, and this is where the German fighters normally 'nibbled' in their early probing attacks in an attempt to draw off the escort.

The briefing over, the pilots made their way to the dispersals for kitting out, and signing up for aircraft they were to fly and the last minute check of the aircraft itself; oxygen, reflector gun-sight and the gun camera, all must be serviceable to ensure a successful operation. Around the airfield in their protecting pens stood the expectant Spitfires, and near or on them the yellow-vested pilots prepared for strapping-in. A thumbs-up signal from the squadron commander and all twelve pilots in George's squadron reached forward to press their starter buttons.

As the twelve Merlins around him fired into life, George was assailed by that sick sort of feeling that all pilots experience prior to an operation. This momentary touch of fear soon passed in the excitement and jostle as he taxied out from the dispersal to the take-off point.

On the far side of the airfield the other squadron in the wing, led by the Wing Commander Flying, was already taxiing out in a long line of single Spitfires, which filled the twisting taxiway leading to the down-wind end of the airfield. They moved into and down the runway to make more room behind for the following aircraft until twelve pairs of Spitfires, the noise of their revving engines drowning all other sound, were poised to take-off.

'Brutus leader, opening up, opening up – Go.' Thus the wing leader signalled the start of the operation for the Biggin Hill Wing; and his aircraft, accompanied by the

No.2 danced down the runway on its take-off run.

In quick succession pair followed pair into the sky until the airfield circuit was crowded with Spitfires chasing each other around in a wide, circling movement as the pilots closed in on their leaders, and the leaders on the squadron until finally the wing, now a cohesive formation, turned over the airfield and started its long climb towards the east and enemy territory.

On the ground, the ground crews, having watched the form-up pantomine (as they always did) turned to their various tasks in preparation for the wing's return.

Snugly seated in his cockpit and leading the rear section of his squadron George gazed about and below him as the wing climbed higher and higher. Ahead of him the leading squadron, now spread out in open formation, climbed steadily into the pale-blue winter's sky. All around him the perfectly spaced sections of his own squadron followed as though towed along by invisible strings so perfect was their displacement below and behind the leading squadron. Underneath, the patterned fields and familiar landmarks of Kent slipped by, the dark shades of green contrasting strikingly with the whiteness of the scudding cloud banks between the fighters and the ground.

Out over Dover, a slight southerly change of course, and the wing leader was taking up his position above the close-escort fighters, which had formed themselves around the Fortresses.

Land gave way to sea, the white cliffs of Dover to the not-so-white cliffs of Cap Gris Nez and the patterned fields of an enemy-occupied France. The air was now alive with tension. Over France there was a generous amount of medium-altitude cumulus cloud but, mused George, 'none of that drifting cirrus which makes our job of escort so difficult'. With the bombers flying upwards of 20,000 feet the escorting fighters were usually stacked to about 30,000 feet, and drift cirrus between these two heights made station-keeping very difficult. Also, it meant that the defending fighters could sneak in in small numbers using the cirrus cloud to hide their approach.

'Brutus Leader from control: formations of enemy aircraft reported ahead and above.'

The Wing Leader made no reply to this ominous warning from the ground controller; radio silence was never broken unless to report enemy aircraft sightings, and even wing leaders observed this rigid rule. Pilots, who had not already done so, now reached forward to switch on their reflector sights, turned firing buttons to 'fire', and with a last look around the cockpit to check fuel and temperatures, each in his own individual way prepared himself mentally for battle.

George was ready – he had been ever since sighting the coast of France – and eagerly he scanned the sky above, ahead and, all-important, behind, where danger usually materialised in the form of isolated pairs of enemy fighters sneaking in undetected. It was ahead of the formation that George spotted the moving specks of black which rapidly became recognisable as Messerschmitt 109Gs.

'Good', muttered George to himself, 'they're easier meat than the Focke-Wulfs.' In the same instant he gave the sighting call. 'Enemy fighters one o'clock above and closing.'

'I've got them,' responded the Wing Leader. 'You take them Turbulent Leader and rejoin if possible. I'll carry on with the escort.'

'Roger, Brutus – Out,' acknowledged George's squadron leader. 'Turbulent aircraft operate in pairs as briefed. Rejoin escort if possible after combat.'

This final order from the squadron leader meant freedom of action for the section leaders in the squadron. George immediately peeled off from the main formation with his section of four aircraft and commenced a climbing turn into the sun with the intention of meeting the enemy fighters at least on equal terms so far as height was concerned. The enemy pilots however, had other ideas. No sooner had George's section started to climb than they broke into pairs, preparatory to giving battle with the high escort fighters. In response, George broke his section of four into pairs and with his number two keeping a watching brief behind he sped into the attack, now at the same height as the enemy.

He had picked out his target, two ME109s on the right of the fast-closing attackers and on the inside now of his wheeling turn. He realised that preliminary manoeuvring would not be possible.

In a matter of seconds the opposing fighters closed and it now became merely a question of who could out manoeuvre who, and in this respect the turning circles of the contesting fighters was all important. Here the Spitfire was the master, and George had no difficulty in slipping in behind the 109 he had selected to attack. Throttle fully forward, stick hard back and both hands firmly gripping his control column, George juddered his Spitfire into a firing position.

For a second or two, he chased the bead of his reflector sight, caught and steadied it on the target, waited until his range/scale was filled with the wing-span of the Messerschmitt and then pressed the firing button. In response his two 20 mm cannon and four machine-guns spouted flame and lead. In what seemed the same instant yellow flashes, signifying hits, danced along the fuselage and on the wings of the enemy fighter which bucked violently, either under the impact of fire or in response to its frightened pilot's reaction on the controls.

A fleeting second's fire from the deadly Spitfire's guns was enough. At one moment the enemy was clearly recognisable as a ME109 and the next it was but a mass of flame and disintegrating metal which, caught in the dying aircraft's slipstream, trailed out across the sky and in the path of the pursuing Spitfires. Just in time they pulled up and away and the exultant George shouted into his microphone, 'One confirmed, Brutus Leader – Turbulent Yellow rejoining formation.'

With his section of four again together George called for a report from his sub-section leader. 'Any luck, Yellow three?' 'You bet, Yellow one,' came the immediate response, 'this baby never misses. I got me a fat, juicy 109 and I didn't waste much ammunition in doing it either.'

George smiled at the light-hearted boast of the New Zealander who was his number three, an up-and-coming ace who had already proved that he was a brilliant shot when, in an earlier raid, he shot down in one burst a Focke-Wulf 190 using an almost impossible angle of deflection.

Back with the wing and the bombers, which for the time being at least were free from enemy fighter attack, George settled again into watchful alertness, systematically searching the sky around as the 'beehive' (a collective term used by fighter pilots to refer to the bombers and their close-escort fighters) moved majestically on.

As the raid approached the target so did the anti-aircraft fire increase but there were no further attacks from fighters and the bombers, after an uninterrupted run into the dropping point, released their load as planned.

George watched the bombs as in their hundreds they tumbled from the bellies of the Fortresses and curved away in their downwards path to be lost eventually against the background of the countryside below.

Eagerly he awaited the result, his gaze directed at the now clearly discernible airfield on the outskirts of Amiens whose close-packed houses nestled unsuspectingly nearby. The aim was good: one, two, three and then in such quick succession that it became impossible to count them the well-directed bombs cascaded onto their target and burst into thousands of mushroom puffs of smoke completely obliterating the airfield.

'Nothing can live on that,' mused George as the wheeling bombers, their mission accomplished, turned for home.

On the way out the formation moved unmolested through a temporarily quiet French sky, not far to the north and in view of the village of Tours-en-Vimeu.

Near the village a small boy gazed up intently at the British aircraft and wondered if the English aviator he knew was in one of the Spitfires.

He was indeed; and as he gazed down George wondered if Pierre was watching and, although aware that the gesture would not and could not be seen from the ground, he lifted his gloved hand in acknowledgement of help given and spoke aloud his thoughts, 'Your father is avenged, Pierre.'

AIR COMMODORE ALAN DEERE
DSO, OBE, DFC & BAR

ROYAL AIR FORCE RECORD OF SERVICE AND DECORATIONS

28th October 1937	Civil Flying School Training, White Waltham
9th January 1938	No.1 Depot Uxbridge
22nd January 1938	No.6 Flying Training School, Netheravon
20th August 1938	No.54 Squadron, RAF Hornchurch
12th January 1941	Controller Ops at RAF Catterick
6th May 1941	No.602 Squadron
2nd August 1941	Commander of No.602 Squadron
4th March 1942	Duty with RAF Delegation, Washington USA
25th April 1942	Posted to command of No.403 Squadron, North Weald
13th August 1942	Posted to HQ 13 Group
26th October 1942	Course at Staff College, Gerrards Cross
25th January 1943	HQ 13 Group
11th February 1943	Posted as Supernumerary Flying to RAF Biggin Hill
24th February 1943	HQ 13 Group
14th March 1943	Posted as Wing Commander Flying to RAF Biggin Hill
27th September 1943	Sent to HQ 11 Group
21st October 1943	Posted as Chief Instructor to Central Gunnery School
20th March 1944	HQ 11 Group
1st May 1944	Posted to command HQ 145 Airfield, 84 Group
21st July 1944	Posted to No.484 Group Control Centre, 84 Group
5th June 1945	Posted to Biggin Hill as Supernumerary
17th June 1945	Station Commander at Biggin Hill
2nd July 1945	Posted to command St Andrews Field aerodrome
1st December 1945	Station Commander of RAF Duxford
24th August 1946	Air War College Course at Maxwell Field, USA
14th June 1947	Posted to No.5 Personnel Despatch Centre
17th July 1947	Posted to AHQ Malta on air staff
12th September 1949	Posted to HQ No.61 Group
26th September 1949	Temporary Duty at School of Land/Air Warfare
5th November 1951	Posted to Northern Sector HQ 12 Group
7th May 1952	Posted to command RAF North Weald
23rd June 1953	Posted to 2nd TAF, Wildenrath, Germany
7th March 1957	RAF Staff College, Bracknell on Directing Staff
17th October 1959	HQ Transport Command on liaison and lecture duties
4th January 1960	Air Secretary Department
16th October 1961	Posted to Air Ministry
3rd February 1963	Posted as Assistant Commandant at RAF Cranwell
23rd March 1964	Posted as Commander of HQ 12 (East Anglian) Sector
31st December 1965	Posted to Neatishead as supernumerary
27th January 1966	Posted to 1 School of Technical Training, RAF Halton
12th December 1967	Placed on Retired List

Decorations

14th June 1940	Distinguished Flying Cross
6th September 1940	Bar to DFC
4th June 1943	Distinguished Service Order
18th January 1944	Distinguished Flying Cross (USA)
3rd March 1944	Croix de Guerre (France)
1st January 1946	Order of the British Empire (Military)

Appendix B

EXCAVATION RECOVERY OF CRASHED SPITFIRES
FLOWN BY ALAN DEERE
AND FURTHER HISTORICAL INFORMATION

Appendix B was researched with information supplied from Mr David Smith of the Medway Aviation Research Group.

Spitfire N3180 – The aircraft undertook its first test flight on 13th November 1939 before being delivered to No.11 Maintenance Unit from where it was delivered to No.54 Squadron at Hornchurch on 16th January 1940. On 28th May 1940, Deere force-landed the aircraft on a beach near Calais after return fire from a Dornier Do17 damaged the glycol tank. He clambered out of the aircraft and set fire to it.

When the wreckage of a Spitfire was discovered on a beach in the 1980s it was thought that it might be Alan Deere's aircraft; however it turned out to be Spitfire P9374 of No.92 Squadron, which had been flown by Flying Officer Peter Casanove. The aircraft was recovered from its sandy grave and still awaits restoration.

Spitfire R6832 – This aircraft first flew on 27th June 1940 and was taken to No.9 Maintenance Unit on 29th June 1940 before going operational with No.54 Squadron on 19th August 1940. On 28th August, Deere was again forced to bale out, when he was shot down, this time apparently by another Spitfire. This aircraft came down at Pond Field, Vinson Farm, Oad Street, Boreham near Sittingbourne, Kent. Deere landed by parachute in a plum tree in the village of Bredgar. In the 1980s the tree was still there. At the time of the crash Ronald Spink was in the field and saw the aircraft go in. The field was full of blackcurrants, but is now a wheat field, which can be seen easily from the M2 motorway. Mr Spink's son is Clifford Spink who later became a squadron leader with No.111 Squadron flying Phantom jet fighters. He served with the Battle of Britain Memorial Flight and is now Air Vice-Marshal Spink CBE.

The Spitfire was excavated by Mike Llewellyn and members of the Kent Battle of Britain Museum in October 1973 and the remains can now be seen on display in the museum.

Spitfire R6981 – This aircraft was first flown and tested by George Pickering on 19th July 1940. It was then sent to No.6 Maintenance Unit on 20th July, before going to No.72 Squadron on 24th July. It went to Hornchurch to No.54 Squadron on 9th August 1940. It was destroyed after combat with Me109s on 15th August, when Deere was forced to bale out, having followed some 109s back across the Channel. Deere later described this as 'A very silly thing to do.' He got back as far as Chilham in Kent before having to vacate the aircraft.

Spitfire R6895 – Undertook its first flight on 5th July 1940 and was flown to No.6 Maintenance Unit on the same day. It arrived at Hornchurch and No.54 Squadron on 9th July. It suffered Category 2 damage on 2nd August and was totally written off due to bomb damage, whilst trying to take off on 31st August 1940, when the airfield came under attack. Pilot Officer Deere miraculously survived.

Spitfire X4276 – First flown on 27th August 1940, it was delivered the same day to No.6 Maintenance Unit. It was taken on charge with No.54 Squadron on 29th August.

Following the collision with Sergeant Squire's aircraft during a dogfight practice on 28th December 1940, Deere baled out of the aircraft, which crashed at Town End Farm, Kirk Leavington, North Yorkshire. Years later in July 1987 Dave Smith tracked down an eyewitness to the crash, John W. Hodgson, who pinpointed the crash site. On 15th September that same year, Dave Smith excavated the site with other local enthusiasts. The complete aircraft with the exception of the tail was still in the ground. The collection of items recovered included a complete Merlin engine, gun sight, cockpit instruments and harness buckles etc.

The following written account of the crash was sent to Dave Smith by John Hodgson in July 1987.

Dear Mr David Smith

In reply to your letter, I have been in contact with Mr Tom Watson of Fir Tree House. He did not see the two aircraft collide, as at the time he was in a farm building, but on hearing the planes crash, he went outside and saw a pilot descending by parachute. I have marked the landing place by a red circle in field 154. (See Map)

I saw the two planes when I was ploughing with two horses at High Forest Farm, where I lived with my father and mother. I have marked the field with a letter P.

Both aircraft had been in the air for 15 minutes or more, combat flying. It was a beautiful clear day for December. One plane seemed to fly very close to the other one's tail and I saw a piece fall off as the plane came straight down.

One pilot jumped out very quickly, I saw the parachute open, then I looked for the other plane, which seemed to be flying quite normally, but then the other pilot jumped out too. The aircraft seemed to lose height quickly and disappeared out of sight. I was told later it had crashed in the Leven Valley. The pilot came down in a farm at Hilton. I have marked the place where the first aircraft crashed with an X. The engine of that is still buried in the ground.

I am very pleased that both pilots are still alive after going through the war. I'm also pleased that I have been able to assist in your enquiries, as I never knew what happened to the pilots.

Yours faithfully

J.W. Hodgson

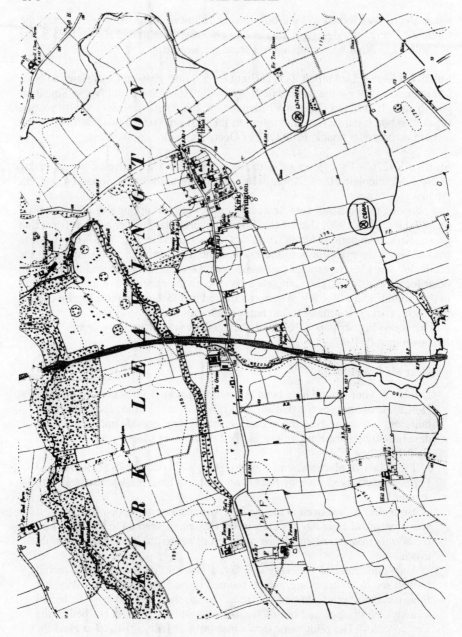

Above: Map of Kirk Leavington showing crash site and witness (ringed).
Opposite top: The Rolls-Royce engine recovered at Kirk Leavington.
Opposite middle: Wartime eye-witness John Hodgson at Al Deere's crash site in December 1940.
Opposite bottom: Caked in mud – the propeller boss of Al Deere's aircraft.

SPITFIRE AIRCRAFT FLOWN BY ALAN DEERE

Spitfire MkIA, No.54 Squadron
L1042	Arrived on 3.7.39, to 19 Sqdn 19.6.40, back to 54 Sqdn on 26.7.40. sent to operational training unit on 25.9.40.
N3180	Arrived on 16.1.40, force-landed at Dunkirk on 28.5.40, P/O Deere.
N3183	Arrived on 10.12.39, lost on 9.7.40, P/O Evershed missing.
N3192	Arrived on 20.3.40, damaged on 24.7.40, Sgt Collett injured.
P9367	Arrived on 12.6.40, sent to 57 OTU on 1.2.41.
P9390	Arrived on 25.4.40, damaged by Me109s over Deal on 7.7.1940. P/O Coleman slightly wounded.
R6812	Arrived on 12.7.40, lost on 24.7.40, P/O Allen killed.
R6814	Arrived on 12.7.40, engine failed and destroyed by fire on 24.10.40.
R6832	Arrived on 19.8.40, lost on 28.8.40, F/Lt Deere baled out.
R6895	Arrived on 9.7.40, hit by bombs on take-off 31.8.40, F/Lt Deere safe.
R6901	Arrived on 17.7.40, lost on 7.9.40, P/O Krepski missing.
R6981	Arrived on 9.8.40, shot down on 15.8.40, F/Lt Deere baled out.
R7017	Arrived on 24.7.40, sent to No.234 Sqdn on 9.9.40.
X4019	Arrived on 1.8.40, damaged on 24.8.40, went to 603 Sqdn on 7.10.40.
X4235	Arrived on 25.8.40, damaged during enemy raid on airfield on 31.8.40.
X4276	Arrived on 29.8.40, struck off charge on 4.1.41.

Spitfire MkI, IIB, Vb, No.602 Squadron
P9510 MkI	Arrived on 13.7.40, sent to 61 OTU on 20.4.41.
R7071	Arrived on 28.4.41, sent to 61 OTU on 28.7.41.
X4336	Arrived on 4.1.41, sent to 61 OTU on 20.4.41.
X4829	Arrived on 26.2.41, sent to 52 OTU on 18.7.41.
P7601 MkII	Arrived on 29.5.41, sent to No.313 Sqdn on 13.8.41.
P7818	Arrived on 15.7.41, sent to 71 Sqdn on 6.8.41.
P7838	*Fermanagh*, arrived on 4.7.41, sent to 122 Sqdn on 19.9.41.
P8718 MkV	Arrived on 2.8.41, sent to No.485 Sqdn on 7.12.41.
P8724	Arrived on 2.8.41.
W3638	Arrived on 25.3.42.
AB185	*Kolhapur III*, arrived on 7.12.41, sent to No.457 Sqdn on 2.4.42.
AB849	Arrived on 9.8.41, sent to No.340 Sqdn on 4.5.42.
AB862	Arrived on 30.7.41, sent to No.316 Sqdn on 11.10.41.
AD251	*Willenhall*, arrived on 22.9.41 sent to Farnborough Aircraft. Establishment on 23.11.41.
BL288	Arrived on 15.12.41, sent to No.222 Sqdn on 30.3.42.

Spitfire Mk Vb, No.403 Squadron
W3324	*Newcastle on Tyne II*, arrived on 5.5.42, listed as missing on 2.6.43.
AA862	*Blackburn II*, arrived on 8.6.42.
AD208	Arrived on 12.9.41, listed as missing on 2.6.42.
AD324	No further information.
AD328	*Saugre Charrua*, no further information.
AD329	Arrived on 24.4.42, sent to No.416 Sqdn on 2.6.43.
AR389	Arrived on 15.4.42, failed to return from operations.

Spitfire Mk Vb, IX, No.611 Squadron

BM328 MkV	Arrived on 11.12.42, sent to No.308 Sqdn on 16.3.43.
BS547	Arrived on 10.11.42, sent to No.341 Sqdn on 21.4.43.
BS556	Arrived on 10.11.42, sent to No.315 Sqdn on 9.4. 43.
EN572 Mk IX	Arrived on 30.4.43, sent to No.485 Sqdn on 4.7.43, failed to return from operations on 6.9.43.
EN575	Arrived on 6.5.43, sent to No.485 Sqdn on 4.7.43.
JK762	Arrived on 17.4.43, sent to No.485 Sqdn on 4.7.43, failed to return from operations on 20.10.43.
JK767	No information.
JK769	Arrived on 1.4.43, sent to No.485 Sqdn on 4.7.43, failed to return from operations on 3.10.43.
JK860	Arrived on 1.4.43, sent to No.485 Sqdn on 4.7.43.

Spitfire MkIX, No.485 Squadron

EN573 MkIX	Arrived on 1.7.43, failed to return from operations 15.7.43.
MH473	Arrived on 27.8.43.

Spitfire Mk IX, Headquarters Biggin Hill Wing

EN568	Arrived on 17.4.43, sent to No.485 Squadron on 23.9.43.

WARTIME CARICATURE BY MEL DATED 1940

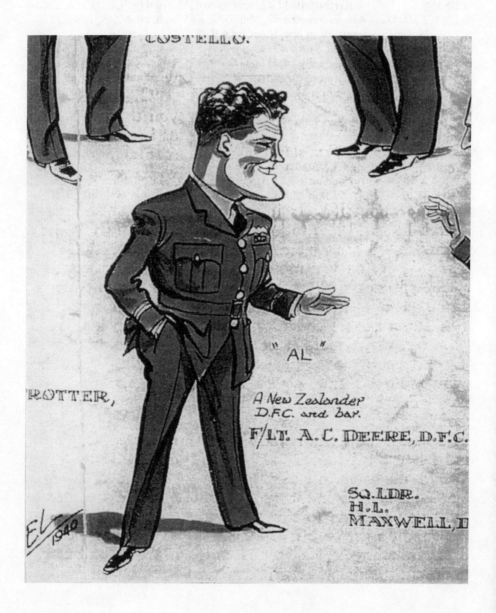

DISTINGUISHED SERVICE ORDER WARRANT
SIGNED BY KING GEORGE VI 1943

George R I

George the Sixth by the Grace of God of Great Britain, Ireland and the British Dominions beyond the Seas, King, Defender of the Faith, Emperor of India, Sovereign of the Distinguished Service Order, to our Trusty and Well beloved

Alan Christopher Deere, Esquire,

on whom has been conferred the Decoration of the Distinguished Flying Cross, Acting Wing Commander, in Our Royal Air Force

Greeting

Whereas We have thought fit to Nominate and Appoint you to be a Member of Our Distinguished Service Order We do by these Presents Grant unto you the Dignity of a Companion of Our said Order And we do hereby authorize you to Have, Hold and Enjoy the said Dignity as a Member of Our said Order, together with all and singular the Privileges thereunto belonging or appertaining.

Given at Our Court at St James's under Our Sign Manual this Fourth day of June 1943 in the Seventh Year of Our Reign.

By The Sovereign's Command.

Acting Wing Commander
A. C. Deere, D.F.C,
Royal Air Force

Archibald Sinclair

CITATION AWARD CERTIFICATE GIVEN BY
FREE FRENCH AIR FORCE 1943

PEACETIME CARICATURE

CERTIFICATE OF GRADUATION
OF AMERICAN AIR WAR COLLEGE 1946

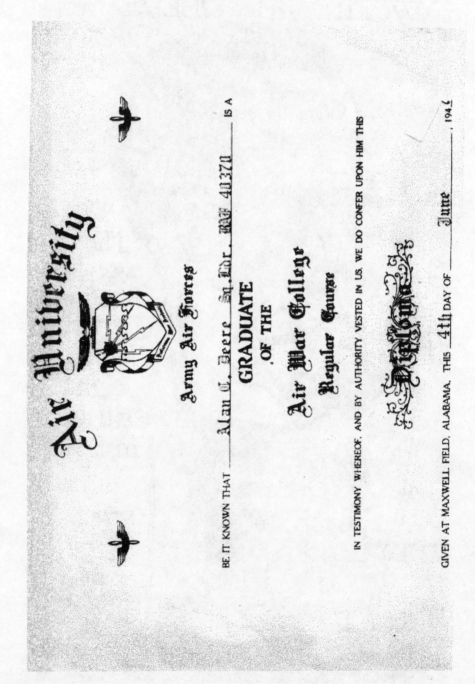

OBE WARRANT SIGNED BY KING GEORGE VI 1946

George R.I.

George the Sixth by the Grace of God of Great Britain Ireland and the British Dominions beyond the Seas King Defender of the Faith Emperor of India and Sovereign of the Most Excellent Order of the British Empire to Our trusty and well beloved Alan Christopher Deere Esquire Companion of Our Distinguished Service Order on whom has been conferred the Decoration of the — Distinguished Flying Cross acting Wing Commander in Our Royal Air Force Reserve of Officers **Greeting**

Whereas We have thought fit to nominate and appoint you to be an Additional Officer of the Military Division of Our said Most Excellent Order of the British Empire We do by these presents grant unto you the Dignity of an Additional Officer of Our said Order and hereby authorise you to have hold and enjoy the said Dignity and Rank of an Additional Officer of Our aforesaid Order together with all and singular the privileges thereunto belonging or appertaining.

Given at Our Court at Saint James's under Our Sign Manual and the Seal of Our said Order this   day of January 1946 in the   year of Our Reign

By the Sovereign's Command

Grand Master

Grant of the dignity of an Additional Officer
of the Military Division of the Order of the British Empire
to acting Wing Commander Alan Christopher Deere, D.S.O., D.F.C. & bar

205

PEN PORTRAITS

The following pages give a brief biography of some of Al Deere's friends and RAF colleagues who have generously contributed their time, memories and photographs during the research of this book.

Squadron Leader Douglas Brown M.I.D was born in Auckland, New Zealand on 6th February 1919. He entered into the Royal New Zealand Air Force in December 1940 and underwent elementary flying training at Whenuapai from February to April 1941. Brown was then sent to Canada to continue his training at the SFTS at Moosejaw, Saskatchewan, from May to August 1941 before journeying to the UK and going to an operational training unit at Grangemouth, Scotland between September and December 1941. He joined 485 New Zealand Squadron at Kenley and remained with it until September 1943, when he was hospitalised due to illness. Afterwards he was sent to the Fighter Leader School at Aston Down, then to the Pre-Invasion School at Milfield, Northumbria as an instructor until May 1944. He was then posted to command 130 'Punjab' Squadron flying Spitfire Vbs before the unit was given Spitfire Mk XIVs during August. The squadron became part of 2nd Tactical Air Force during the end of September. Douglas Brown left the squadron in December 1944 and returned back to New Zealand. He retained the rank of squadron leader.

After the war he returned to civilian life and became a successful businessman eventually being a director on the board of several public and private companies including New Zealand Oil and Gas, National Mutual Life, New Zealand Express and Lees Industries Limited. His other involvements have included the Auckland Medical Research Foundation, Riding for the Disabled and the National Heart Foundation.

Wing Commander John Milne Checketts DSO, DFC, was born on 20th February 1912 in Invercargill, New Zealand. He joined the RNZAF in October 1940 and underwent initial flying training; on completion he was sent to Britain in July 1941 and on arrival went to No.56 OTU at Sutton Bridge. In November 1941 after becoming a pilot officer he was posted to 485 New Zealand Squadron at Kenley. During an engagement with enemy fighters on 4th May 1942, he was shot down and wounded and forced to bale out over the Channel. Fortunately, he was picked up by an air sea rescue launch after spending nearly an hour in the cold water. He was promoted in rank to flying officer on 14th June 1942 and was sent to the Central Gunnery School at Sutton Bridge to undertake a course there. Following this he was posted to Martlesham Heath in Suffolk as an instructor with 1488 Fighter Gunnery Flight, where he stayed until being posted back to operations as a flight commander during the spring of 1943 with 611 Squadron at Biggin Hill. He was given command of 485 Squadron in July 1943 and began to claim many enemy aircraft during sweeps over France. He was awarded a DFC that month and had claimed at least 12 enemy aircraft destroyed.

The 6th September 1943 however, was not a good day and while in combat with FW190s, Checketts was shot down. He survived, but was wounded and burnt. Fortunately, he was rescued immediately by members of the French Resistance and hidden from the Germans. After recovering from his ordeal he was secretly transported to Brittany, where he was put aboard a fishing vessel and ferried to meet a Royal Navy ship at a predetermined rendezvous in the Channel. After time off, he was posted to command an air-to-air combat squadron at the Central Gunnery School at Sutton Bridge, where he met up again with his old friend Al Deere. It was while at CGS that he was awarded the DSO.

In May 1944, Checketts was given command of a Spitfire wing at Horne, near Biggin Hill. He led the wing during the invasion of Normandy on 6th June 1944, after the landings, when Hitler launched his new V1 flying bombs against the south coast of England; Checketts claimed two of the weapons destroyed in the first three days of the German attack. He also participated in the Arnhem operation, 'Market Garden', whereafter he was taken off operations. His final wartime score stood at 14 destroyed, 3 probables, 8 damaged and 2 V1s.

In November 1945, he transferred to the Royal New Zealand Air Force and held a series of appointments until he left the service in 1955. He became a sales representative for an agricultural chemical company until 1963 before moving on to other employment; he finally retired from business in 1982. A biography on Checketts' life was written in 1986 by New Zealand author Dr Vincent Orange, titled *The Road to Biggin Hill.*

Flight Lieutenant Pierre H. Clostermann DFC & Bar, was born in Curitiba, Brazil on 28th February 1921. His enthusiasm for aviation was such that he obtained his private pilot's licence in November 1937 at the age of 17. When war broke out in 1939, he wanted to enlist for the French Air Force, but the French Ambassador in Brazil refused this. He therefore travelled to the USA and attended the Ryan Flying School to become a commercial pilot. He finally applied and joined the Free French Air Force in March 1942. Arriving in Britain, he attended the RAF College at Cranwell and afterwards was sent to 61 OTU at Rednall; from here he was posted as a sergeant pilot to 341 'Alsace' Squadron in January 1943; he flew with the squadron when it operated from Biggin Hill. Here he claimed two enemy aircraft destroyed and two damaged.

In September 1943, he was posted to 602 Squadron and remained with it until July 1944, being awarded a DFC during that month. He was from there posted to French Air Force Headquarters as a staff officer, but soon afterwards was sent to CGS at Catfoss on a course. In December 1944, he underwent conversion to fly Hawker Tempest aircraft and was posted to join 122 Wing in Holland in January 1945. He also flew with 245 Squadron during this period as a supernumerary flight lieutenant.

He was posted yet again in the March to 56 Squadron as a flight commander where he served until April, when he transferred to 3 Squadron just weeks before the war ended. He was released from the RAF in August 1945.

After the war he became an engineer with the Société Aubry et Cie, Paris, and he also sought a career in politics, becoming a member of the House of Representatives in 1958. He also became one of the first post-war fighter pilots to publish their memoirs on the air war of WW2. His first book *The Big Show,* published in 1948, was a great success and since then it has sold over two and half million copies in its various editions worldwide. He followed this success with a second volume titled *Flames in the Sky.* His wartime score of enemy aircraft stands at 11 destroyed, 2 probables, 9 damaged, 2 destroyed on the ground.

Lieutenant General Baron Michael Libert Marie Donnet CVO, DFC, C de C, FR, AE was born in Richmond, England, on 1st April 1917 of Belgian parentage. He was educated at the College St Michel and entered into the Belgian Air Force as an officer cadet on 1st March 1938, where he was awarded the Pilot's Brevet on 24th March 1939. He served with the 9th Reconnaissance Squadron during the early stages of the war flying Renard R 31 aircraft, but was captured on 1st June 1940 and taken to Germany as a prisoner of war. He repatriated to Belgium on 10th January 1941.

Wishing to carry on the fight against the Nazis, Donnet, together with fellow pilot Leon Devoy and a couple of other patriots, made plans to escape to Britain, and found the means when they discovered a Stampe biplane in a hangar in the grounds of a heavily guarded German depot. The aircraft was almost completely airworthy apart from a few missing parts. They spent three months replacing the missing parts by making new ones themselves and then refitting them at night under the noses of the Germans. They also managed to attain enough petrol for the aircraft by purchasing it on the black market. After a couple of false starts due to the Germans changing the locks on the hangar doors and a petrol leak, they finally succeeded in their escape on the night of 4th/5th July 1941, when Donnet and Devoy crept into the hangar, wheeled out the aircraft, started the engine and took off for England.

They successfully landed in England and joined the RAF on 26th July; after finishing operational training at 61 OTU, Donnet joined 64 Squadron on 6th September 1941. He was promoted to flight lieutenant in September 1942 and awarded a DFC and was given command of 64 Squadron in March 1943. In November of that year he was taken off operations and sent as an instructor to the Fighter Leader School at Aston Down. In March 1944 he was appointed to command 350 Belgian Squadron and led it in support operations during the Normandy landings, the Arnhem operation and in fighter escort for strategic bombing.

In November 1944, he was promoted to wing commander and given the appointment of commander of the Hawkinge Wing which comprised four squadrons, 432 and 440 Canadian, 450 Australian and 611. In February 1945, Donnet was given command of a Mustang wing at RAF Bentwaters. During this time he led the wing as fighter escort against the raid on the Gestapo Headquarters in Copenhagen.

At war's end, Donnet had flown 375 operations and was credited with four victories and five enemy aircraft damaged. In September 1945 he became a student at the RAF Staff College and in February 1946 was appointed Chief of the Organization and Provisioning Staff of the Belgian Air Force with the rank of lieutenant colonel. In December 1952, he was assigned as senior air staff officer of 83 Tactical Group (Anglo-Belgian). In August 1959, Donnet was appointed as Deputy Co-ordinator of the Air Defence of Central Europe at the Headquarters, ADCE, Fontainebleau.

In October 1960, he became Chief of Staff of the 2nd ATAF at Monchen-Gladbach, Germany. In June 1963, he commanded the Instruction and Training Group of the Belgian Air Force and in that same year was also appointed Deputy to the Chief of Air Staff. In May 1967, Donnet became chairman of the NADGE Policy Board, taking over from General Den Toom, the Netherlands Minister of Defence. Donnet was promoted to lieutenant general on 26th June 1967. In 1970, he was made the Belgian Defence Attaché in London, where he remained until July 1972, when he returned to NATO as the Belgian representative to the NATO Committee. Michael Donnet retired from the armed services on 1st July 1975. He wrote a book about his wartime career entitled *Flight to Freedom*, which was published in November 1974 by Ian Allan Ltd. He has also written other historical books.

Air Commodore John Lawrence Wemyss Ellacombe CB, DFC & Bar was born on February 28th 1920 in Livingstone, North Rhodesia. He joined the RAF on a short service commission in 1939 and underwent flying training at 2 FTS Brize Norton. After successfully completing the course he was posted to 151 Squadron at Martlesham Heath on 13th July 1940. He scored his first air victory on 24th August, when he shot down a Heinkel bomber near Hornchurch. On 30th August, he claimed another Heinkel, but was himself obliged to force-land his Hurricane after receiving return fire from the enemy, which damaged his aircraft. The following day he was again in the thick of the action and had to bale out of his aircraft when its gravity tank exploded. On landing, he was taken to the Southend General Hospital in Essex suffering from burns. He remained in hospital but on recovery returned to his squadron in December 1940.

He remained with 151 until February 1942, when he was posted to 253 Squadron at Hibaldstow as a flight commander and promoted to flight lieutenant. He was awarded the DFC on 7th April 1942. He took part in the Dieppe raid in August 1942, and during this operation was shot down by German anti-aircraft fire. He parachuted down into the sea and was fortunately picked up by a British rescue craft. In July 1943, he returned to his old squadron, 151, before moving to 487 RNZAF Squadron in 2 Group, during which time he was awarded a Bar to his DFC on 29th December 1944. He remained within the service after the war and attained the rank of air commodore. He was made a CB in 1970 before he finally retired from the RAF on 16th April 1973.

Flight Lieutenant Walter Leslie Harvey, was born in London on 22nd May 1920. Always known as 'Les', he joined the RAF Volunteer Reserve in October 1938 as an airman-under-training. On the declaration of war, Harvey was sent to complete his flying training at 8 EFTS and 10 FTS before going to 5 OTU at Aston Down in early August 1940, where he crashed in a Miles Master aircraft on 6th August, but escaped uninjured. He was posted to 54 Squadron at Hornchurch on 22nd August, but was sent back to Aston Down to receive further training, returning to 54 Squadron at the beginning of September. On 22nd September, Harvey was posted to 245 Squadron at Aldergrove and was with the squadron when he suffered a badly injured leg in a motorcycle accident. Following his recovery, he was posted to 56 OTU on 13th July 1941 and remained there until he was posted to 601 Squadron at Duxford on 18th August. While with the squadron he flew the American aircraft, the Bell Airacobra.

On 17th November, he was posted to 94 Squadron and was sent to North Africa in 1941. During his time there, Harvey was flying Hurricane fighters and while flying as top cover to aircraft of 260 Squadron, 94 was jumped by Me109Fs. Harvey's aircraft was hit and it went into a spin. With the aircraft burning, he managed to bale out at only 1,000 feet, with the parachute only deploying fully a few seconds before he landed. Although he was burned and badly bruised, Harvey was able to walk and was picked up soon after by men of the 11th Hussars Regiment. After making a full recovery, he returned to flying duties with an aircraft delivery unit and continued in this work in West Africa and through Italy as the Allies advanced. On 5th April 1944, Harvey was commissioned as a pilot officer and posted back to Britain on 4th May 1944 to 567 Anti-Aircraft Co-Operation Squadron.

He moved to 695 Squadron on 24th July and again to 595 Squadron on 11th September, flying Hawker Hurricane IVs. On 3rd October, Harvey was attached to 597 Squadron and two days later was promoted to flying officer. He was posted back to 595 Squadron on 13th November 1944. On 31st January, he was posted to 290 Squadron, flying Spitfire, Airspeed Oxford and Miles Martinet aircraft. He remained with this unit until October 1945. Harvey was finally released from the RAF in 1946 with the rank of flight lieutenant. In civilian life he held a number of positions as a sales representative with business companies including Sarsons Vinegar and Nestlé Chocolate. Les Harvey passed away on 24th November 2002

Air Commodore James Anthony Leathart CB, DSO, was born in London on 5th January 1915 and was educated at St Edward's, Oxford. He continued his education at Liverpool University where he studied and won a degree in electrical engineering. It was whilst at university that he joined the auxiliary air force and 610 Squadron at Hooten Park on 23rd January 1937, gaining his wings on 2nd May. On 8th May, he transferred to the RAF and was posted to 3 FTS at Grantham, before moving with the school to South Cerney. After completion of the course he was posted to his first operational squadron, No.54 at Hornchurch in late November 1937. During this time with 54, he acquired the nickname of 'Prof' because of his academic background and skills. A month after war was declared in 1939, Leathart was promoted to a flight commander within the squadron. During the Dunkirk evacuation, he led the squadron on its first patrols against the enemy over the beaches and claimed a Heinkel He111 probably destroyed on 21st May 1940. On 23rd May, he led a rescue attempt to Calais-Marck airfield to pick up Squadron Leader White of 74 Squadron, who had landed his damaged Spitfire there an hour or so earlier. Flying the squadron's Miles Master two-seat aeroplane, he was escorted over to Calais-Marck by Al Deere and Johnny Allen and after being attacked by enemy fighters while attempting the rescue, successfully extricated Squadron Leader White and returned back to Hornchurch. For this outstanding rescue, Leathart was awarded the DSO, while Deere and Allen both were awarded DFCs.

He continued to lead the squadron during the Battle of Britain until he was posted away to the Air Ministry on 18th October 1940 to the Deputy Directorate of Air Tactics. On 3rd March 1941 he moved to HQ Fighter Command as Ops 2 night-fighters. In May he was sent to Acklington to form and command the Canadian squadron, 406. Leathart was then posted to HQ Middle East on 8th November 1941 as Wing Commander Air Tactics. Here he remained until he was given command of 89 Squadron on 16th October 1942 and while with this unit he claimed an Italian Cant Z1007 aircraft on 23rd February 1943.

Leathart was posted back to Britain that July and was appointed to 84 Group HQ to prepare for the Normandy invasion. He was appointed Air Chief Marshal Trafford Leigh-Mallory's personal pilot during this period. On 30th May 1944, Leathart volunteered to be part of the Mobile Warning Radar Unit, which would land on the beachhead after the main assault. This unit's job was to control night-fighters on D-Day, and it landed in France on H-Hour + 5. Leathart luckily escaped unscathed when a German stick grenade was thrown and landed a few feet away, but failed to explode.

He was posted to another command in March 1945, when he was given control of 148 Wing, which operated Mosquito night-fighters. His final wartime score was 7 and 1 shared destroyed, and 3 and 1 shared unconfirmed, 2 probables, 3 damaged. Following the end of hostilities, he remained within the service and went on the Directing Staff at the RAF Staff College on 10th July 1945. He was made a CB on 11th June 1960, finally retiring from the RAF at his own request on 24th July 1962, retaining the rank of air commodore. He died on 17th November 1998.

Flying Officer Hugh Glen Niven was born in Canada in 1919. But in 1937, returned to Britain to live in Scotland. On 7th May 1939, Niven joined the RAF Auxiliary Air Force at Abbotsinch with 602 City of Glasgow Squadron, where he underwent flying training on Avro Tutor aircraft. After the outbreak of war he was sent to 11 Elementary Flying Training School at Perth on 25th October 1939; following this on 23rd March 1940, he went to 15 FTS Lossiemouth and then to 5 OTU at Aston Down on 17th August to convert to Hurricane fighters.

On 1st September he was posted back to his first squadron, 602, which was then operating from Westhampnett in Sussex. Three days later however, he was posted to 601 Squadron at Debden. He returned back to 602 again, on 21st September and was to see action during the Battle of Britain. During one engagement with Me109s on October 29th, his Spitfire was damaged while in combat over Maidstone. He remained with the squadron until September 1941 except for a few days when he was with 603 Squadron at Hornchurch in July. On 24th September he was admitted to Horton Emergency Hospital suffering from tuberculosis. He was invalided out of the RAF on 12th March 1942. After the war, Niven rejoined 602 Squadron in June 1946 after it had been reformed. His post was as civilian clerk.

Flight Lieutenant John Donald Rae DFC & Bar, always known as 'Jack', was born in Auckland, New Zealand on 15th January 1917. A year after the outbreak of war, he joined the Royal New Zealand Air Force on 1st September 1940 and after completing flying training was promoted to sergeant and posted to Britain on 1st March 1941.

He was posted to his first operational squadron, 485 'New Zealand' at Redhill, Surrey on 11th July and that October was promoted to flight sergeant. On 21st October the squadron moved to Kenley.

On 12th April 1942, Rae was posted to 603 Squadron and the following day embarked for Malta board the USS aircraft carrier *Wasp*, arriving at the besieged island on 20th April. On 1st May he was shot down by Me109s, but managed to bale out with only a slight wound to the leg. That same day he had been promoted to warrant officer. After making a full recovery, Rae was soon back in action and by the end of July had claimed 4 and 1 shared enemy aircraft destroyed, four probables and five damaged.

Now commissioned as a pilot officer he returned to Britain on 22nd August 1942 and took up the role of an instructor at 57 Operational Training Unit. Rae was awarded the DFC on 30th November and promoted to flying officer that December. He resumed his role as an operational fighter pilot when he was sent to 118 Squadron at Coltishall on 3rd May 1943, but his stay with the squadron was only brief and on 25th May he was sent back to his old squadron, 485, now operating from Merston. 1st July saw the squadron transferred to become part of the Biggin Hill Wing.

Rae's luck ran out on 22nd August when his Spitfire's engine failed during a sweep over France. He force-landed his aircraft but was captured and became a prisoner of war until his release on 28th April 1945. His final wartime score as a fighter ace was of 11 and 2 shared destroyed, 8 and 1 shared probable and 6 damaged.

After the war, Rae returned home to New Zealand where he ran a successful clothing manufacturing company with his wife. He also became involved with the Red Cross Association at executive level and worked with the Rotary on a voluntary basis during his spare time. Grub Street published Rae's autobiography *Kiwi Spitfire Ace* in 2001.

Flight Lieutenant Stuart Nigel Rose, was born on 21st June 1918 and after leaving school was employed as a trainee quantity surveyor. It was at this time also that he joined the RAFVR at Southampton to learn to fly in March 1939. He underwent flying training at 3 E & RFTS at Hamble in Hampshire, where he managed to attain 87 hours' flying time before the outbreak of war. Rose was sent to No.1 Initial Training Wing, Cambridge, in November 1939, and then to 14 FTS, Kinloss on 3rd February 1940, and from there to 14 FTS, Cranfield on 19th April.

On completion of training, Rose was commissioned as a pilot officer on 17th June 1940, and the next day joined 602 Squadron up at Drem in Scotland. During the Battle of Britain he claimed 2 and 1 shared, enemy aircraft destroyed. He remained with 602 until the beginning of September 1941, when he was posted to 54 Squadron at Hornchurch where he stayed, until he was posted to 57 OTU, Hawarden, as an instructor in November. A year later in November 1942, he was sent to CFS Hullavington to undertake a course before return to 57 OTU, which had moved by then to Eshott. Rose remained as an instructor throughout the remainder of the war before being finally released from the RAF in February 1946. In 1948, he qualified to become a chartered quantity surveyor.

Flying Officer Howard Squire joined the RAFVR in September 1939 for pilot training at Padgate. In December he went to the Initial Training Wing at Bexhill and from there in June 1940 went to 10 EFTS at Yatesbury on Tiger Moths. That July, he went on a pre-fighter course and passed out as 'above the average'. In August he was sent to 5 SFTS at Sealand and passed out top of ground studies and above average flying. He declined an invitation to go the Central Flying School for instructor training, which probably cost him a commission, because he had been selected at FTS as a cadet officer.

In October 1940, he was sent to 7 OTU at Hawarden to convert to Spitfires, and was posted in November to 54 Squadron at Catterick in Yorkshire. It was on 28th December 1940, that Squire and Al Deere were both almost killed in an air collision during a dogfight practice. He remained with the squadron until 26th February 1941, when he was shot down during a sweep operation over northern France by the German ace, Hauptmann Herbert Ihlefeld of Jagdgeschwader 77.

He successfully crash-landed his aircraft but was taken prisoner and became a prisoner of war. In March, Squire was sent first to Dulag Luft, then to Stalag Luft I at Barth, where he remained until 1943 before moving to Stalag Luft III at Sagan. In 1944, he moved camp again to Stalag Luft VI at Heidekrug in East Prussia and finally to Stalag 357 in Thorn, Poland and Luneberg Heath, Germany. On 26th April the advancing British 7th Armoured Division liberated him and those in the camp.

In 1948, Squire re-enlisted into the RAFVR as a flight sergeant at 5 RFS, Castle Bromwich, operating Tiger Moth and Chipmunk aircraft. During 1951, he completed a QFI Course and was commissioned as a pilot officer. He finally left the RAFVR in 1956 as a flying officer.

Air Commodore David Malcolm Strong CB, AFC was born on 30th September 1913 and was educated at Cardiff High School. He underwent pilot training in 1936 and afterwards joined a bomber squadron in 1937. He was with 166 Squadron at the outbreak of war, flying Whitley aircraft and was then posted to 104 Squadron which operated Vickers Wellington aeroplanes. In 1941, Strong was awarded the Air Force Cross, but whilst returning from a bombing raid his aircraft was struck by lightning causing it to lose altitude; Strong managed to pull the aircraft out at 200 feet over the North Sea, but was forced to ditch. All the crew survived the ordeal, but they were captured by the Germans and spent the remainder of the war in prison camps. Strong was himself sent to Stalag Luft III.

After the war Strong remained in the RAF and had a distinguished career. He became station commander at RAF Jurby and RAF Driffield between 1946 and 1948 then spent a year at the RAF Staff College. He was a staff officer at the Rhodesian Air Training Group between 1949-51 before returning to a position on the Directing Staff of the RAF Staff College, between 1952 and 1955. He was made the chairman of the RAF Rugby Union, a post he held from 1954-56. In 1956, he was sent to the Air Warfare College before he was given the appointment of station commander, RAF Coningsby in 1957. In 1959, Strong was made Director of Personnel, Air Ministry, where he remained until he was made Senior Air Staff Officer, RAF Germany in 1962. His final appointment was as officer commanding RAF Halton in 1964 where he remained until his retirement in 1966. During his time at Halton he was made a CB and also chairman of the RAF Golf Society. He retired from the service in 1966.

Squadron Leader Harvey Nelson Sweetman DFC was born on 10th October 1921 in Auckland, New Zealand. In April 1940, he joined the RNZAF and after completing training was posted to Britain to join 485 Squadron at Driffield, Yorkshire, in early March 1941. He claimed two enemy aircraft during this period, one Me 109 destroyed and one probable. After receiving a commission, he was posted to the newly formed New Zealand squadron, 486 in early 1942, flying Hawker Hurricane and Typhoon aircraft. In June 1943 he was awarded a DFC and later that year was asked to become a production test pilot for Hawker Aircraft. In June 1944, he returned to operations rejoining 486 Squadron as a flight commander flying Hawker Tempest aeroplanes. When Hitler's V1 rockets threatened the south-east of Britain, Sweetman became an ace against these weapons, claiming 11 and 1 shared destroyed between June and August of 1944. In September 1944, Sweetman was given command of 3 Squadron in the same wing until January 1945. His final enemy aircraft score stood at 1 and 2 shared destroyed, 1 and 1 shared probable, 2 and 1 shared damaged together with the V1 rockets he accounted for and a German Me262 jet fighter which he damaged during a ground attack. After the war, he attended the Empire Test Pilots' School, but soon after returned home to New Zealand.

Group Captain Edward Preston Wells DSO, DFC & Bar, was born on 26th July 1916 in Cambridge, New Zealand. He joined the RNZAF in October 1938 and was accepted in April 1939, being given a short service commission. It was not until 26th October, however, that he undertook training at Weraroa. In November that year he went to 2 Flying Training School at New Plymouth, before moving to another school at Woodbourne on 15th January 1940, where he completed his training. Wells sailed for Britain aboard the RMS *Rangitata* on 7th June and was sent to 7 Operational Training Unit at Hawarden on 4th August 1940.

After successfully converting to Spitfire aircraft, he was posted to 266 Squadron at Wittering on 26th August. He remained with this squadron until 2nd October, when he was transferred to 41 Squadron at Hornchurch. It was during this month that he claimed his first successes against the enemy and earned the nickname of 'Hawkeye' because of his extremely good vision in detecting and shooting down enemy aircraft. In November, he was the first pilot to engage and shoot down an Italian aircraft over Britain, when the Italians sent a small force against England towards the end of the Battle of Britain.

At the beginning of March, Wells was posted to join the newly formed New Zealand Squadron, 485, at Driffield in Yorkshire. He was to claim the squadron's first victory, when he destroyed a Me109 on 5th July 1941. Wells was awarded the DFC on 7th August. His score continued to increase while serving with 485, and on 6th November 1941, he was awarded a Bar to his DFC. On 22nd, he was given command of the squadron.

During February of 1942, he led the squadron, when the German battle-cruisers *Scharnhorst* and *Gneisenau* made their escape through the Channel from Brest to Wilhelmshaven in Germany. On 5th May, Wells was appointed Wing Leader at Kenley and promoted in rank to acting wing commander. He received the award of the DSO on 28th July 1942 and was posted to New Zealand on loan to the Government. Nine months later he arrived back in Britain and was sent to the RAF Staff College to undertake a course before returning to lead the Kenley Wing, which he did until November 1943; he was then sent to HQ 11 Group as Wing Commander Training.

He returned to operations on 20th March 1944, as commander of the Tangmere Wing, and also led the Detling and West Malling Wings. He was posted away on 1st November 1944 to take command of the Day Fighter Leaders' School at the Central Flying Establishment at Wittering.

His final wartime score of enemy aircraft destroyed was 12 destroyed, 4 probables, 6 and 1 shared damaged, 1 destroyed on ground. After the war, Wells was released from the RNZAF and took up a permanent commission in the RAF. He finally retired from the service on 15th June 1960 retaining the rank of group captain.

Air Commodore Sir Archie Little Winskill, KCVO, CVO, DFC & Bar, was born on 24th January 1917 in Penrith, Cumberland. In April 1937, he joined the RAFVR to undertake flying training and when war was declared in September 1939, he was called up immediately for service, and was sent to Bombing Gunnery School at Catfoss as a staff pilot. He was commissioned in August 1940 as a pilot officer and attended 7 OTU at Hawarden to convert to Spitfire aircraft.

Winskill was posted on 4th October 1940 to 72 Squadron, but was sent to 603 at Hornchurch on the 17th of that month. He made his first enemy claim an Me109, on 28th October and then a shared claim, of a Heinkel on 21st November and two Italian CR42 biplanes on the 23rd.

In January 1941 Winskill was posted from 603 to 41 Squadron at Hornchurch, where he had been appointed earlier as flight commander. He destroyed a Me109 on 14th August, when the squadron was operating as part of the Tangmere Wing, but was himself shot down over France. He survived and managed to avoid capture and with the help of the Resistance, he made his way to Spain and to Gibraltar, before being transported back to Britain in December 1941. He was awarded the DFC on 6th January 1942.

Winskill was given command of the newly formed 165 Squadron at Ayr in April 1942 and led it until August, when he was posted to take over command of 222 Squadron at Drem in Scotland. He held this post only until September, when he was sent to command 232 Squadron at Turnhouse. That November he led the squadron to North Africa. On 18th January 1943, Winskill was again shot down while undertaking a sweep operation over the Mateur area, when his aircraft was attacked by FW190s. He managed successfully to ditch his aircraft in the sea without injury to himself and then swim ashore. He was awarded a Bar to his DFC on 27th July 1943 and on completion of his tour was sent back to Britain.

From September 1943 till December 1944, he commanded the Central Gunnery School at Catfoss. Archie Winskill's wartime score stands at 4 and 2 shared enemy aircraft destroyed, 1 probable, 1 damaged, 2 destroyed on ground and 1 damaged on ground. He was posted to Air Ministry in June 1945 and remained in the service until his retirement as an air commodore in December 1968. He became Captain of the Queen's Flight in 1968 and was made a Commander of Victorian Order in 1973 and then Knights Cross of the Victorian Order in 1980.

ALAN DEERE'S AIRCRAFT COMBAT CLAIMS

Date	Total	Type	Own A/C	Serial No.	Area of combat	Sqn
1940			Spitfire Ia			
23rd May	2	Me109Es		N3180	Calais-Marck	54
,,	1	Me109E u/c		N3180	,,	,,
24th May	1	Me109E		N3183	20 m NE St Omer	,,
25th May	1	Me110		N3183	Gravelines	,,
26th May	2	Me110s		N3180	Calais-Dunkirk	,,
27th May	1	Ju88		N3180	15 m SE Calais	,,
,,	$1/3$	Ju88 u/c		N3180	Dunkirk area	,,
28th May	$1/2$	Do 17 damaged		N3180	Ostend-Bruges	,,
17th June	$1/2$	Ju88 u/c		P9390	Abbeville	,,
9th July	1	Me109E		N3183	10 m SE Deal	,,
,,	1 (a)	Me109E u/c		N3183	,,	,,
24th July	1	Me109E		R6895	Thames estuary	,,
12th August	1	Me109E		X4019	Dover Straits	,,
,,	1	Me110		X4019	,,	,,
15th August	1	Me109E		R6981	Dover-Hawkinge	,,
,,	1	Me109E damaged		R6981	,,	,,
,,	1	Me109E		R6981	Maidstone	,,
,,	1	Me109E		R6981	,,	,,
28th August	1	Me109E probable		R6832	North Foreland	,,
30th August	1	Me109E probable		R6895	near Thameshaven	,,
1941			Spitfire V			
1st August	1 (b)	Me109			Channel	602
9th August	3	Me109Fs damaged		AD251	near Béthune	,,
13th October	1	Me109F damaged		AD251	15 m NW St Omer	,,
18th November	1	Me109E damaged		AD251	10 m-N Le Touquet	,,
1943			Spitfire IX			
16th February	1	FW190		BS556	off Calais	611
4th May	1	FW190		JK769	15m W Antwerp	BHW
10th June	1	FW190 damaged		EN568	Ghent coast	,,
23rd June	1	FW190		EN568	3 m-N Rue	,,
14th July	1	FW190 probable		EN568	10 m-W Le Havre	,,

Total: 17 and 1 shared destroyed, 2 and 1 shared unconfirmed destroyed, 3 probables, 7 and 1 shared damaged.

(a) Deere's collision with Oberfeldwebel Johannn Illner.

(b) But see reference to author's findings on page 73.

NB: Combat claim list supplied courtesy *Aces High* by Christopher Shores and Clive Williams.

BIBLIOGRAPHY

Aces High, Christopher Shores & Clive Williams, Grub Street 1994
Battle of Britain Then & Now Mk V, Winston Ramsey, After the Battle 1980
Hornchurch Scramble, Richard C. Smith, Grub Street, 2000
Illustrated History of No.485 New Zealand Squadron, Kevin Wells, Hutchinson Group
   of New Zealand 1984
Kiwi Spitfire Ace, Jack Rae, Grub Street, 2001
Lights of Freedom, Walter Graebner & Allan A. Michie, George Allen & Unwin Ltd
   1941
New Zealanders in the Air War, Alan Mitchell, George Harrap & Co 1945
Nine Lives, A/Cdr Alan Deere, Hodder & Stoughton Ltd 1959
Spitfire The History, Morgan and Shacklady, Key Publishing Ltd 1987
Wing Leader, G/Capt J.E Johnson, Chatto & Windus 1956

Documents
Station, Squadron Operations Books and Pilots' combat reports etc, consulted at the
Public Record Office, Kew, London.

No.54 Squadron	Operations Book	Air 27/511
	Combat Reports	Air 50/21
No.602 Squadron	Operations Book	Air 27/2075
	Combat Reports	Air 50/166
No.611 Squadron	Operations Book	Air 27/2110
	Combat Reports	Air 50/173
No.403 Squadron	Operations Book	Air 27/1781
No.485 Squadron	Operations Book	Air 27/1933
RAF Hornchurch	Operations Book	
RAF North Weald	Operations Book	
RAF Biggin Hill	Operations Book	

Documents and other source material from the Alan Deere Collection, now held at the
Royal Air Force Museum, Hendon since the sale of Alan Deere's medals and
memorabilia at auction on 2nd April 2003.

INDEX